BEYOND
STALINGRAD

The Stackpole Military History Series

THE AMERICAN CIVIL WAR

Cavalry Raids of the Civil War
Ghost, Thunderbolt, and Wizard
Pickett's Charge
Witness to Gettysburg

WORLD WAR I

Doughboy War

WORLD WAR II

After D-Day
Armor Battles of the Waffen-SS, 1943–45
Armoured Guardsmen
Army of the West
Australian Commandos
The B-24 in China
Backwater War
The Battle of Sicily
Battle of the Bulge, Vol. 1
Battle of the Bulge, Vol. 2
Beyond the Beachhead
Beyond Stalingrad
The Brandenburger Commandos
The Brigade
Bringing the Thunder
The Canadian Army and the Normandy Campaign
Coast Watching in World War II
Colossal Cracks
A Dangerous Assignment
D-Day Deception
D-Day to Berlin
Destination Normandy
Dive Bomber!
A Drop Too Many
Eagles of the Third Reich
Eastern Front Combat
Exit Rommel
Fist from the Sky
Flying American Combat Aircraft of World War II
Forging the Thunderbolt
Fortress France
The German Defeat in the East, 1944–45

German Order of Battle, Vol. 1
German Order of Battle, Vol. 2
German Order of Battle, Vol. 3
The Germans in Normandy
Germany's Panzer Arm in World War II
GI Ingenuity
Goodwood
The Great Ships
Grenadiers
Hitler's Nemesis
Infantry Aces
Iron Arm
Iron Knights
Kampfgruppe Peiper at the Battle of the Bulge
The Key to the Bulge
Kursk
Luftwaffe Aces
Luftwaffe Fighter Ace
Massacre at Tobruk
Mechanized Juggernaut or Military Anachronism?
Messerschmitts over Sicily
Michael Wittmann, Vol. 1
Michael Wittmann, Vol. 2
Mountain Warriors
The Nazi Rocketeers
No Holding Back
On the Canal
Operation Mercury
Packs On!
Panzer Aces
Panzer Aces II
Panzer Commanders of the Western Front
Panzer Gunner
The Panzer Legions
Panzers in Normandy
Panzers in Winter
The Path to Blitzkrieg
Penalty Strike
Red Road from Stalingrad
Red Star under the Baltic
Retreat to the Reich
Rommel's Desert Commanders
Rommel's Desert War
Rommel's Lieutenants
The Savage Sky
The Siegfried Line

A Soldier in the Cockpit
Soviet Blitzkrieg
Stalin's Keys to Victory
Surviving Bataan and Beyond
T-34 in Action
Tank Tactics
Tigers in the Mud
Triumphant Fox
The 12th SS, Vol. 1
The 12th SS, Vol. 2
Twilight of the Gods
The War against Rommel's Supply Lines
War in the Aegean
Wolfpack Warriors
Zhukov at the Oder

THE COLD WAR / VIETNAM

Cyclops in the Jungle
Expendable Warriors
Flying American Combat Aircraft: The Cold War
Here There Are Tigers
Land with No Sun
Phantom Reflections
Street without Joy
Through the Valley

WARS OF THE MIDDLE EAST

Never-Ending Conflict

GENERAL MILITARY HISTORY

Carriers in Combat
Cavalry from Hoof to Track
Desert Battles
Guerrilla Warfare
Ranger Dawn
Sieges

BEYOND STALINGRAD

Manstein and the Operations of Army Group Don

Dana V. Sadarananda

STACKPOLE
BOOKS

Copyright © 1990 by Dana V. Sadarananda

Published in paperback in 2009 by
STACKPOLE BOOKS
5067 Ritter Road
Mechanicsburg, PA 17055
www.stackpolebooks.com

BEYOND STALINGRAD: MANSTEIN AND THE OPERATIONS OF ARMY GROUP
DON, by Dana V. Sadarananda, was originally published in hard cover by Praeger, an
imprint of Greenwood Publishing Group, Inc., Westport, CT. Copyright © 1990 by
Dana V. Sadarananda. Paperback edition by arrangement with Greenwood Publishing Group, Inc. All rights reserved.

Cover design by Tracy Patterson
Cover photos courtesy of Scott Pick/Summit Photographics

Printed in the United States of America

Distributed by NATIONAL BOOK NETWORK

ISBN 978-0-8117-3574-2 (Stackpole paperback)

The Library of Congress has cataloged the hardcover edition as follows:

Sadarananda, Dana V.
    Beyond Stalingrad : Manstein and the operations of Army Group Don / Dana V.
Sadarananda.
       p.   cm.
    Includes bibliographical references.
    ISBN 0-275-93440-3 (alk. paper)
    1. World War, 1939–1945—Campaigns—Soviet Union. 2. Manstein, Erich von,
1887–1973. 3. Germany. Heeresgruppe Don—History. 4. Soviet Union, Southern—
History.   I. Title.
D764.3.S66S23 1990
940.54'2147—dc19   89-16261

Contents

Preface

Until now, it has been the habit of English-speaking historians study-ing World War II to deal almost exclusively on the European Theatre of Operations and to ignore the war on the Eastern Front. Those who have studied the war in Russia have generally done so by offering sweeping observations of the Russo-German war as a whole. With the notable exceptions of the battles of Leningrad, Stalingrad, and per-haps Kursk, individual battles and campaigns have been ignored. In the case of Stalingrad and Leningrad, the classic accounts of these two battles (William Craig's *Enemy at the Gates, The Battle for Stalingrad* and Harrison Salisbury's *900 Days: The Siege of Leningrad*) focus as much on the human misery and suffering of the soldiers and civilians as on the military and operational aspects of the campaigns. The military events serve only as a background for the more memorable human drama.

Even as the battle was being waged, Stalingrad was viewed as a decisive turning point. Indeed, its significance cannot be discounted. Unfortunately, this impression of the battle has led many to see it as an event unto itself, without relating its significance to the larger picture. That Stalingrad represented a strategic setback and a deep psychological blow to Adolf Hitler and the German Army cannot be denied. However, as future events would show, the German Army at least was able to recover. On the other hand, little mention is made of the equally desperate battles that occurred on the flanks of Stalingrad as the struggle for the city reached its climax. The outcome of the battle for Stalingrad would decide the fate of the 6th Army. The battles raging along the flanks, which would continue well into March 1943, would decide the fate of the entire German strategic position on the Eastern Front.

It is the aim of this book to help fill the void in the study of individual battles and operations on the Eastern Front. It is my hope in writing this book that historians will rediscover the "drums and bugles" form of military history that has been recently neglected and in particular, to stimulate an interest in discovering the individual engagements and operations that were fought on the Eastern Front.

Of all the land campaigns conducted during World War II, there were only three that could have dramatically changed the course of the war. The first occurred in the fall and winter of 1941 as the Germans approached Moscow. Only indecision and a difference of opinion within the German high command kept the *Wehrmacht* from marching through the Kremlin. With Russia out of the war, Hitler would have been free to use his resources in the West, possibly making "Fortress Europe" a reality. The second decisive campaign took place in June 1944, when the Anglo-American Allies landed in Normandy and subsequently broke out of their lodgement areas in July and August. Had the initial amphibious landings failed, or the stalemate in the Normandy hedgerow country not quickly broke, Hitler would have been spared a two front war and allowed to use his resources against Russia.

The third campaign of such great importance was the campaign in southern Russia during the winter of 1942–1943. Had the Russians succeeded at any time in overrunning Army Group Don, they would have been free to wheel northward into the flank of the German Army, producing the collapse of the Eastern Front in 1943, rather than 1944.

In 1942, the steppes of southern Russia became the critical area of operations on the Eastern Front as both Germany and the Soviet Union sought a decisive victory. It was in the south that Hitler made his main effort during the summer of 1942, driving ever closer to Stalingrad and disaster. Stalin, too, was drawn to the south. The destruction of the 6th Army would not only clear Stalingrad, but would pave the way for more decisive operations.

From mid-November 1942 to March 1943 the *Wehrmacht* and Red Army remained locked in mortal combat. Although the 6th Army in Stalingrad was initially the main focus, much larger issues were at stake. For the Russians, there was the prospect of cutting off the German southern wing and driving the enemy out of the Ukraine. If successful, the entire German position in the East would be exposed from the south and made ripe for collapse in 1943. For the Germans, it could no longer be a matter of victory, but mere survival. In short, the future course of the war hung in the balance and would be determined by the outcome of the winter campaign of 1942–1943.

That the south had become the decisive battleground was reflected by the fact that active operations along the remainder of the front were greatly reduced. The Red Army was able to maintain pressure against the Germans on other sectors, but it was only in the south that the Soviets undertook major offensive operations. The only exception involved attacks by the Leningrad and Volkhov Fronts to pierce the Leningrad blockade in January 1943.

South of Leningrad, the Germans evacuated the Demyansk pocket in February 1943, in part under Russian pressure, but more significantly to reduce the front. The Vyazama salient, to the east of Smolensk, was also abandoned for similar reasons in March 1943.

Events in the south had a more profound effect on German operations. Both sides poured massive reinforcements into the southern sector, the Russians in hopes of producing victory, the Germans to stave off disaster. From November 1942 to March 1943, the Soviets committed four fronts totaling fourteen armies, approximately 1.75 million men (exclusive of the forces investing Stalingrad), along a 300-mile sector from Voronezh to Rostov. While the Germans could not hope to match the Russian numbers, they increased their strength considerably. Army Group Don grew from barely corps strength in November 1942 to a formidable army group of twelve panzer and motorized divisions (including four SS divisions) and eighteen infantry divisions. Of these reinforcements, fourteen divisions, including five panzer divisions, came from France.

The battles that Manstein directed from November 1942 to March 1943 were among the most critical of the entire war. Significantly, the initial battles of this period are cast in the background of the events of Stalingrad from November 1942 to February 1943. Indeed, Manstein was given command of the 6th Army and Army Group Don, the latter created with the responsibility of not only the rescue of 6th Army in Stalingrad but "to bring the enemy attacks to a standstill and recapture the positions previously held by us."

Manstein, however, was quick to recognize that more than the fate of the 6th Army was at stake, and that the rapidly deteriorating positions along the flanks of Stalingrad threatened with collapse not only the southern wing but the entire Eastern Front. Army Group Don was the only force available to stem the Russian tide.

In fact, shortly after the Red Army entombed the 6th Army in Stalingrad, Stalin was planning even more decisive operations which, if successful, would trap the three German army groups in the south and liberate the Ukraine, thus precipitating the collapse not only of the German southern flank but the entire German strategic position in the East.

It was Manstein who recognized this danger and who, for nearly four months, struggled not only to keep the Red Army at bay but with Hitler who, by his orders and indecision effectively complicated Manstein's task by denying him any degree of freedom that would have made his job considerably less difficult and risky. Manstein's foresight in dealing with the enemy as well as his determination in dealing with Hitler were major factors that enabled Army Group Don to survive the winter of 1942–1943 and deliver an effective counterblow in February 1943.

Fortunately for the historian, the course of a given battle or campaign is easy to follow. There is generally a clearly recognizable beginning and end, and the turning points are readily apparent as the battle progresses. The winter campaign in southern Russia can be conveniently separated into four distinct phases. The first was from November 27, 1942, to late December, when the 4th Panzer Army aborted its relief drive on Stalingrad. The second phase began with the withdrawal of the 4th Panzer Army on December 24, 1942 and continued throughout most of January 1943. This period was marked by the withdrawal of Army Group Don from the Don River to the Donets River, during which time Manstein struggled with Hitler as much as the Red Army. The third phase began in early February 1943 with the arrival of the 1st Panzer Army on the middle Donets. During this period Manstein again had to argue his viewpoints with Hitler, pressing him for timely decisions. The third phase ended with the destruction of the Russian 6th Army and Mobile Group Popov. Much of the fourth phase occurred simultaneously with events of the third, but for clarity is dealt with separately. During this period, from late February until mid-March 1943, Manstein completed the elimination of Russian forces, recaptured the line of the Donets River, and regained the initiative for the German side.

Throughout the campaign there were many turning points. In fact, each phase seems to have its own critical moment. The Russians were so intent on encircling the German 6th Army in Stalingrad, then forming an impenetrable outer ring, that they failed to exploit the initial shock of their offensive by pushing farther west against crumbling, and in some places nonexistent resistance. By exploiting this opportunity, the initial Soviet blow could have wrecked the German front beyond repair.

The Germans also lost their share of opportunities. Could Paulus have disobeyed Hitler and fought his way out of Stalingrad? The question will never be answered with certainty because Manstein, despite plans for a breakout, never issued the codeword that would have put it into effect. The Russian defense of Verkhne Kumsky, the withdrawal of the 1st Panzer Army from the Caucasus, Hitler's meetings with Manstein, and the failure of Soviet intelligence are but a few of the events on which the fate of Army Group Don and the German position in Russia hung.

There are two threads that run continuously from November 1942 to February 1943, crisis and uncertainty. From the moment he took command of Army Group Don on November 27, 1942, in the wake of the Soviet attacks on November 19, until February 28, 1943, Manstein and his army group were faced with a series of crises. It would be more appropriate to say that the entire period was of a singular crisis and that at times the crisis became more acute. Time after time one reads in Manstein's messages of the "critical situation" or "urgent necessity," of the "insufficient forces" or "inadequate supplies."

These phrases repeat like a dull refrain for nearly four months. The situation faced by Manstein and Army Group Don was indeed critical, but this situation was in part symptomatic of another factor, uncertainty: uncertainty not on Manstein's part, but on Hitler's. Manstein's initial assessment of the situation upon assuming command of Army Group Don remained essentially unchanged and was the basis for all of his subsequent actions. Hitler, on the other hand, could not bring himself to accept the situation. Time and again Army Group Don found itself in a more serious position than necessary because of Hitler's indecision. Hitler was unwilling to let Paulus abandon Stalingrad: Manstein was forced to maintain his army in exposed positions while the 4th Panzer Army made a relief sortie; Hitler delayed in bringing the 1st Panzer Army out of the Caucasus: Manstein was compelled to fight a protracted delaying action during which Army Group Don was repeatedly threatened with encirclement. As a result of Hitler's indecision, Manstein found himself faced with an uncertain situation again and again.

In spite of Hitler's indecision, the constant enemy pressure, the countless breakthroughs, the inadequate supplies, the lack of reinforcements, and all the other difficulties that plagued Army Group Don, Manstein was able to rise above it all and bring firm, decisive, inspiring, energetic, and most important, farsighted guidance to Army Group Don. All of these attributes, as well as all of Manstein's experience and skill as a commander, would be called upon to rescue Army Group Don and save the southern wing.

Manstein's foresight enabled him to assess his own and the enemy's capabilities and intentions and to develop both short-term and long-range priorities and a long-range plan of operations. Without Manstein's foresight, his ability to divine enemy intentions and to look beyond the immediate and into the future, the German position in Russia would have been lost in 1943. Manstein's firmness, decisiveness, and energy allowed him to choose his course of action and carry on his arguments with his own high command until Hitler could be made to face the increasingly dangerous situation.

Acknowledgments

Although the words are mine, many people contributed to make this book possible. My graduate advisor, Russell F. Weigley, who, in addition to shaping my education, has offered words of encouragement on many occasions. Nicole O'Neil typed most of the manuscript and supervised the work on the remainder. Thanks to her efforts, I was able to meet my teaching responsibilities and meet the publication deadline.

I am especially greatful to Steve Newton, who also gave freely of his time. The two of us spent many hours of friendly conversation thrashing out ideas and his insights and editorial assistance have been invaluable. Steve was also kind enough to allow me to incorporate material from an unpublished manuscript into my book.

Last but not least, I would like to thank my parents, who always impressed upon me the value of education, and my wife Michele, whose patience, sacrifices, and unwavering support over the years enabled me to devote myself full time to earning my degree.

While I am indebted to all those who had input, I assume all responsibility for any errors of fact or translation.

CHAPTER 1

The Front Collapses . . . Manstein Is Called

As the train rolled through the Russian countryside, a group of uniformed men stood huddled around a large table, peering intently at a map. Dressed in identical field-gray tunics and trousers, the men also wore the same grim expressions. Scattered about the table were various reports and radio messages. Once in a while, one of the men would pick up a report, briefly scan it, then return his attention to the map. Occasionally, he would turn to the man standing next to him or say something to someone across the table, focusing on the map or gesturing for another report.

One of the men circling the table was Colonel Theodor Busse, Chief of Operations for the 11th Army. The white piping on his epaulets identified him as a common infantryman but the wine red stripes on his trousers distinguished him as a member of the general staff, the elite graduate school of the German Army. Solidly built, the spectacled Busse was a tireless worker who might have gone unnoticed except for two accidents of timing. Busse started the war as a staff officer on the Oberkommando des Heeres (OKH) staff and thus failed to gain any combat experience in either Poland or France. In September 1940, he was selected as the Operations Officer to the 11th Army, which at the time was primarily a training headquarters.

However, when the Balkan campaign delayed Operation *BARBAROSSA*, the 12th Army was retained in Greece and the 11th Army was upgraded and sent to Rumania to command the combined German-Rumanian offensive across the Dneister River. This was Busse's first lucky break. Without the Balkan interlude, Busse would not have been in the field when the Russian campaign opened.

Busse's assignment to 11th Army also enabled him to gain valuable experience with the German Army's Rumanian allies. As a result, Busse was more familiar with the training, weapons, and capabilities of Rumanian troops—or lack thereof—than almost any other German staff officer.

Busse was again in the right place when an airplane accident killed General Ritter von Schobert. The 11th Army's new commander,

1

General Erich von Manstein, was not initially pleased with his staff. For Busse it was a confusing and trying time, especially while he learned to meet Manstein's exacting standards.

Nevertheless, Busse survived—and learned. His most constructive qualities were his endless patience with detail, a refusal to panic under any conditions, a hardy constitution, and an instinctive feel for the morale and capability of the troops in the field.

By the end of the Crimea campaign, Busse had earned Manstein's trust and confidence as his indispensable right-hand man. As the Operations Officer of Army Group Don it was Busse who would have to turn the strategic insights of his brilliant commander into reality.[1]

It had been several days since the initial reports had reached him, but he was no closer to forming a clear picture of the situation now than he had been then. Staring out at the scarred landscape, Field Marshal Erich von Manstein was slowly attempting to piece together the fragmentary information at his disposal. While specific details were still lacking, there were enough reports to allow him to form a general picture of the events in the last week. The picture that was beginning to take shape was far from encouraging.

On November 19, 1942, the Red Army launched a major counterattack against the German front north and south of the city of Stalingrad. By November 23, Colonel General Friedrich von Paulus and his 6th Army, more than a quarter of a million men and their equipment, were trapped. In addition, the German lines north and south of Stalingrad were shattered, and Russian spearheads were racing into the German rear.

This was a far cry from the situation envisioned the previous April, when Hitler issued Directive No. 41 outlining the goals for the 1942 campaign against Russia. The main objectives were to be Leningrad in the north and a breakthrough into the Caucasus in the south, while the central sector of the front was to remain static. Since the Soviet counteroffensive from December 1941 to March 1942 had left only limited forces available, these objectives would be obtained in stages. Initially, all resources would be allocated for the primary operation in the southern sector, the goal "being to destroy the enemy before the Don in order to gain the oil region in the Caucasian area and to cross the Caucasus mountains."[2]

Even this phase of the campaign was to take place in stages. The first attacks would be launched in the area south of Orel toward Voronezh. Subsequent attacks were designed to achieve a breakthrough in the Kharkov area. In the final phase of the operation German forces would advance on Stalingrad by moving along the Don River and from the Taganrog-Artemovsk area between the Lower Don and Voroshilovgrad. As far as Stalingrad itself was concerned, the directive stated: "We must try to reach Stalingrad or at least subject this city to bombardment of our heavy weapons. . . ."[3] At this point Stalingrad had not been critical to future German plans.

Indeed, much more emphasis was placed on providing strong flank protection to the northeast along the Don River, especially strong anti-tank defenses. Because this sector of the line would be held by forces of Germany's allies, plans were made to stiffen the Don Front by adding German troops as support between Orel and Stalingrad while German divisions would also be held in reserve behind the front.[4]

By November 1942, Hitler had developed an obsession with the city bearing Stalin's name and long since reversed the priorities of Stalingrad and northeast flank along the Don, stripping German units from the flank and reserve and sending them into Stalingrad. By this time the German front in southern Russia reached far into the Caucasus and the eastern Ukraine. The right flank touched the Black Sea at Novorossik and ran along the front of Army Group A (17th Army and 1st Panzer Army) into the northern Caucasus. Holding the open flank toward the Volga River was the 16th Motorized Division, east of Elista in the Kalmyk Steppes.

Further north, the continuous front of Army Group B began south of Stalingrad, following the Don River northward to Voronezh. Although a "German" army group, Army Group B was composed mostly of allied armies. While most of its German forces were engaged in the fighting around Stalingrad, the greater part of the front, particularly the line of the Don, was held by non-Germans. To the north, farthest from Stalingrad, was the German 2nd Army around Voronezh. To its right, holding the line of the Don, were the Hungarian 2nd Army, the Italian 8th Army, and the Rumanian 3rd Army. South of Stalingrad, the Rumanian 4th Army front stretched into the Kalmyk Steppes.

Thus, the German front in southern Russia stretched some 800 miles, covered by Army Groups A and B with only the 16th Motorized Division to screen the broad gap between them. Inherent in this situation was the danger that the Russians would attack in this area and threaten the Germans with dislocation, a danger that was aggravated by the distances involved.

From the Rumanian 3rd Army's position along the Don River, which was overrun on November 19, to the Don crossings at Rostov, it was a little more than 185 miles. Rostov was a critical crossing, because through it ran the lines of communications for Army Group A, the 4th Panzer Army, and the Rumanian 4th Army. The left flank of Army Group A lay some 330 miles from Rostov, while the 4th Panzer Army, south of Stalingrad, was 250 miles distant. The lines of communications of virtually the entire German southern wing lay farther back at the Dnieper River crossings of Dnepropetrovsk and Zaporozhye, which were only 260 miles from the Russians on the Don but 440 miles from the 6th Army at Stalingrad and 560 miles from the 1st Panzer Army. The capture of these vital crossings would threaten the entire Eastern Front with collapse.[5]

The strung-out position of Army Group B, and the weak state of the Rumanian units did not go unnoticed by the Soviet high command. On September 12, Stalin had overheard Marshals Georgi Zhukov and A. M. Vasilevsky discussing the possible solutions to the desperate situation at Stalingrad. The solution favored by both Zhukov and Vasilevsky was an operation on a major scale, the outcome of which would have a fundamental effect on future operations.

The marshals told Stalin that a new front in the vicinity of Serafimovich, just south of the Don opposite the Rumanian 3rd Army, would have to be formed with the mission of mounting a blow into the rear of the German forces in the Stalingrad area. This new plan was a phased operation: First, it would be necessary to breach the enemy's defenses and isolate the German forces in Stalingrad and to establish a solid ring to seal off any relief attempt. Second, they had to destroy the encircled enemy forces and ward off attempts to break into the ring.[6]

Until the time when the counteroffensive could be launched, the main effort of the Red Army was to hold Stalingrad. Stalingrad became critical to the Russians not merely because it was the city of Stalin's name or because it represented a major geographical objective, but because it now became the hinge on which the coming offensive would swing.

The initial idea for a strategic counteroffensive called for attacks from the right wing of the Stalingrad Front, to cut through the Rumanian units on both flanks so as to cut off the Germans in the Stalingrad area. Soviet bridgeheads north of Stalingrad, at Kletskaya and Serafimovich, offered the best possibilities. Serafimovich was a key area for maneuvering troops—the bridgehead there was out of range of German artillery. Further up the Don at Kletskaya, the southward bulge of the river offered the possibility of pressuring the enemy flank northwest of Kletskaya itself.[7]

The most immediate decision, however, was an administrative one affecting the combined Stalingrad-Southeastern Fronts and the disposition of troops in the Stalingrad area. General A. I. Yeremenko's Southeastern Front officially became the Stalingrad Front on September 28. The Stalingrad Front was redesignated Don Front and immediately divided. A new front, Southwestern, was formed from the right flank of the old Stalingrad Front. Lieutenant General Konstantine

Rokossovsky was nominated as the new commander of the Don Front; Yeremenko remained as the head of the Stalingrad Front, and Lieutenant General N. Vatutin filled the post as commander of the Southwestern Front.

This reorganization served to assist both the deployment of forces for the coming offensive and the defense of Stalingrad. At the end of September, Russian forces in the Stalingrad area (Stalingrad and Don Fronts) totaled seventy-eight rifle divisions, six cavalry divisions, five tank corps, and eighteen tank brigades: 771,000 men, 8,100 guns, 525 tanks, and 448 aircraft. The Don Front, with thirty-nine rifle divisions, three cavalry divisions, three tank corps, nine tank brigades, and two motorized rifle brigades, occupied a 200-mile front from Pavlosk in the north to the Volga south of Yerzovka. At the center of this front were the Soviet bridgeheads on the southern bank of the Don.

The new Southwestern Front formed its junction with the Don Front at Kletskaya. Running north along the Don to Verkhne Mamon, it was composed primarily of the two right flank armies of the old Stalingrad Front (63rd and 21st Armies) and a tank army from STAVKA reserve.[8] The main force of this front was concentrated in the bridgehead area west and southwest of Serafimovich. The Stalingrad Front ran along the Volga, from Rynok in the city itself, through the bridgehead of the 62nd Army in Stalingrad, then southward past the Volga bend into the steppe. It had a total of five armies, 62nd, 64th (both in Stalingrad), 57th, 51st, and 28th, the latter two covering Malay Bebert and the approaches to Astrakhan.

The basic concept behind the planned offensive involved two attacks: one from the middle Don striking southward; the other, south of Stalingrad, driving in a northwesterly direction toward the Don bend where the two pincers would meet. Both blows were initially aimed at the satellite divisions holding the German flanks. South of Stalingrad, between Tundutovo and Lake Barmantsak, the lower Russian hook would sweep through the Rumanian 4th Army. The final phase of the counteroffensive envisioned the encirclement and destruction of the German 6th Army and the 4th Panzer Army. This plan was accepted by STAVKA in late September, and contained the basic form of the Red Army's major counteroffensive. Codenamed URANUS, it would assume its complete and final form in mid-October.[9]

Rokossovsky (Don Front) first learned of the planned offensive from Zhukov in early October. Vasilevsky also instructed Yeremenko (Stalingrad Front) and Rokossovsky to prepare their own proposals. Yeremenko was concerned about the dimensions of the offensive, arguing that the blow from the northwest of Stalingrad should be conducted on a broader front and in greater depth. He also urged that the attack be shifted farther to the northwest to reduce the possibility of resistance. These changes would make it more difficult for the enemy to check Russian mobile units committed to the encirclement operation. These alterations also would trap a larger enemy force than a shallow penetration aimed only at German troops engaged directly in Stalingrad. These modifications were adopted in the second half of October. Now the attack from the northwest of Stalingrad was shifted from the center of the Don Front to the area southwest of Serafimovich. Not only was the size and the scale of the operation increased, but the roles of the Don and Southwestern Fronts reversed, with the latter now mounting the main attack from the north.[10]

The attacks by the Don and Southwestern Fronts would begin on November 9, the Stalingrad Front on November 10. Because of delays in troop movements and shifting of supplies, the offensive was postponed for a week. It was delayed once again because it was necessary to reinforce the Russian position in Stalingrad in the face of furious German assaults to reach the Volga. Nevertheless, to arrive at the Kalach area in time, the Southwestern Front would have to travel sixty to seventy miles in three days, the Stalingrad Front fifty miles in two days. Once in the Kalach area, Soviet troops would be in the rear of the main German force driving on the Volga, and would isolate them from their supply bases on the Chir River.[11]

In discussing the outer encirclement front, it became evident that it would develop into an undertaking of its own. At the end of the first week in November, it was given the codename SATURN. The SATURN plan called for two fronts, Voronezh and Southwestern, to strike deep blows in the direction of Rostov. The destruction of the Italian 8th Army would be followed by an advance to the line Kanteminovka-Chertkovo-Millerovo. This attack would be carried out by the left flank of the Voronezh Front (6th Army) and the 1st Guards Army (Southwestern Front) reinforced by the 17th, 18th, and 25th Tank Corps. Moving from the Chertkovo-Millerovo line, with the addition of STAVKA reserves, the Southwestern Front would drive for Rostov, striking into the rear of the entire German southern front, cutting off its escape route.[12] However, before this plan could be developed further, the Russians had to deal with the situation at Stalingrad.

To carry out Operation URANUS the Red Army deployed 1,000,500 men on the Stalingrad axis. These troops were supported by 13,542 guns (exclusive of anti-aircraft guns and 50mm mortars), 894 tanks, and 1,115 aircraft. The Southwestern Front (1st Guards, 5th Tank, 21st, and 17th Armies) had eighteen rifle divisions, three tank and two cavalry corps, one tank and one motorized rifle brigade, and eighteen artillery regiments. The Don Front (65th, 24th, 66th Armies, and 16th

Air Army) deployed twenty-four rifle divisions, seventeen rifle and motorized brigades, one mechanized and one tank corps, seven tank brigades, and sixty-seven artillery and mortar regiments.[13]

Against this array of men and steel, Army Group B had little to offer in the way of resistance. Holding the sector along the Don River opposite the Soviet Southwestern Front was the Rumanian 3rd Army, composed of the I, II, IV, and V Rumanian Corps. Over the entire course of its nearly seventy-five mile front, it could muster only sixty 50mm or larger anti-tank guns. The remainder of its heavy equipment was an assortment of captured Czech, French, and Russian pieces, as well as inferior Rumanian guns. There was virtually no armor except the German XLVIII Panzer Corps, which was being held in reserve behind the front in the area of Medveshi.[14]

A potentially formidable force, the XLVIII Panzer Corps was composed of parts of the 14th and 22nd Panzer Divisions as well as the Rumanian 1st Panzer Division. But together they totaled only 182 tanks capable of combat.[15] In the 14th Panzer Division only seven of the thirty-six tanks were the more powerful *Panzerkampfwagen* IV (PzKw) tanks, while in the 22nd Panzer Division, just eleven of the thirty-eight tanks were PzKw IVs. The worst situation was in the Rumanian 1st Panzer Division, where eighty-seven of its 108 tanks were Czech 38ts, the remainder being PzKw IIIs. By the end of the first week of fighting, the 22nd Panzer Division had been reduced to nineteen tanks and the 1st Panzer Division to only thirteen. Most of the 14th Panzer Division would end up trapped in the Stalingrad pocket.[16]

Opposite the Soviet Don Front was the German 6th Army, composed of the XI Corps, holding the line of the Don; VIII Corps holding the stretch running southeast of the Don bend; and the XIV Panzer Corps, holding the area immediately north and west of Stalingrad. The LI Corps occupying the city of Stalingrad faced the Soviet Stalingrad Front. The nearly seventy-five-mile front between the XI Corps and the XIV Panzer Corps was held by a thin screen of five understrength infantry divisions. Twelve divisions were concentrated in the area north of Stalingrad and within the city itself, including two motorized and three panzer divisions. None of these units would escape the encirclement.[17]

South of Stalingrad, the 4th Panzer Army was deployed opposite the Russian Stalingrad Front. Although a panzer army in name, the 4th Panzer Army had very little tank strength. Its two motorized divisions, the 16th and 29th, counted only 104 tanks between them, and, after the Soviet breakthrough, would be of little value. The 29th Motorized Division was trapped in the Stalingrad pocket, and the 16th Motorized Division was the only unit holding the flank with the 1st

Panzer Army. The 4th Panzer Army's two German infantry divisions, the 371st and 297th, would also become trapped in Stalingrad. The remaining units of the 4th Panzer Army were Rumanian troops of the VI and VII Corps. These forces were deployed along a line south of Stalingrad stretching toward Elista, a distance of over seventy-five miles. The four infantry and two cavalry divisions covering this area could count only twenty-eight anti-tank guns between them.[18]

Thus, with most of the German forces concentrated in the immediate vicinity of Stalingrad, and with ill-equipped allies holding the long flanks north and south of the city, the Soviets were easily able to surround the 6th Army. By November 23, the Rumanian 3rd Army ceased to exist as a coherent formation, while Russian troops of the 5th Tank Army poured through the shattered front.

From the opening of the Soviet offensive until well into the new year, the German position in southern Russia would continue to deteriorate. The 6th Army was encircled at Stalingrad with little prospect for relief. The loss of the 6th Army in February 1943 doubled the total losses on the Eastern Front up to that time. By March, the German Army in Russia would be nearly 500,000 men below establishment, to say nothing of the hardships of the men and machines who had been fighting their way across the Soviet Union since 1941.

In a desperate effort to restore the situation, Hitler called upon Field Marshall Erich von Manstein. A better choice could not have been made. Manstein had all the necessary skills, experience, and temperament required for such a delicate yet awesome task. He came from a family with a long tradition of military service: sixteen of Manstein's male relatives were general officers under either the Kaiser or the Tsar.

In October 1907, Manstein received a commission in the 3rd Guards Regiment of his uncle, Colonel Paul von Hindenburg. In 1913 he attended the *Kriegsakademie*. During World War I he served in several capacities as *Oberleutnant* and regimental adjutant, most notably in the 2nd Guards Reserve Regiment, which saw action both against the French at Namur and at the Battle of the Masurian Lakes in East Prussia. Throughout the remainder of the war he served in several staff positions on both the Western and Eastern Fronts.

After the war he was retained in the *Reichswehr*. Promoted to major in 1927, by 1929 he was serving in the *Reichswehr* Ministry as head of the Operations Staff of the *Truppenamt*, responsible for the operations staff of the commander in chief, arranging wargames and instructional tours for senior commanders and their staff officers.

When Hitler came to power in 1933, Manstein was in command of the 4th Infantry Regiment. One year later he was appointed Chief of Staff of the Third Military District in Berlin. In July 1935, he became

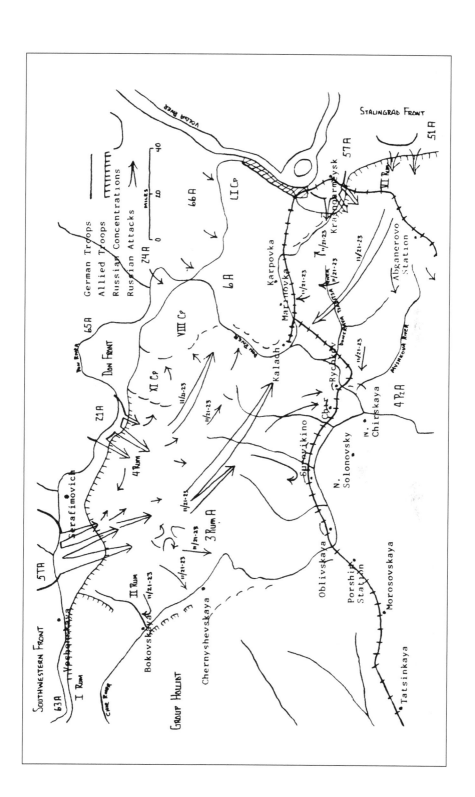

head of the Operations Branch at army headquarters. Promoted to
Major General in 1936, he filled the post of Quartermaster General of
the Army. He also acted as Deputy Chief of the Army General Staff to
both Colonel General Werner von Fritsch and Colonel General Lud-
wig Beck.[19]

Manstein was a brilliant staff officer. General Adolf Heusinger,
Chief of Operations of the army general staff, recalled that he "could
accomplish in a single night what other military leaders would take
weeks to do."[20] The rapidly changing political climate that accompanied Hitler's rise to power and the volatile international situation
of the mid-thirties made this ability an almost necessary prerequisite.
Plans for both the reoccupation of the Rhineland and the occupation
of Austria were drawn up literally within hours.

Despite his obvious ability, Manstein's personality seems to have
kept him from being fully accepted by his superiors. General Hans
Speidel, Chief of Staff to Field Marshall Erwin Rommel, commander
of Army Group B in the West in 1944, observed that while Manstein
was often genial toward his subordinates he was frequently abrasive
and arrogant toward his equals or those above him. Even his operations officer, Busse recalled that "During the first few weeks I hated
his guts; I never left his presence without smarting."[21] After assisting
Beck in drawing up plans for the invasion of Austria, Manstein was
posted to command the 18th Infantry Division. During the occupation
of the Sudetenland he was briefly assigned to Colonel General Ritter
von Leeb's 12th Army as chief of staff, and again during the 1939
mobilization he was appointed chief of staff to General Gerd von
Rundstedt's Army Group South prior to the war against Poland.

In February 1940, Manstein was promoted to command the XXXVIII
Corps. It was at this time that Manstein was given the opportunity to
voice his advocacy of the Ardennes plan for the invasion of France.
The original plan envisaged a two pronged attack with the heavier
blow being delivered by General Fedor von Bock's Army Group B in
the north into the Netherlands and Belgium, while von Rundstedt's
Army Group A, to the left of Bock, advanced toward the Meuse
between Namur and Sedan. The revised plan reversed the role of the
two army groups, giving Army Group A the decisive role of enveloping the Anglo-French and Belgian forces from the south. Postwar
mythology, cultivated by Manstein and Colonel General Heinz
Guderian, attributed the Ardennes plan entirely to Manstein. In fact,
the plan had many authors, including Hitler. Nevertheless, Manstein's
vocal support for the revised plan was instrumental in its final approval.

Manstein's opportunity to voice his opinion regarding the revised
plan came on February 17, when he was called to Hitler's head-

quarters to be congratulated for his appointment as commander of the XXXVIII Corps. Three days latter the plan was adopted. Shortly afterward Manstein was removed from Army Group A, ostensibly for his outspoken support of the Ardennes plan.

Manstein believed that his transfer from Army Group A was punishment. However, the diary of Colonel General Franz Halder, the Chief of the General Staff, indicates that the decision to transfer Manstein predated the planning controversy and that the transfer was nothing more than a normal career progression. In fact, Manstein had even been considered for the command of the panzer group being formed to lead the operation. He was passed over in favor of General Ewald von Kleist because Kleist was senior to two of the corps commanders in the group, while Manstein was junior to them. Halder felt that he would have enough on his hands in dealing with Guderian without precipitating a rank controversy. Manstein also did not receive command of either of the two newly formed panzer corps because these positions were being reserved for Generals Schmidt and Georg-Han Reinhardt. While both of these men were junior to Manstein, they had one qualification and advantage that he lacked: each had commanded a panzer division in Poland. There was a concerted effort by the Army Personnel Office to keep the panzer commands in the hands of those who had trained for them before the war or who had exercised command in combat.[22]

In any event, Manstein's part in the French campaign as commander of the XXXVIII Corps was little different from that of any other commander. However, during the final phase of the campaign Manstein demonstrated the same flare for leadership as Guderian and Rommel. While his headquarters staff was left to handle routine matters in the rear, Manstein could be found conducting operations at the front from a radio truck. Manstein often "turned up at the all critical points during action among the most forward elements so as to see the situation at first hand. He then usually gave any necessary orders on the spot, which frequently interfered ruthlessly with the normal chain of command within individual units."[23]

That he had not been intentionally snubbed for his role in advocating the Ardennes plan was later demonstrated by his subsequent assignment to the LVI Panzer Corps for the campaign against Russia. In his first experience commanding panzer troops Manstein distinguished himself by seizing the Divna River bridge at Divnsk intact, operating 200 miles from the frontier and eighty miles from the nearest German unit.

Further evidence that Manstein had not been punished for his support of the Ardennes plan came in September 1941, when he was chosen to lead the 11th Army. In this case, Manstein had been chosen ahead of eighteen more senior corps commanders. From September 1941 to July 1942, the 11th Army was engaged in the Crimea in a campaign that climaxed with the surrender of the Russian fortress at Sevastopol. For this accomplishment Manstein was promoted to field marshal.[24] By now his success and fame were such that the very mention of his name was enough to inspire troops. At this point, Hitler decided to appoint him as commander of Army Group Don, which was created specifically to deal with the situation at Stalingrad.

Thus, all of Manstein's experience made him an ideal choice for his new assignment as commander of Army Group Don. As a staff officer he had demonstrated his ability and competence at the highest level. Having commanded both an infantry and armored corps, Manstein was familiar with the capabilities and limitations of German troops. While not alone in his support of the revised plan for the French campaign, Manstein's advocacy of this operation demonstrated his boldness and willingness to accept the unorthodox and explore alternative solutions to an operational or strategic challenge. Finally, as the commander of the 11th Army, Manstein proved himself capable of directing large bodies of troops and earned a reputation as an inspirational leader.

On November 21, 1942, Manstein received orders at 11th Army headquarters at Vitebsk instructing him to travel south to the headquarters of Army Group B at Starobelsk. At the juncture of Army Groups A and B, he was to form a new army group, Army Group Don, whose task was "to bring the enemy attacks to a standstill and recapture the positions previously held by us."[25]

The condition of Manstein's command was hardly encouraging. The 6th Army, bottled up in Stalingrad, was virtually useless. The remainder of his units were only skeletons of the corps and armies they represented. The Rumanian 3rd Army had been decimated by the Russian attacks of November 19. The XLVIII Panzer Corps had been roughly handled in an unsuccessful counterattack against the Soviet perimeter around Stalingrad. Colonel General Hermann Hoth's 4th Panzer Army, to the south of Stalingrad, had itself been cut by the southern arc of the Russian pincer, losing most of its tank force into the Stalingrad pocket. Any strength that remained was in the form of service and communication troops. The only full strength formation, the 16th Motorized Division, was 150 miles away and responsible for protecting the left flank of Army Group A and the right flank of the main front.

Meanwhile, before Manstein could reach his new headquarters, the Red Army had moved thirty-four divisions across the Don, their mobile formations wreaking havoc in the German rear. Against this wave, Army Group Don was incapable of any serious resistance, especially if the Russians should shift their attack westward or south-ward to cut the communications of Army Group A. Excluding the 6th Army, Army Group Don had barely the strength of a corps and was stretched over a 200-mile front.

Under these conditions, Manstein's problems seemed insurmountable. The Russian offensive had shattered the entire German southern front. Without reserves or immediately available reinforcements to stabilize the situation, much of the German "front" was being held by *ad hoc* battlegroups formed from the remnants of shattered units, stragglers, and support personnel rallied around a local commander who, on his own initiative, attempted to organize resistance. Except for the fact that there had been major breakthroughs along the flanks of Stalingrad, the situation was unclear, especially to Manstein, who would be unable to form a complete picture of the situation until he reached Army Group Don headquarters at Novocherkassk on November 27.

These problems were compounded by the fact that in the weeks that followed the initial Russian breakthroughs on November 19, Hitler remained inflexible in his decisions. It was also characteristic that in a crisis such as now faced the German Army in southern Russia, Hitler postponed making decisions for as long as possible.[26] Once the Red Army had routed the Rumanians along the Don, it was clear that the existing front could not be held. There were only two options: Either pull the 6th Army out of Stalingrad west of the Don to reinforce the position in the Don bend, or, as Manstein proposed, undertake a strategic withdrawal of all German forces from the Don bend and the Caucasus to defensive positions behind the Lower Dnieper. Either alternative would have shortened the front and allowed the German forces to be more concentrated. It would have then been possible to strike a blow against the exposed flank of the advancing enemy. However, Hitler's refusal to yield ground ruled out both alternatives. Thus, the Russians gained the initiative while all the Germans could do was to react to the moves of the Red Army.[27]

Stalingrad had been cut off on November 23. In three weeks the Russians were able to drive more than 100 miles. On December 17, the Italians of Army Group B broke and ran. Rostov lay only 125 miles away. The situation deteriorated further when the Russians broke through the Chir Front and the Kalmyk Steppes on Christmas Eve in the direction of Rostov. By New Year's Day, the attack had advanced another seventy miles, with only Hoth's 4th Panzer Army to bar the way.[28]

With the southern flank collapsing along its entire length, and in light of Hitler's refusal to allow the 6th Army to move, Manstein's problems magnified. One of Army Group Don's original tasks was the relief of the 6th Army. But this was now made more difficult because the Soviets had closed the ring around Stalingrad on November 23. In addition, it now became Army Group Don's responsibility to contain the Russian breakthrough.

Notes

1. Steven A. Newton, *Hitler's Generals: A Biographical Register of German Generals, 1939–1945, Including Senior Luftwaffe and Waffen SS Commanders* (unpublished), no page numbers.
2. Hugh Trevor-Roper, *Blitzkrieg to Defeat: Hitler's War Directives, 1939–1945* (New York: Holt, Reinhart and Winston, 1964), p. 118.
3. Ibid., p. 119.
4. Ibid., pp. 19–20.
5. Erich von Manstein, *Lost Victories*, ed. and trans. by Anthony G. Powell (Novato, California: Presidio Press, 1982), pp. 368–369. Matthew Cooper, *The German Army, 1933–1945* (New York: Stein and Day Publishers, 1978), pp. 343–346.
6. John Erickson, *The Road to Stalingrad: Stalin's War With Germany* (London: Westview Press, 1975), pp. 388–390.
7. Ibid., p. 423.
8. STAVKA was the general headquarters of all Soviet forces. It would eventually evolve into something like the combined chiefs of staff. It included the Marshals of the Soviet Union, the Chief of the General Staff, the head of the naval and air forces, and the heads of arms and services. Ibid., pp. 136–137.
9. Ibid., pp. 425–426.
10. Ibid., p. 429.
11. Ibid., pp. 445, 465, 460.
12. Ibid., pp. 459–460.
13. Ibid., p. 462.
14. Manfred Kehrig, *Stalingrad: Analyse und Dokumentation einer Schlact* (Stuttgart: Deutsches Verlags-Anstalt, 1974), pp. 667–668. Also map, **Die Lage am 19 November 1942**. Historical Division Headquarters, USA, Europe, Foreign Military Studies, Ms P114c, Part 4, *Die Operationen der deutschen Heeresgruppen an der Ostfront, 1941 bis 1945, Sudliches Gebiet: Die russiche Gegenoffensive bis zum Mius und bis zum Donets, November 1942–March 1943,* vol. 1, by F. W. Hauck Gen. d. Art. a.D., p. 54. Cited henceforth as Ms P114c.
15. Authorized tank establishment for an armored division was approximately 160.
16. XLVIII Panzer Corps Ia, Anlagen z. KTB, November 1–30, 1942, Microcopy T 314, Roll 1160, Frames, 192, 445. (The usual method of citing these captured German documents is of little assistance to the reader in locating them. The method used here, although unconventional, allows quicker identification of the source material.) Kehrig, p. 668.

17. Manstein, pp. 365–366. F. W. von Mellenthin, *Panzer Battles: A Study in the Employment of Armor in the Second World War* (New York: Ballantine Books, 1971), pp. 225–226. Kehrig, map,**Die Lage am 19 November 1942.** Ms P114c, p. 54.

18. Kehrig, p. 667, also map, **Die Lage am 19 November 1942.** Ms P114c, p. 54.

19. R. T. Paget, *Manstein: His Campaigns and His Trial* (London: Collins, 1951), pp. 1–35 *passim*. F. W. von Mellenthin, *German Generals of World War Two as I Saw Them* (Norman, Oklahoma: University of Oklahoma Press, 1977), pp. 19–28 *passim*. Albert Seaton "Field Marshall Erich von Manstein," in *The War Lords: Military Commanders of the Twentieth Century*, ed. by Michael Carver (Boston: Little, Brown and Company, 1976), pp. 237–240. While Paget and Mellenthin are generally favorable to Manstein, Seaton's account is considerably less so.

20. Newton.

21. Ibid.

22. Ibid.

23. Ibid.

24. Ibid.

25. Heeresgruppe Don Ia, Anlagenband 2 u. 3 z. KTB, November 27–December 14, 1942, Microcopy T 311, Roll 268, Frames, 871–874.

26. David Irving, *Hitler's War* (New York: Viking Press, 1977), vol. 2. p. 499. David Downing, *Devil's Virtuosos: German Generals at War, 1940–45* (New York: St. Martins Press, 1977), p. 278. Cooper, p. 436.

27. Cooper, pp. 436–437. Manstein, p. 372.

28. Cooper, p. 437.

CHAPTER 2

Winter Storm and the Crisis on the Chir Front

From the time he assumed command of Army Group Don in late November 1942, until the end of December, Manstein had three concerns: stabilizing the front to keep the Russians from threatening his line of communications; gathering enough forces to make this possible; and simultaneously, to relieve the beleaguered 6th Army in Stalingrad. Attempting to accomplish one of these tasks was a monumental effort, to tackle all three perhaps was beyond even Manstein's ability.

During the nearly one week it took to complete the rail journey to their new headquarters at Novocherkassk, Manstein and his staff had ample time to assess the situation, although much of what they learned was based on second-hand information. At their first stop at Orsha on the night of November 21, Manstein met with Field Marshal Gunther von Kluge, the commander of Army Group Center. Kluge painted a dim picture of the situation and concluded by telling Manstein: "You will find it impossible to move any formation larger than a battalion without first referring back to the Führer."[1] Kluge's words were prophetic.

Regardless of what Kluge had said, it was clear that active measures would have to be taken to restore the front. One of Manstein's first acts, therefore, was to request reinforcements from *OKH*. In a teleprinter message to the Chief of the General Staff, Colonel General Kurt Zeitzler, Manstein estimated that "The situation in the army group area depends on the insertion of powerful forces of army size. None of these forces should be committed, if possible, until fully assembled for a counterattack."[2] Several days later Manstein received Zeitzler's reply indicating that the 3rd Mountain Division, the 306th Infantry Division, and the 17th Panzer Division would arrive in the Army Group Don area shortly after the beginning of December.[3]

By the time he arrived in Starobelsk on November 24, the unpromising situation that Manstein was about to inherit had become critical. From here he again contacted Zeitzler, this time to discuss the plight of the 6th Army. Manstein felt that the 6th Army "should not at present attempt a breakout so long as sufficient supplies can be maintained,

especially fuel, anti-tank and infantry ammunition."[4] A relief operation could be launched with the forces scheduled to arrive at the
beginning of December, but it was necessary to ensure a steady flow
of reinforcements to counter any Russian buildup. An independent
breakout by the 6th Army might still be necessary as a last alternative
"if enemy pressure were to prevent us from deploying these forces."[5]

The Soviet offensive which had shattered the German southern
front was limited to the encirclement and destruction of the 6th Army
at Stalingrad. However, at the time Manstein did not know this. After
meeting with his staff on November 24, Manstein concluded that the
Russians would do everything in their power to destroy the 6th Army.
In addition, there was a possibility that they would try to exploit the
collapse of the Rumanian 3rd Army by pushing mechanized forces
across the large bend of the Don River toward Rostov to threaten the
communications not only of Army Group Don, but of Army Group A
in the Caucasus as well. Manstein also believed that by reinforcing the
forces already engaged, the Soviets could pursue both aims simultaneously.[6]

While his conclusion regarding Russian intentions to destroy the 6th
Army were accurate, Manstein's assessment of a simultaneous drive
on Rostov was only partially correct. Nevertheless, his overall assumption was sound and remained the basis for all of Army Group
Don's subsequent operations. More significantly, Manstein's evaluation represented the first independent and rational approach to the
situation since the Russians launched their attacks on November 19.

Thus, even before he took active command of Army Group Don on
November 27, Manstein had correctly assessed the overall strategic
situation. This was the first time, but would not be the last time, that
Manstein would accurately anticipate Soviet intentions. Indeed, from
the time he assumed command of Army Group Don in November
1942, until the 4th Panzer Army's counterstroke in February 1943,
Manstein never lost sight of the fact that the Russians were making
their main effort against Army Group Don with the aim of amputating
the southern flank from the rest of the front. All subsequent operations
of Army Group Don were founded on this principle, despite the
enemy's attempts to divert Manstein's energy elsewhere. Manstein's
foresight and resolve not to be distracted from his primary task, the
maintenance of the southern flank, were the single most important
factors in determining a successful outcome for the Germans.

For Manstein, however, this was nothing new. General F. W. von
Mellenthin, chief of staff of the XLVIII Panzer Corps, recalled that as
the commander of the 18th Infantry Division in the 1930s, Manstein
would invariably command the "German" forces in staff wargames.
Younger officers "who knew his [Manstein's] capability would lay

bets whether or not he would once again confidently produce the Staff College solution. Those who managed to find takers for their bets always won."[7]

After taking command of Army Group Don on November 27, Manstein received a teleprinter message replying to the appreciation he had submitted on the 24th. Hitler refused to abandon Stalingrad on the grounds that it would mean the renunciation of the year's offensive success and would allow the Russians to regain the essential communications of the Volga River. He was also determined that every effort should be made to reestablish contact with the 6th Army. Hitler also believed that the Russians would soon be experiencing supply difficulties and envisioned a German attack to blunt the Soviet drive and achieve a quick breakthrough to Stalingrad.[8]

The following day Manstein sent a detailed appraisal to Hitler, telling him that the best that could be expected was to cut a corridor through to the 6th Army to replenish its fuel and ammunition stocks thus restoring its mobility. The 6th Army would then have to be immediately extricated from the pocket. Furthermore, Manstein told Hitler that it was strategically impossible to continue tying down German forces in such a restricted area while the enemy enjoyed freedom along hundreds of miles of front. Maneuverability had to be regained at all costs.[9] Meanwhile, Manstein worked to collect sufficient forces for a relief drive on Stalingrad and to reestablish a coherent front. During the first weeks after the Russian breakthrough, Army Group Don managed to hold its front with ad hoc *Kampfgruppen* composed of headquarters staffs, service and communications personnel, and troops returning to their parent units from furlough and sick leave. The Russians, however, were concerned with tightening the ring around Stalingrad and as a result did not press aggressively against these units. This allowed the Germans enough time to stiffen their line and fill in some of the gaps. The Rumanian 3rd Army even managed to hold its bridgehead at Nizhne Chirskaya, at the confluence of the Chir and Don rivers.

The Rumanians' success was due largely to the efforts of Lieutenant Colonel Walther Wenck. Too young to serve in World War I, Wenck's first military experience came as an officer cadet in the *Freikorps* in August 1919. Carried into the *Reichswehr*, he was later commissioned as a lieutenant in Infantry Regiment 9 in February 1923. In 1928, the regiment participated in the first exercises in motorized tactics, during which Wenck's abilities impressed Guderian.

In 1936, Wenck was posted to the General Staff College in Berlin. Graduated in 1938, he soon found himself serving as the Chief of Mobile Troops and in April 1939, he was named operations officer to the 1st Panzer Division.

After three years with the 1st Panzer Division, Wenck then served as an instructor at the *Kriegsakademie*. However, in September 1942, he was named chief of staff to the LVII Panzer Corps where he was reunited with Lieutenant General Friedrich Kirchner, his old commander at the 1st Panzer Division. During the Soviet Stalingrad offensive Wenck was assigned as Chief of Staff to the Rumanian 3rd Army, the remnants of which merged with *Armee Abteilung* Hollidt and in March 1943, a new 6th Army, serving as chief of staff each time. He subsequently served as chief of staff at 1st Panzer Army in April 1943, and as Chief of Staff to Army Group South Ukraine in April 1944. When Guderian was appointed Chief of the Army General Staff in July 1944, he chose Wenck as his Chief of Operations.

Wenck was recognized early in his career as a talented staff officer. During the last three years of the war he also proved himself a brilliant tactical improviser and is credited by Manstein as the man most responsible for reestablishing a defensive front after the rout of the Rumanian 3rd Army:[10]

> Needing troops and equipment, the colonel instituted his own set of rules. He rode the highways and dragooned stragglers into ad hoc units. He played movies at intersections and when exhausted soldiers stopped to watch, Wenck brusquely marched them back to war. One of his noncommissioned officers found an abandoned fuel dump and put up signs reading: "to the Fuel-Issuing Point." Hundreds of cars, trucks, and tanks drove into this oasis only to become part of Wenck's new army.[11]

In fact, Wenck was so successful as an improviser that he even managed to secure his own panzer battalion. After being forbidden by Manstein to collect stray tanks on his own authority, Wenck recalled, "We passed some of our tanks to the 6th and 23rd Panzer Divisions, and from then onward employed our own armored units in no more than company strength so that they should not attract attention from higher headquarters."[12]

Wenck's commander, General Karl Hollidt, was similarly capable and equal to the task. In an army where glamor and glory were found in the panzer arm, Hollidt was the archetypal infantrymen. As such, his early career was one marked by obscure commands, and it was not until after the Polish campaign that he served with an active headquarters, when the 9th Army was sent to the west during the second phase of the French campaign.

After the campaign he took command of the 50th Infantry Division, another low status division, composed of *Landwehr* troops. Hollidt supervised the division's conversion to a full-strength unit and fought with the division in the Balkans and southern Russia, primarily under Schobert's (then Manstein's) 11th Army. In January 1942, Hollidt was rewarded for his performance and elevated to command the XVII Corps.

His experience with low priority divisions early in the war turned out to be extremely valuable. By late 1942, Hollidt was experienced at quickly organizing untrained, half-trained, overaged troops for battle, like those he had scavenged to patch up the line on the Chir Front.[13]

It was the bridgehead of the Rumanian 3rd Army, southwest of the Chir, that was the first to be reinforced. By December 4, three fresh divisions had been assembled. The 336th Infantry Division had been brought over from the Hungarian 2nd Army in Army Group B's sector and deployed around Verkhne Solonovsky, Farm 2 of Collective Farm 78, and Axenovsky to support the bridgehead. The 7th Luftwaffe Field Division was concentrated around Morosovskaya, and the 11th Panzer Division was deployed in the Morosovskaya-Krapinvin-Skassyrskaya area.[14]

The 11th Panzer Division had been *OKH* reserve since October and had its full complement of tanks and assault guns. Its commander, Major General Hermann Balck, had learned his trade with the 1st Motorized Infantry Regiment in the 1st Panzer Division. He was promoted to command the 2nd Panzer Brigade in the 2nd Panzer Division in Greece and in the early stages of the Russian campaign. During the winter of 1941–1942, he served as Chief of Motorized Troops at *OKH*, before taking command of the 11th Panzer Division in May 1942.

Balck had by this time completely mastered the principles of mobile warfare, maneuver, and surprise. He was also resourceful, flexible, and an experienced panzer leader who was demanding of his subordinates.[15] By the time the 11th Panzer Division reached Army Group Don, Balck had molded it into one of the finest and most dependable armored divisions in the *Wehrmacht*. This was mainly because, in Balck's words, "We were fortunate that after the hard fighting in the previous campaigns, all commanders whose nerves could not stand the test had been replaced by proven men. There was no commander left who was not absolutely reliable."[16] In the coming weeks, the 11th Panzer Division would be fortunate to have such leaders.

Also arriving in the Army Group Don sector were the headquarters of the LVII Panzer Corps, the 6th and 23rd Panzer Divisions, and the 15th Luftwaffe Field Division. The headquarters of the LVII Panzer Corps, brought over from the 17th Army in the Caucasus, would have under its command the 6th Panzer Division arriving from France, and the 23rd Panzer Division from the 1st Panzer Army. Both of these units were assembled around Kotelnikovo. The 23rd Panzer Division had only sixty-nine tanks when it arrived and suffered delays in its movement because of poor road conditions in the Caucasus region. The 6th Panzer Division, having been just reequipped in the West, was a full-strength unit.[17]

Three other units that had been promised, the 3rd Mountain Division, the 306th Infantry Division, and the 17th Panzer Division, either failed to arrive at all or would arrive too late to be of any major consequence. Half of the 3rd Mountain Division was diverted to Army Group A to deal with a local crisis; the second half was kept by Army Group B for similar reasons. The 306th Infantry Division, which had been promised on November 21, and was scheduled to arrive in early December, was not released until December 6, and had to travel all the way from France. The 17th Panzer Division, promised at the same time, was retained by *OKH* as a reserve around Orel and was not released until December 3. When it finally reached the LVII Panzer Corps on December 17, it was too late to matter.[18]

Originally, Manstein had intended to attempt the relief of the 6th Army from two different directions, the 4th Panzer Army from Kotelnikovo east of the Don, and *Armee Abteilung* Hollidt from the Chir toward Kalach.[19] The shortage of forces now made this impracticable. Under the circumstances, only the LVII Panzer Corps (6th and 23rd Panzer Divisions and the 5th and 8th Rumanian Cavalry Divisions) of the 4th Panzer Army had sufficient strength to launch an attack. It was farther from Stalingrad than *Armee Abteilung* Hollidt, but there were fewer obstacles to cross between Kotelnikovo and the 6th Army. Manstein also hoped that this was the last place that the Russians expected an attack, as was indicated by the fact that the Soviets had only five divisions opposite the 4th Panzer Army, but fifteen on the Chir Front.[20]

On December 1, Manstein issued orders for Operation WINTER STORM. On a date still to be fixed, but in any case not sooner than December 8, the main force of the 4th Panzer Army west of the Don was to push through the Russian defenses with the objective of pushing back the enemy forces on the south and southwest fronts of the 6th Army from the south or west. At the same time, the XLVIII Panzer Corps (11th Panzer Division, 336th Infantry Division, and 7th Luftwaffe Field Division) was to clear the high ground west of the Don and hold the Kalach crossing open for the 6th Army. After receiving orders from Army Group Don, the 6th Army was itself to breakout to the southwest toward the Donskaya Tsariza River to link up with the 4th Panzer Army. In addition, the 6th Army was also to push back the Russian forces on its west front and breakout toward Kalach.[21]

The right flank of the attack was to be covered by the Rumanian 4th Army, while the Rumanian 3rd Army and *Armee Abteilung* Hollidt were to hold the Chir Front and cover the left flank.[22] It was a measure of the desperate situation of Army Group Don that the only forces available to cover the relief attack were the very troops who had collapsed only weeks earlier.

Several days later, Hoth issued more detailed instructions to his forces charged with carrying out the plan. The task of reaching Stalingrad fell to Lieutenant General Friedrich Kirchner and the LVII Panzer Corps. Kirchner had entered the *Reichswehr* in 1906 as a cavalry officer. In October 1933, he was given command of *Reiter* Regiment 11, which one year later was converted into a motorized regiment for the 1st Panzer Division. Thereafter, Kirchner's promotions followed the usual pattern—brigade commander in November 1938 and in the Polish campaign, and divisional commander in November 1939. During the attack on France Kirchner's 1st Panzer Division formed part of Guderian's XIX Corps and played a leading role in the assault on the Meuse, resulting in the collapse of the Allied front.

In November 1941, Kirchner was promoted to command the LVII Panzer Corps and served in that capacity until the end of the war. The corps was in the vanguard of the German drive into the Caucasus in the summer of 1942. In December 1942, Kirchner was called upon to lead the 4th Panzer Army's relief drive to Stalingrad and was thereafter continuously engaged in all the battles on the southern wing.

While he remained on active service throughout the war, Kirchner never rose above corps commander. Despite playing a prominent role in the relief attack on Stalingrad, Manstein makes little more than a passing reference to him and even in Guderian's account of the French campaign Kirchner appears only twice. This anonymity was at least in part due to his demeanor. A quiet, competent man, Kirchner appears never to have attracted the attention needed to get promoted. In addition, his superiors apparently recognized that he had reached his potential as a corps commander and simply left him there.[23]

The LVII Panzer Corps was given the task of breaking through the Jesaulovsky-Aksay sector and splitting the Soviet forces on both sides of the line Pimen Tsherny-Shutov Station. After driving the enemy back, the corps was to occupy the north bank of the Aksay River and, without regard for its west flank, continue its thrust across the steppe to the north to seize the high ground at Sety and Verkhne Tsaritsynsky. This advance would be followed by a thrust into the enemy rear in the Karpovka sector. The entire attack was to be covered by the Rumanian 5th and 8th Cavalry Divisions bringing up the right rear. It was also their task to clear the east flank on both sides of Plodovetoy to prevent a Russian advance from the lakes on either side of Tsatsa.

While the XLVIII Panzer Corps was to cover the advance of the 4th Panzer Army west of the Don the 11th Panzer and 7th Luftwaffe Field

Divisions would break through the Russian defenses between Rut-shov and the Chir railroad station. Thrusting to the northeast, between the Don and Liska, the 11th Panzer and 7th Luftwaffe Field Divisions were to cross the Don at Kalach and await the 6th Army. Meanwhile, the 336th Infantry Division would attack out of the Verkhne Chirskaya bridgehead and establish a link with the XLVIII Panzer Corps between Nish Petrovsky and Businovka.

The 336th Infantry Division was to launch its attack simultaneously with the bulk of the 4th Panzer Army. The 11th Panzer and 7th Luftwaffe Field Divisions would not attack until the LVII Panzer Corps turned north across the Jesaulovsky-Aksay sector. Once contact was established with the 6th Army at Kalach, the LVII Panzer Corps would open a corridor and guide through the supply convoy being held in readiness around Nizhne Chirskaya.[24]

While waiting for the 4th Panzer Army to assemble, Manstein was forced to deal with developments on the Chir Front. Ever since the initial Russian attack on November 19, *Armee Abteilung* Hollidt and the Rumanian 3rd Army had been forced to deal with local breakthroughs and penetrations along the Chir Front. Every day, the Soviets launched numerous, small-scale attacks that the Germans always managed to contain. As a result, the Russians were kept to the north and east of the Chir River. However, by early December, in-creased enemy reconnaissance activity, as well as movement and troop concentrations in the Don-Chir triangle, indicated preparations for a major Soviet attack against the Rumanian 3rd Army in the Chir bridgehead. On December 4, Manstein reported to *OKH* that the purpose of the attack was "... to collapse the Chir Front to increase the distance between the Army Group and the 6th Army."[25]

On December 6, the 336th Infantry Division took up positions along the Chir between Nizhne Chirskaya and Surovikino. One day later, elements of the Russian 1st Tank Corps of the 5th Tank Army broke through the left flank of the division at Ostrovsky. By nightfall, fifty to seventy tanks had penetrated approximately fifteen miles to State Farm Number 78.[26]

Luckily, General Balck and the 11th Panzer Division were moving up from Rostov at about the same speed at which the 1st Tank Corps were moving south. By afternoon, the 15th Panzer Regiment had checked any further Soviet advance.

As he formulated his plan of action, Balck remembered a similar situation in 1940 that would later be described by Guderian:

Early on the 16th of May, I went to the headquarters of the 1st Panzer Division. . . . All that was known was that there had been heavy fighting during the night in the neighborhood of

Bouvellmount.... In the main street of the burning village I found the regimental commander, Lieutenant-Colonel Balck, and let him describe the events of the previous night to me. The troops were overtired, having had no rest since the 9th of May. Ammunition was running low. The men in the front lines were falling to sleep in their slit trenches. Balck himself, in wind jacket and with a knotty stick in his hand, told me that the capture of the village had only succeeded because, when his officers complained against the continuation of the attack, he had replied: "In that case I'll take the place on my own!" and moved off. His dirty face and red-rimmed eyes showed that he had spent a hard day and sleepless night. For his doings on that day he was to receive the Knights Cross.[27]

While the Russians sought shelter from the winter night in the surrounding far buildings, the 11th Panzer Division was on the move. Balck decided to make his main effort along the heights to the west and north of the farm and fall on the enemy rear. The attack was led by the 15th Panzer Regiment with support from the 11th Panzer Grenadier Regiment. A holding attack was to be launched by the 110th Panzer Grenadier Regiment from the southwest. To the south, Balck placed an engineer battalion and a screen of 88mm anti-aircraft guns.

By dawn, the 15th Panzer Regiment was blocking the Russian approach route and could see a long column of enemy trucks and infantry. Charging down from the heights, the 15th Panzer Regiment destroyed the column at close range with machine gun fire. Without pause, the tanks continued to move south, arriving at the farm just as the Russian T-34s were moving off to attack the flank of the 336th Infantry Division. Balck's panzers hit the Russian rear just as the first T-34s ran into a screen of 88s. By nightfall, forty-six enemy tanks had been destroyed.[28]

This action eliminated the threat to the rear of the 336th Infantry Division, but did little to stem the crisis on the Chir Front. During the next two days a series of small bridgeheads were made opposite the 336th Infantry Division, making it clear that the Russians were increasing their strength against the Chir position, both as a spoiling move against any concentration for a relief force and with the more ambitious purpose of capturing the airlift bases at Tatsinkaya and Morosovskaya.[29]

The Germans were clearly incapable of sustaining a static defense along the whole length of the Chir and dealing with numerous Russian bridgeheads. However, Lieutenant General Otto von Knoblesdorff, the new commander of the XLVIII Panzer Corps, decided that it was more important to maintain the bridgehead at Nizhne Chirskaya and restrained Balck from action. Instead, the 11th Panzer Division was positioned for an counterattack against the Russians who had just broken through the defense perimeter. Just as the leading elements of the 11th Panzer Division were about to cross their start lines, however, a message arrived from the 336th Infantry Division indicating that its front had been penetrated at Nizhne Kalinovsky and also at Lissensky.[30]

Unlike Balck, Knoblesdorff lacked any specific training in armored warfare and had actually received a panzer command only after his 19th Infantry Division was converted prior to the attack against the Soviet Union. Nevertheless, as part of Hoth's *Panzergruppe* 3, Knoblesdorff shared in the thrilling dash across Russia and in the bitter fighting in front of Moscow. He also learned his trade quickly and gained a reputation for leading from the front.

Perhaps his greatest strength was a complete understanding of infantry tactics and, more importantly, the proper coordination of infantry and panzer divisions—a trait particularly indispensable on the defense.

After a brief consultation between Balck and Knoblesdorff, the German counterattack was called off and the 11th Panzer Division spent the night marching to Lissensky. Here there was a mixed force of Soviet tanks, cavalry, and anti-tank guns. By midday the bridgehead had been eliminated, and that afternoon, the 11th Panzer Division marched fifteen miles northwest to Nizhne Kalinovsky, attacking as it had done earlier in the day, with neither preparation nor reconnaissance.

At Nizhne Kalinovsky, the Russians had time to gather their strength. Nearly sixty T-34s had crossed the river. Two companies had swung east during the night toward the sound of firing from the Lissensky battle. This group took the brunt of the 11th Panzer Division's attack, giving time for their comrades to prepare hull-down positions. Against this defense, the 11th Panzer Division made little progress, and in the morning its attack was silhouetted against the rising sun. By evening the division had been reduced to half of its November strength. Unable to eliminate the bridgehead, the 11th Panzer Division dug in to contain the Russian position. After moving by night and fighting by day for over a week, the 11th Panzer Division had finally ground to a standstill.[31]

The action of the 11th Panzer Division in the Chir bend during the second week of December 1942 would be repeated again and again throughout the coming months. Lacking sufficient infantry forces, Manstein relied on his panzers to act as "fire brigades" to deal with the most serious Russian penetrations along the front. Because of the panzer division's mobility and firepower, it was ideally suited for this role. Mobility allowed the panzer division to reach the threatened area quickly, while firepower enabled it to deal with almost any enemy breakthrough.

Manstein's use of his panzer divisions, in the Chir bend, and later south of the Don and in the Donets bend, enabled him to use what few superior resources he had to great advantage. Not only did the panzer division's mobility allow it to react quickly, it also enabled it to cover larger frontages. While it had been done earlier, Manstein's employment of his armored formations as mobile fire brigades made a virtue out of necessity, and in many ways pioneered the mobile defense tactics on which the German Army was forced increasingly to rely.

Thrust into an unpromising situation, which continued to deteriorate on a daily basis, Manstein made the most of his few resources, although from the outset there was no question that he could " . . . recapture the positions previously held by us." Actually, Manstein had few choices in dealing with the Russian counteroffensive. The enemy held the initiative and, at best, all that he could do was to react to the most immediate threat and trust in the ability of his local commanders and troops on the spot. Even in this regard, Manstein was fortunate to have energetic and resourceful army commanders like General Karl Hollidt and Hoth, not to mention divisional commanders such as General Erhard Raus and Balck or regimental commanders the caliber of Huhnersdorff, who were able to rally their men and sustain some semblance of resistance against overwhelming odds.

By 1942, Hoth was a seasoned veteran of virtually every campaign of the war. His previous commands included the XV Corps (later motorized) in Poland and France, the 3rd Panzer Army in the initial invasion of Russia, and the 17th Army in southern Russia. Hollidt was also a seasoned veteran of the Eastern Front, having commanded the 50th Infantry Division in the Crimea and later the XVII Corps on the southern sector in Russia.[32]

While the 11th Panzer Division was acting as a fire brigade in the Chir bend, the Russians began to build up their forces along the Northern Chir opposite *Armee Abteilung* Hollidt, where the front was being held by the Rumanian 14th Infantry and 7th Cavalry Divisions. Daily reports reaching Army Group Don headquarters indicated that the Russians were continuing to bring reinforcements into this area and that numerous enemy concentrations had been identified. Furthermore, the Rumanian 3rd Army reported that "At present, the forces of the XLVIII Panzer Corps are not enough to clear up both the breakthrough and to begin the counterattack on December 12."[33] Because the Chir Front was vital for covering the main thrust on

Stalingrad by the 4th Panzer Army, Manstein was forced to tell *OKH* that "the release of the 11th Panzer Division is not in sight."[34]

Farther south, the 4th Panzer Army was concentrating for its relief drive. Because of the delay in the arrival of the LVII Panzer Corps, the date for the final assembly was pushed back from December 3 to the eighth, then again to the twelfth. These delays afforded the Russians the opportunity of advancing through the gap between the Rumanian VI and VII Corps. By early December, the remnants of the Rumanian units (primarily the Rumanian 4th Infantry, and 5th and 8th Cavalry Divisions) had been pushed back and now formed a rough arc around Kotelnikovo. This arc, with Kotelnikovo as its focal point, stretched from Budarka in the southeast, then curved northeastward to Dorganov. Here, the arc curved northwest until it reached Nebykov, where it continued westward to Verkhne Kuromarsky.[35]

Since December 1, there had been growing indications of an impending renewal of Soviet attacks. On November 30, the Russians had advanced as far as Pokhlebin, barely ten miles from Kotelnikovo, where they were stopped by the 6th Panzer Division. All evidence pointed to a Russian attack on December 3 or 4, with the aim of capturing Kotelnikovo.[36] Kotelnikovo was vital to the Germans because it was the closest major railroad station to the front.

The Russians had nearly destroyed it in late November while the first elements of the 6th Panzer Division were unloading. During the next several days the 6th Panzer Division fought off repeated attacks to take the station.[37]

Despite their earlier failures to capture Kotelnikovo, the Soviets were planning future attacks on the 4th Panzer Army, and from December 7 on, there were signs of a major buildup northeast of Kotelnikovo around Aksay, where the Russian 13th Tank Corps was concentrating.[38]

Manstein had already resigned himself to postponing the relief drive because of delays in moving the 23rd Panzer Division. He also anticipated that the XLVIII Panzer Corps, presently engaged on the Chir Front, would not be released in time to assist the drive as intended. Even his initial hope that the 4th Panzer Army would not be opposed by strong Russian forces faded as he wrote to *OKH* that "The Army Group expects the enemy to mount a major effort in the area east of Kotelnikovo and on the Chir Front before the assembly of our forces necessary for the relief of the 6th Army."[39]

On December 9, Manstein sent a detailed appraisal to *OKH* in which he outlined the situation of both the German and Russian forces. On the Chir Front, the attack on Stalingrad was being covered by the 5th Tank Army with twelve rifle divisions, five cavalry divisions, two motorized divisions, four tank brigades, one tank regiment, and two motorized brigades. There were also two rifle divisions, four tank brigades, and one motorized brigade in reserve. Opposite the left and center of *Armee Abteilung* Hollidt were three more rifle divisions. To the south, east of the Don, was the 51st Army, composed of four rifle divisions, four cavalry divisions, one tank brigade, and one motorized brigade.

In addition to these forces, unloading operations east of Stalingrad and troop movement across the Don to the south had been observed by reconnaissance. Manstein continued noting that while the front east of the Don remained passive, this was only because the concentration of Russian motorized forces was not yet complete. Nevertheless, strong attacks had been made across the Chir on the German bridgehead at Nizhne Chirskaya and to the west of the Chir railroad station. Furthermore, the continuous north-to-south movement of Russian forces across the front of *Armee Abteilung* Hollidt led Manstein to believe that these attacks would be extended farther to the west.

He conceded that the Russians had suffered considerable material losses, especially tanks, but this was being offset by the continuous arrival of new forces. He also noted that Russian artillery had been substantially increased, particularly east of Stalingrad.

Manstein's assessment of the Rumanian units under his command was equally discouraging. The Rumanian 4th Army could not be expected to withstand an attack of any strength, especially as it had been ordered by Marshal Ion Antonescu, the commander in chief of the Rumanian forces, to avoid being cut off. In the case of the Rumanian 3rd Army, apart from the reasonably intact Rumanian I Corps forming part of *Armee Abteilung* Hollidt, the strength of the rest of the Rumanian divisions holding the front amounted to no more than one to two battalions.

As far as the restoration of units to the rear was concerned, these were of little value because of the lack of heavy weapons. The remainder of the Rumanian 3rd Army front was being held by various units which lacked artillery and anti-tank weapons. Manstein warned his superiors that ". . . there must be no illusion that the front can be held for any length of time against strong attacks, especially by armored forces."[40]

Outlining German intentions, Manstein urged an attack by the 4th Panzer Army as soon as possible. There was also the question of the XLVIII Panzer Corps. It was still uncertain if it would be released from the Chir Front by December 11. Since it appeared that the Russians would attempt to extend their attacks toward Morosovskaya shortly, he pointed out that it would be necessary for *Armee Abteilung* Hollidt to cooperate to relieve the pressure on this front either by attacking east toward Perelasovsky or by surrendering a German division to the Rumanian 3rd Army.

Manstein also observed that "The weight of forces brought in by the enemy against Army Group Don makes it clear that he sees his main effort here. He will carry on the struggle here as long as possible by bringing over forces from other fronts."[41]

Regardless of how the 6th Army's position might develop in the future, Manstein emphasized that a steady flow of reinforcements to Army Group Don was necessary to offset Russian reinforcements and that it was critically important to increase their rate of arrival if the Germans were not always to lag behind the Russians. He also considered it essential to restore the usefulness of the Rumanian Army, especially its will to fight and its confidence in the German command.[42]

It appears that by this time Manstein was not quite certain as to the proper course of action once contact had been reestablished with the 6th Army. Previously he had advocated the breakout of the 6th Army as a necessary prerequisite for solidifying the southern flank. However, in his appraisal of December 9, he wrote:

Should the army be left in the fortress area, it is entirely possible that the Russians will tie themselves down here and gradually fritter away their manpower in useless assaults. At the same time it must be faced that the 6th Army is being forced to live and fight under particularly unfavorable conditions in the fortress and that if the present ratio of strength continues much longer, contact may well be lost again. At best it must be assumed that there will be no decisive change in the next few weeks.

On the other hand, one must also allow for the possibility that the Russians will take the proper action and, while maintaining their encirclement of Stalingrad, launch strong attacks against the 3rd and 4th Rumanian Armies with Rostov as their target. If this happens our most vital forces will be operationally immobilized in the fortress area or tied down keeping the link with it open, whereas the Russians will have freedom of action along the whole of the Army Group's remaining front. To maintain this situation throughout the winter strikes me as inexpedient.[43]

In other words, despite the desperate need for German troops to support Army Group Don, Manstein now believed that the 6th Army would play a more valuable role by continuing to tie down Russian forces around Stalingrad. Releasing the 6th Army from Stalingrad would free more Soviet forces than could possibly be desirable.

One of the few decisions that Manstein had any control over was the planned relief drive and the breakout of the 6th Army. His first impression, communicated to Zeitzler on November 24, was that the 6th Army should not be allowed to break out of Stalingrad as long as it could be adequately supplied. An immediate breakout by the 6th Army would unleash four full Soviet armies and considerable elements of two others. To keep these forces tied down, Manstein preferred instead a relief operation to reestablish contact with the 6th Army, an independent breakout being a last alternative.

However, by November 9, Manstein was beginning to feel some doubt as to the proper course of action once contact was made. By this time, he was beginning to fear the possibility of a Soviet attack on the Rumanian 3rd Army and 4th Panzer Armies with Rostov as their final objective.

Manstein later claimed that the fact that the 6th Army was tying down considerable Russian strength played no part in making his assessment of November 24, but that saving the 6th Army was "urgently needed to give the maximum possible help in stabilizing the situation on the southern wing sufficiently to bring us through the winter."[44] Furthermore, an immediate breakout was out of the question because:

Most probably the army would sooner or later have no choice but stand and fight out in the steppes without adequate supplies or ammunition, fuel, or food! Some elements, such as tank units, might possibly get away, but the fate of the army as a whole would be sealed. The Soviet forces it had been engaging till then would be released, and this in turn was likely to lead to the destruction of the German armies' entire southern wing—including Army Group A, which was still out in the Caucasus.[45]

These two statements illustrate the dimensions of the choice that Manstein was faced with. On the one hand the release of the 6th Army was essential if the Germans were to make it through the winter. On the other hand, a breakout, even if successful, would probably result in the elimination of the army anyway as well as freeing major soviet forces from the immediate Stalingrad area.

For this reason Manstein decided to leave the 6th Army in Stalingrad until it could be assisted by relief groups. It was hoped that the attack by the relief forces would alleviate some of the Russian pressure on the encirclement to facilitate the initial breakout. The danger here was that any delay would give the Soviets time to consolidate their siege front. In any case, it was absolutely necessary to guarantee adequate supplies for the 6th Army if it were not to make an immediate breakout.[46]

On December 10, final preparations for the LVII Panzer Corps thrust were made. By now, the situation had changed from the time of the original order for WINTER STORM on December 1. The LVII Panzer Corps would now have to face hostile forces on both of its flanks in the Jesaulovsky-Aksay sector, of which the eastern group was the most dangerous. Advancing toward the Jesaulovsky-Aksay sector, the panzer corps was to keep its left flank free and not be drawn west by the Russian forces at Verkhne Kurmoysrsky. The 6th Panzer Division would attack between Gremyatshy and Verkhne Yablotshny and to drive the Russians north.

This attack would be covered by the 23rd Panzer Division between Pimen Tsherny and Nebykov to the right rear of the 6th Panzer Division. Together they would cross the Aksay River between Generalov and the Shutov railroad station and continue their drive northward.[47]

Almost simultaneously with Manstein's arrival at Army Group Don headquarters, Stalin was reviewing a proposal submitted by Vasilevsky for Operation SATURN. This proposal called for the reorganization of forces on the Southwestern Front. The 1st Guards Army was to be split, with its forces on the line formed by the Don, Drivaya, and Chir Rivers, as far as Chernyshevskaya, creating the 3rd Guards Army. The 5th Tank Army was then assigned the sector from Chernyshevskaya to the junction with the Stalingrad Front at the mouth of the Chir.

The immediate aim of the operation was the destruction of the Italian 8th Army and *Armee Abteilung* Hollidt. To do this, the Southwestern Front had two assault groups: one on its right flank with the 1st Guards Army of six rifle divisions, one tank corps, plus five rifle divisions, three tank corps, one mechanized corps, six tank regiments, and sixteen artillery and mortar regiments in reserve, to attack the bridgehead from the south of Verkhne Mamon toward Millerovo; the second group was on the 3rd Guards Army front east of Bokovskaya with five rifle divisions and one mechanized corps and was to attack simultaneously from the east toward Millerovo.[48]

Stalin had the highest hopes of gaining a decisive strategic success against the entire German southern flank, but everything depended on the quick reduction of the 6th Army in Stalingrad to release Soviet troops for the new offensive operation. Meanwhile, Stalin had built up the 2nd Guards Army as a powerful reserve for use against Rostov when the situation turned in his favor. This was one of the most potent formations in the Red Army and was ordered to move to the

Stalingrad area at top speed. However, the 2nd Guards Army was soon the center of a serious Russian dilemma: where to strike first—Paulus in Stalingrad, or Manstein and the relief force.[49]

When the Russian attack on December 2, failed to crack Stalingrad, Stalin decided to use the 2nd Guards Army against the city and ordered Vasilevsky, Rokossovsky, and Yeremenko to prepare a new plan to be ready no later than December 18. A new formation, the 5th Shock Army, would take the place of the 2nd Guards Army between the 5th Tank and the 51st Armies. Commanded by Lieutenant General M. M. Popov, the 5th Shock Army was composed of three guards rifle divisions, and one guards cavalry corps.[50] On December 9, Stalin reviewed the revised plan, which envisaged a three-stage operation to split up and eliminate the German 6th Army. On the Don Front, the 2nd Guards Army was to destroy the enemy forces west of the Rossosh River, then turn southeast of Voroponov in conjunction with the 6th Army from the Stalingrad Front, to liquidate the southern sector of the pocket. A final assault by both fronts would then be directed at Gurmak.[51]

The 4th Panzer Army's attack on December 12, forced another revision of the SATURN plan, which was now postponed until December 16, to allow for final preparations and troop movements. The 5th Tank Army had also failed to clear the Lower Chir which, if successful, would have isolated the 6th Army from the southeast and established good jumping off points for a later drive on Rostov.

The 5th Tank Army opened its attack on December 30, along a thirty-mile stretch of front between Oblivskaya and Rychkovsky with 50,000 troops, 900 guns and mortars, and seventy-two tanks. It was this force that compelled Manstein to commit the XLVIII Panzer Corps to hold the Chir Front.[52]

To crush the stiffening German resistance on the Chir Front, Popov's 5th Shock Army was formed to bolster the 5th Tank Army. This additional force included five rifle divisions, one tank corps, one mechanized corps, and one cavalry corps, totaling 71,000 men, 252 tanks, and 814 guns.[53]

While the 5th Tank and 5th Shock Armies were attempting to collapse the Chir Front, Yeremenko began to suspect a major German armored concentration at Kotelnikovo. Two cavalry divisions from the 4th Corps had already been severely mauled by the 6th Panzer Division in early December. On December 11, Vasilevsky decided on a new attack to split the German groups at Kotelnikovo and Nizhne Chirskaya using the 7th Tank Corps and two rifle divisions in a surprise assault on the German bridgehead at Rychkovsky. The 4th Corps and the 13th Mechanized Corps were pulled into reserve and the 58th Army was ordered to hold its position on the Stalingrad siege front to prevent a breakout by the 6th Army. The 51st Army was ordered to cover Kotelnikovo although it was a relatively weak formation.[54]

The German attack on December 12, forced yet another change in Russian plans. The thrust by the LVII Panzer Corps across the Aksay River threatened to expose the rear of the 57th Army covering Stalingrad. Something had to be done until reinforcements arrived. An improvised battlegroup of the 13th Tank Corps and the 4th Mechanized Corps was sent to block the path of the 6th and 23rd Panzer Divisions moving across the Aksay. On the night of December 12–13, the 4th Mechanized Corps, reduced to 5,600 men and seventy tanks (thirty-two T-34s and thirty-eight T-70s) took up its position at Verkhne Kumsky.[55] It was this force that would cause the most serious delay in the advance of the LVII Panzer Corps.

More significantly, Vasilevsky requested permission to move the 2nd Guards Army from the Don to the Stalingrad Front to block the German relief drive. This move, on December 13, effectively postponed the Russian assault to reduce the Stalingrad pocket. The 51st Army had already been ordered to hold the LVII Panzer Corps advance with its rifle divisions while the armor attacked the flanks. An immediate attack by the 5th Shock Army on the German bridgehead at Nizhne Chirskaya was also ordered. The next day, the 7th Tank Corps opened the assault, forcing the German troops out of the bridgehead and destroying the bridge over the Don behind them.[56]

The most substantial change that occurred as a result of Manstein's attack took place on December 14, when the Voronezh and Southwestern Fronts received new orders relating to SATURN. Rather than a single attack southward as originally intended (BIG SATURN), the attack was now to be directed southeast, into the rear of the approaching relief forces (LITTLE SATURN). The main blow, coming from the 5th Tank and 3rd Guards Armies, would be aimed in the direction of Nizhne Astakhov. The 1st Guards Army, with five rifle divisions and three tank corps, would attack through Mankovo, Kalitvenskaya, Degevo, Tatsinkaya, and Morosovskaya to destroy the Italian 8th Army and *Armee Abteilung* Hollidt. The 3rd Guards Army's task was to break through at Bokovskaya along the lines Bokovskaya-Nizhne Astakhov-Kashara and Bokovskaya-Verkhne Chirskaya-Tormosin area. The Russian 6th Army (Voronezh Front) was responsible for attacking Kantemirovka and reaching the line Golubaya-Krinitsa-Pasyubkov-Klenovy by the fifth day. Total forces on the approximately 200-mile front from Novaya Kalitva (6th Army) in the north to Nizhne Chirskaya (5th Tank Army) included thirty-six rifle divisions, 425,476 men, 1,030 tanks, and almost 5,000 guns and mortars.[57]

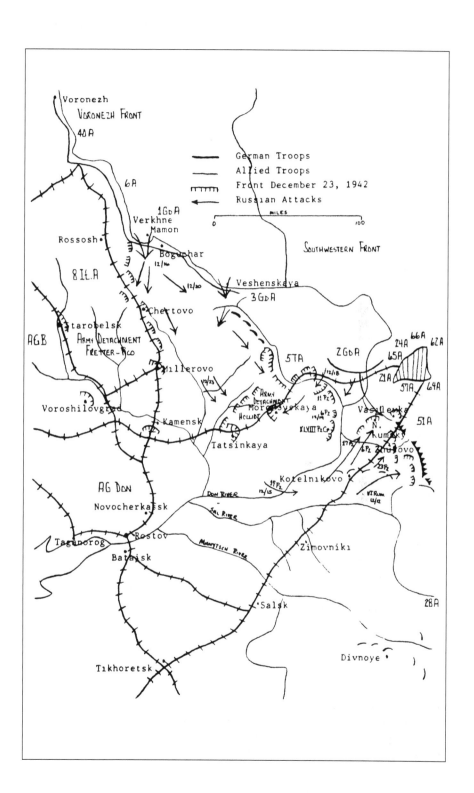

Led by the 6th and 23rd Panzer Divisions, the drive by the LVII Panzer Corps made initially good progress. By the end of the first day, the 6th Panzer Division had advanced to Samchin, about two-thirds of the way to the Aksay River. Early reports also indicated that except for two previously identified rifle divisions (126th and 302nd), no new forces had been introduced into the battle area west of the railroad in the Jesaulovsky-Askay sector.[58] The attack continued to make good progress on the second day, although Russian resistance was becoming more determined. Led by the dashing and energetic Colonel Huhnersdorff, the 11th Panzer Regiment, 6th Panzer Division (*Kampfgruppe* Huhnersdorff) crossed the Aksay at Salivesky and advanced as far as Verkhne Kumsky, where it was met by the Russian 4th Mechanized Corps.[59]

The village of Verkhne Kumsky lies in the Aksay Valley about seven miles north of the river at Salivesky. Approximately three miles south of the village the road passes through a rise. To the west of the road is Point 140, to the east is Hill 147. As the Germans approached, the Russians intended to push into the flank of the column from a depression south of Hill 147. As they reached the edge of the depression, however, they began to receive fire from German tanks that had taken up positions behind a low ridge of hills. Almost immediately, twelve Russian tanks were set ablaze, bringing the advance to a halt. The remainder of the tanks withdrew into the depression, where they were pursued by the Germans, who soon formed a ring around the depression. Caught in a tight pocket, the Russians formed a hedgehog but were unable to escape the withering fire being poured down on them by the German tanks.[60]

As the battle south of Hill 147 raged, German armored elements began to enter Verkhne Kumsky, but were soon engaged by Russian tanks hurrying to assist their encircled comrades. The Russian advance forced the Germans back to the northern edge of the village where, with the arrival of reinforcements, they were able to hold. When a Soviet armored brigade emerged on the eastern flank, the situation became critical, as it appeared that the German forces already at Verkhne Kumsky would be cut off.[61]

Suddenly, the sounds of battle coming from the hills south of the village ceased. At almost the same moment, the German units in Verkhne Kumsky received a message from Colonel Huhnersdorff to hold out until help arrived. Soon the familiar outline of German tanks appeared on both sides of Hill 147 as four wedge-shaped formations raced down the slopes.

It was now the Russians who found themselves in a critical situation as they sent out urgent pleas for help. It was clear that the Germans were attempting a double envelopment of their position. As the German tanks compressed their position, the Russians countered by bending back their flanks. But as the pressure along their flanks increased, the Russian position became more and more drawn out and vulnerable. When German tanks nearly blocked their last escape route, the Russians decided to withdraw rather than face elimination. As the Russian rearguard was being overrun, the main body escaped to the northeast.[62]

Despite having already defeated two enemy armored groups, the Germans knew that the battle was far from over. Radio intercepts indicated that the Russians were preparing a concentric assault on Verkhne Kumsky with numerically superior mechanized and armored forces. Huhnersdorff, who had advanced some twelve miles northeast of the village, was informed of the situation. Realizing that the Russian group approaching from the west would not reach him for at least one to two hours, Huhnersdorff decided first to strike a mechanized brigade moving from the east. The first attack hit the Russians on their west flank. As the Russians turned to meet this attack, they were struck by a second attack in the rear by a German force that approached undetected along a depression. In the confusion of battle, the motorized infantry following the Soviet tanks withdrew to the northwest and escaped.[63]

Delayed by German armored reconnaissance units, the Russian force moving from the west arrived too late to save the mechanized brigade. Turning northeast, the newly arrived tanks tried to attack the German battle group from the rear. They promptly ran into a German defense front that had been detached from the main body. During the tank duel that followed, the Germans were attacked in the rear by a Soviet motorized infantry. Meanwhile, Huhnersdorff had wheeled his panzers 180° back toward Verkhne Kumsky, where enemy tanks were already engaged with the garrison. These tanks were quickly destroyed, allowing the Germans to push through the village into the flank of the Russian western group, forcing them to retreat.[64]

While the opposing armored forces were engaged, Soviet infantry had managed to press in on the village from the northeast, bringing it under mortar fire. Some of these forces actually entered the village but were quickly driven back or destroyed by the Germans. The situation changed suddenly when several T-34s broke into the village, destroying a number of artillery and anti-tank pieces before they could be eliminated by German anti-tank teams. The garrison also received reports from reconnaissance tanks that strong Soviet armored forces were advancing on Point 140 southwest of the village with the intention of cutting it off. Once again Huhnersdorff had to turn his tanks 180°. Breaking through the Russian encirclement, the German tanks engaged the Russians on Point 140. Despite repeated efforts, the

Russians were unable to break German resistance. The Germans, however, had maintained an armored reserve that was now used in a counterattack against the Soviet flank, forcing the main body back.[65]

In the meantime, the defenders of Verkhne Kumsky had been surrounded. Responding to their calls for help, Huhnersdorff turned his tanks and for a second time broke through the Russian encirclement to free the garrison.[66]

Despite destroying over one hundred Russian tanks, as well as severely weakening parts of three armored and two mechanized brigades, the 11th Panzer Regiment was forced to abandon Verkhne Kumsky and retreat to the bridgehead at Salivesky.[67] This was primarily because the bridgehead there was not entirely secure. Ever since the 11th Panzer Regiment had advanced across the Aksay, the bridge at Salivesky had been threatened by Soviet forces from the area east of the bridge and around the Shutov railroad station. Part of the 6th Panzer Division was also covering Verkhne Yablotshny to the west.[68]

Shortly after *Kampfgruppe* Huhnersdorff had crossed the river to the north, Russian infantry, supported by several tanks, appeared along a dried out riverbed on the western flank of the bridgehead south of the Aksay River. This dry riverbed stretched for a few miles along the supply route of the German forces engaged at Verkhne Kumsky. Unable to cross the riverbed, which was approximately twelve feet deep and fifteen to thirty feet wide, the Russian tanks fired through gaps in the shrubbery at the German convoys moving toward Salivesky. This forced the Germans to shift their supply route to the east, out of range of the Russian tanks.[69]

Determined to halt the flow of supplies, two Soviet infantry battalions advanced across the riverbed while the tanks supported them from the bank. This attack was met by German small arms fire and driven back. During the afternoon, a Russian attack reached the east bank of the riverbed. Shortly afterward, eight to ten Soviet tanks also advanced from the riverbed. This was managed by using field improvisations and caught the Germans by surprise. Overrunning the German position, the tanks pushed across the bridge into the village. However, without the infantry to support them, the tanks were quickly destroyed.

Despite their previous failures, the Russians attacked Salivesky twice more on December 14, and again on the following day. Each time, the Russian tanks were allowed to pass by the German infantry, who were dug into trenches and foxholes. Once the tanks had passed, the Germans would emerge with devastating machine gun fire and force the infantry following the tanks back to their starting lines. Once the tanks entered the village, they became easy prey for the expert German tank-hunting teams.[70]

Almost immediately after the Germans withdrew to the Salivesky bridgehead, the Russians occupied Verkhne Kumsky and the hills to the south. On December 16, the 6th Panzer Division was ordered to make an assault on the Soviet position situated on these hills. Moving off from Kryloff, Huhnersdorff and the 11th Panzer Regiment were to clear and occupy the hills. To hold this extended range he was given the 2nd Battalion, 114th Infantry for support.[71]

The 11th Panzer Regiment easily overran the Russian position, but was unable to force the defenders from their foxholes. Using anti-tank rifles, the Russians opened fire at close range on the lightly armored personnel carriers following behind the tanks. As a result, the Germans were forced to withdraw without achieving their objective.[72]

On December 17, a second attempt was made to take the hill line, this time with the 6th Motorcycle Battalion and the dismounted 1st Battalion, 114th Infantry. At 0800 hours German artillery began shelling the Soviet positions. A few minutes later, the first assault groups advanced behind a cloud of dust, capturing the observation post and penetrating into the Russian defenses. Meanwhile, dive-bombers silenced the Russian artillery.[73]

By noon, the motorcyclists had cleared the enemy from their sector. An hour later the infantry did the same. This combined effort opened a gap about two miles wide which could now be exploited.

German reserves assembled for an attack on Verkhne Kumsky, which was reported to be strongly occupied. Air reconnaissance had identified numerous anti-tank guns and dug-in tanks along the edge of the village and the hills to either side. Given the usually high quality of Russian camouflage the Germans knew that there must be dozens of hidden guns. Soviet tanks were also observed to be moving toward the village from the west.

Because the area between the hills south of Verkhne Kumsky and the village itself was devoid of any natural cover, the Germans decided to wait until nightfall to make the final assault. In preparation, German artillery and aircraft bombarded the Russian positions that had been identified earlier. That night the Germans struck the village from three sides and forced the Russians back to the hills to the north.[74]

While the LVII Panzer Corps struggled east of the Don, the Russians intensified their efforts against the bridgehead at Nizhne Chirskaya. On December 12, air reconnaissance spotted approximately one thousand Soviet vehicles moving along the Don toward the Don-Chir bridge. It was also apparent that the Russians were increasing their artillery strength in the Chir bend and that they had stepped up their patrol activity and probing attacks. On December 13, the Russians introduced new tank and motorized forces along the front (5th Tank Army). The Rumanian 3rd Army reported that there were indications of a major enemy attack against the north front of the Chir. Throughout the day, the Russians launched numerous attacks between the Chir bridge at the Pershin railroad station and Nish Kalinovsky in an effort to expand their bridgeheads. For the most part, the Germans managed to contain the Soviet attacks in this area, but in the area north of the Don-Chir triangle, the Russians succeeded in capturing the northern end of the Rytshov bridge. There were also strong Soviet tank concentrations in this area.[75]

On December 14, the Russians inserted the 7th Tank corps into the battle in the Don-Chir triangle. This action proved to be decisive. By the end of the day, they had succeeded in overrunning Verkhne Chirskaya and cutting off the German garrison from the bridgehead. While the German forces there prepared the bridge for demolition, Manstein informed Hitler that it was essential to withdraw the forces that were still east of the Don because there were no other units available to stabilize the situation. Not even the 11th Panzer Division could be relied upon, because it was tied down farther west.[76]

By now, too, there were signs of a major Soviet buildup in the large bend of the Don on the left flank of Army Group Don. *Armee Abteilung* Hollidt had reported increased enemy movement and concentrations on both sides of the Chir opposite the Rumanian 14th Infantry Division in the area of Tshistyakovka. Concentrations were also spotted around Warlmov, Tshsyaka, and Astachov. On December 12, heavy vehicle and troop traffic was observed all along the front of *Armee Abteilung* Hollidt. This movement was accompanied by an increase in air and ground reconnaissance in the area opposite the Rumanian 14th and German 294th Infantry Divisions, between Demin and the heights east of Belavinsky. In addition, Soviet reinforcements were being moved through the Tustkan Valley toward Kamenka and the high ground east of the Kriusha Valley. There was also considerable movement in front of the German 62nd Infantry Division and the Rumanian I Corps around Yayodny and Nish Krivsky.[77]

While they were both concerned about the Russian activity, neither Hollidt nor Manstein seems to have felt alarm over this buildup or its implications. Reports from *Armee Abteilung* Hollidt stated only that "The conspicuous enemy movement indicates that it is perhaps a deceptive measure. On the other hand, it must be recognized that this concentration could be for an attack from the southwest or possibly northwest of Bokovskaya against the Rumanian 14th and 294th Infantry."[78] One day later Manstein reported to *OKH* that "A major attack does not yet appear imminent, because in the past days forces have been released and brought to the Chir Front."[79]

Whatever they may have felt about the situation developing along the Upper Chir, there was little that either Hollidt or Manstein could do. Hollidt had already taken the few countermeasures available to him. The sector held by the Rumanian 14th Infantry Division was subordinated to the command of the 294th Infantry Division. The little strength that was left in the 22nd Panzer Division (fourteen tanks) was assembled as a combined arms reserve behind the front at Marochin. A panzer grenadier regiment and an anti-tank detachment were concentrated west of Krasnoktskava, and a flak detachment was placed around Bokovskaya to stiffen the Rumanian I Corps.[80] Even with these measures, Hollidt knew that his forces were inadequate for carrying out their task, writing to Manstein that the "Holding of the Chir Front and the Kriusha Front as well as the defense of the deep flank of Army Group Don and the 8th Italian Army cannot be guaranteed."[81]

On December 16, the Russians launched their LITTLE SATURN attacks against *Armee Abteilung* Hollidt and the Italian 8th Army in Army Group B's sector. Three divisions broke through against the Rumanian 14th Infantry Division, but the situation was restored by inserting the 22nd Panzer Division and parts of the 294th Infantry Division. In the area of Bokosovskaya, the Russians attacked with three to four regiments supported by forty to sixty tanks and penetrated the main line at several points. Another Soviet group, including about fifteen tanks, hit the Rumanian 7th Infantry Division between Nish Kaliniky and Srel Gremok and created a breach about two and a half miles wide and two miles deep. Heavy air attacks were made against the 294th and Rumanian 14th Infantry Divisions throughout the day. Meanwhile, fresh Soviet forces were arriving from the east. The following day the 294th Infantry Division was attacked by the 14th Guards and 266th Rifle Divisions supported by about one hundred tanks. This attack succeeded in capturing the Kriusha Valley and opening a gap between the 294th and 62nd Infantry Division to the north, a situation that prompted *OKH* to order the left flank of *Armee Abteilung* Hollidt and the right flank of the XXIX Corps of Army Group B to withdraw to prepare blocking positions.[82]

On December 18, the rapidly deteriorating situation in *Armee Abteilung* Hollidt and the Italian 8th Army became highly critical. Italian resistance, which had been weak at best, crumbled, exposing the left flank of *Armee Abteilung* Hollidt. To the south, the German and Rumanian forces were too weak and too few in number to contain the breakthroughs and maintain a defensive front. By the end of the day these forces had been pushed to the west bank of the Chir.[83]

The following day, Hitler issued orders to secure the use of the Rossosh-Millerovo railroad, which ran roughly parallel to the front from just inside Army Group Don's sector to the north. This railroad, which was approximately ninety miles from the front at Millerovo, but only eighteen miles from the front at Rossosh, was in danger of being cut by the Russian breakthroughs. Meanwhile, *Armee Abteilung* Hollidt managed to piece together a thin screen, reestablishing contact with the Italians and the 62nd Infantry Division. Despite this, several Soviet mobile groups roamed the rear areas virtually unopposed.[84]

During the next few days, *Armee Abteilung* Hollidt carried out a series of withdrawals, both in an effort to solidify the front and in response to the mobile groups in its deep flank. This situation was made more difficult by the unauthorized withdrawal of the Italian *Celere* Division as well as the Rumanian 7th Infantry Division and the staff of the Rumanian I Corps. Hitler himself added to the confusion when he ordered *Armee Abteilung* Hollidt to hold a line that had long been overtaken by events. Despite all efforts, *Armee Abteilung* Hollidt was able only to impede the Soviet advance and not to stop it. By December 24, its front had been pushed south to Artemov on the Chir. From there, a thin screen of strongpoints and *kampfgruppen* stretched to the west and south along the Gnilaya-Bystraya River to Tatsinkaya. Here the Russians had captured the airfield, cutting one of the few remaining vital links with Stalingrad.[85]

The LVII Panzer Corps, meanwhile, was still struggling against Russian forces on the hills north of Verkhne Kumsky. This area was finally cleared by the 17th Panzer Division, which had crossed the Aksay at Generalov on December 17. This action eliminated the last significant resistance north of the river. However, at the same time, long columns of Soviet infantry and vehicles were spotted moving across the Donskaya Tsaritsa valley and moving south.[86]

On December 19, elements of the 17th Panzer Division reached the Myshkova sector at Nish Kimsky. The next day, the 6th Panzer Division seized a crossing at Vesilyvka. The Russians, determined to deny the Germans any further advance, continued to move in new forces from the northeast, north, and northwest, including the 6th Motorized Corps. To the south, the 23rd Panzer Division fought off heavy attacks from the east, attempting to cut off the Jesaulovsky-Aksay sector.[87]

Despite now being only thirty miles from Stalingrad, Manstein was not optimistic about the LVII Panzer Corps' chances of reaching the pocket. He had already written to Hitler that "It is impossible for the LVII Panzer Corps alone to establish a land link with the 6th Army, to say nothing of maintaining the link. A breakout by the 6th Army to the southwest is the last alternative. At least most of the troops and mobile weapons of the army will be preserved."[88]

To accomplish this, it was necessary for the forces within the pocket to shift to the southwest, abandoning the northern part of the fortress area in stages. The 6th Army was then to break out and establish a link with LVII Panzer Corps around Yerik Myshkova. Of course, the 6th

Army would have to be adequately supplied by air. In any case, the 6th Army would need several days to regroup and bring up its fuel supplies.[89]

There was already mounting pressure against the north flank of the Rumanian 4th Army, making it urgently necessary to bring up mobile forces from the Caucasus Front to cover the right flank of LVII Panzer Corps. Manstein warned that "In case of further delays, it is foreseeable that the LVII Panzer Corps will bog down on or north to the Upper Myshkova or be tied down by enemy attacks on its right flank."[90]

These misgivings were supported by Hoth, who on December 21, wrote to Manstein to express concern over his threatened positions on the Aksay. Here Hoth feared that "As soon as the enemy realizes the weakness on the eastern flank, he will attack using his less valuable troops to quickly take this region where, just as in November, Rumanian troops are standing without adequate anti-tank defenses and without German forces to back them up.

"These extended dispositions are ripe for a rapid collapse of the entire front that can be expected any day."[91]

After failing to receive a reply from Hitler to allow the 6th Army to break out of Stalingrad, Manstein sent a message to Paulus instructing him to prepare his forces to assist the LVII Panzer Corps in establishing a link with the pocket (i.e., expand the pocket to the southwest). If the LVII Panzer Corps was unable to cover the distance necessary to make contact, then the 6th Army, upon receipt of the codeword THUNDERCLAP, was to break out to meet the approaching relief force.[92]

Paulus, however, was unwilling to execute this plan, arguing that he had only enough fuel to cover fifteen to twenty miles. Furthermore, Hitler, although agreeing that the pocket should be expanded to the southwest, demanded that the northern front be held as well. On December 21, Manstein made one final effort to persuade Hitler to allow the 6th Army to break out. Hitler replied by telling him that Paulus had only enough fuel for fifteen to twenty miles.[93]

By this time Manstein could no longer ignore the threat against *Armee Abteilung* Holliat, and on December 23, the 11th Panzer Division was ordered to the western flank to protect the airfields at Tatsinkaya and Morosovskaya. To make good this loss, the 4th Panzer Army was forced to give up the 6th Panzer Division, without which the Lower Chir could not be held.[94]

Since the relief drive had begun, the Russians had moved in over nineteen divisions, 149,000 men, 635 tanks, and over 1,500 guns to keep the 4th Panzer Army from reaching Stalingrad. Four rifle divisions, five to seven motorized brigades, and four tank brigades had opposed the drive by the LVII Panzer Corps. On the other hand, by December 24, the 23rd and 17th Panzer Divisions had only thirty-five tanks between them and only about 2,000 infantrymen.[95] This weakness, together with the loss of the 6th Panzer Division and the fact that no new reinforcements could be expected in time for a renewed drive, effectively ended the attempted relief drive on Stalingrad and forced the LVII Panzer Corps over to the defensive to hold what it had gained.

That Manstein carried a sense of guilt over his failure to relieve the 6th Army is revealed in his memoirs. Reflecting on the problems that led to failure, namely Hitler's insistence that Stalingrad be held, inadequate air supply of the 6th Army, delays in assembling the relief group, and the Soviet attack on the Italian front that kept *Armee Abteilung* Hollidt from taking any action to relieve Stalingrad Manstein concludes that:

> Anyone who witnessed the subsequent tragedy of Stalingrad
> . . . will conclude that it would have been better to insist on an
> immediate breakout by the Sixth Army.
> It is fair to assume that at least some of the besieged formations
> would have managed to fight their way through to the remnants
> of the Fourth Panzer Army—certainly the tanks and probably a
> number of the infantry battalions as well.[96]

Even if the 6th Army had been successful in its breakout efforts, there was still the very real possibility that it would not reach the German lines, especially as the Russians had by this time launched their LITTLE SATURN offensive, designed to pinch off the relief drive by the 4th Panzer Army. These forces, together with the forces that would have been released from the encirclement once the 6th Army escaped, would probably have trapped not only the 6th Army, but the 4th Panzer Army as well.

In light of these circumstances, and given the fact that Manstein had already expressed fears over a possible Soviet attack to reach Rostov, was there any reason to risk sending a relief force to Stalingrad at all? Certainly the Russians were determined not to let the 6th Army slip away.

The answer to this question is complex. For political and moral reasons Manstein was compelled to make at least an attempt to save the 6th Army. Above this, however, was Manstein's hope that the 6th Army could be brought safely out of Stalingrad to support the southern flank. An immediate breakout by the 6th Army in November would have released a horde of Soviet troops against an already shattered German front. The longer the Russians tied themselves down at Stalingrad, the better chance that the southern flank could be stabilized and solidified. In addition, there was the possibility that the Soviet forces besieging the 6th Army would exhaust themselves and facilitate an attempted German breakout or relief effort. However, Operation LITTLE SATURN routed the Italian 8th Army and ended any hope that the Germans would have time to strengthen their defenses. The critical task now became to reach the 6th army as quickly as possible. This could best be accomplished by a breakout by the 6th Army to meet the approaching 4th Panzer Army.

By this time, however, it was too late. Manstein was justified in allowing the 6th Army to fight on in Stalingrad, but he waited too long to make the decision for Paulus to breakout. Under the circumstances, the timing for the relief/breakout effort was a delicate matter. Manstein had to judge just how long he could allow the 6th Army to remain in Stalingrad: If he acted prematurely, additional Soviet forces would be added to the already overwhelming numbers that were attacking Army Group Don. If he waited too long, the 6th Army might be too weak and unable to fight its way out.

Manstein's failure was a result of a number of factors. While the LVII Panzer Corps made good progress, it was too weak to reach Stalingrad alone. This was especially true after the Russians committed the 2nd Guards Army to block the German relief drive. Manstein had anticipated that some of the forces investing Stalingrad would be diverted to meet the 4th Panzer Army, thus facilitating the 6th Army's breakout. However, Manstein underestimated the Soviet response to meet the German relief effort.

Given Soviet determination to eliminate the 6th Army, perhaps nothing short of a major offensive could have saved it even if the 6th Army made an independent breakout. In December 1942, the Germans were incapable of mounting a major offensive.

The fact that the 6th Army never made a breakout attempt can be traced to four factors. First, Hitler had absolutely forbidden Paulus to attempt a breakout. Second, even though it appeared that Manstein was willing to take responsibility for ordering Paulus to break out, the codeword was never sent. Then there is the question of whether Paulus would have obeyed Manstein and disobeyed a direct order from Hitler. Finally, there was Manstein's opposition to an independent breakout, until December 19, when it was too late, if not impossible.

Paulus had been hesitant to order a breakout of his army when Stalingrad was first surrounded, preferring instead to request permission from Hitler.[97] To obey Manstein now would have been in direct conflict with Hitler's order. Still, there was a chance that he might have done so. After all, SS Lieutenant General Paul Hausser, commanding the II SS Panzer Corps, would later abandon Kharkov despite similar orders from Hitler.

Perhaps the best explanation why Paulus never attempted a breakout is that he had no intention of making an attempt. His arguments concerning his fuel supply were specious. As a rule, military units have more supplies and are more capable of action than they would have their higher headquarters believe. Then there is the fact that, by his own admission, Paulus could have covered the necessary distance to the LVII Panzer Corps by reducing the number of vehicles by thirty percent.[98]

Curiously, Manstein neglects any discussion of why he never sent the codeword, THUNDERCLAP, for Paulus to break out. There are two possible explanations why Manstein never sent the codeword. By November 19, Manstein may have realized that Paulus, broken and dispirited about the condition and eventual fate of his army, was seized by paralysis and therefore was unable or unwilling to act. On the other hand, Manstein may have decided that by this time it was better to sacrifice the 6th Army to keep the Russian forces that were investing Stalingrad from adding their weight to the attacks farther west. However, if Manstein did indeed make a conscious decision to sacrifice the 6th Army, it does not explain why he allowed the LVII Panzer Corps to remain on the Myshkova until December 24, when it was forced to withdraw when threatened with envelopment.

Despite the fact that there was no breakout attempt, and that the relief effort failed, the thrust by the 4th Panzer Army did have a positive effect on the overall strategic situation. Even though it failed, the relief effort was the single most important factor in extending the life of the 6th Army.

One of the reasons Manstein did not immediately advocate a breakout was his belief that this task would be made easier by the approaching relief forces. The original plan for a relief effort was to be carried out by two groups, one east and one west of the Don. By advancing west of the Don, German forces would relieve some of the pressure on the 6th Army by drawing off Russian forces from Stalingrad. The thrust by the second group into the Soviet front east of the Don was designed to draw off forces there, thus improving the chances for a breakout.

This is, in fact, exactly what happened when the 4th Panzer Army started its drive. However, the Russian forces that were initially sent to prevent the advance of the LVII Panzer Corps were only the weak forces of the 51st Army. At the same time, the Soviets were increasing their strength against the Lower Chir by moving in fresh forces. This was in anticipation of a German drive toward Stalingrad from this sector and as a preliminary move for an advance on the airfields at Morosovskaya and Tatsinkaya.

The most decisive action, as far as the 6th Army was concerned, took place on December 13, when Vasilevsky convinced Stalin to transfer the 2nd Guards Army, earmarked for the attack on Stalingrad, to the Stalingrad Front to block the German relief drive. While the reinforced 51st Army threatened the LVII Panzer Corps' right flank, the 2nd Guards Army menaced its left. Together the two Russian armies were threatening to envelop the 23rd and 17th Panzer Divisions.

The mounting pressure against the north flank of the Rumanian 4th Army, which threatened the LVII Panzer Corps right flank, was probably enough to force it to abandon its advance. The introduction of the 2nd Guards Army would eventually compel the LVII Panzer Corps to withdraw from the Myshkova sector and end any hope of reaching Stalingrad.

The shifting of the 2nd Guards Army was the critical factor in postponing the Russian assault on Stalingrad. The decisive factor in keeping the LVII Panzer Corps from making more progress than it did, and perhaps from reaching Stalingrad, was the battle around Verkhne Kumsky. Here, relatively modest Russian forces delayed the 6th and 23rd Panzer Divisions for five days (December 13–18), allowing time for more powerful Soviet forces to be concentrated on the Myshkova to stop the German drive.

Manstein asserts that had the 17th Panzer Division been available from the outset, the LVII Panzer Corps could have reached Stalingrad. This claim can be discounted. According to the commander of the division, General Fridolin von Senger und Etterlin, the 17th Panzer Division had only fifty-four tanks and 2,300 panzer grenadiers when it reached the front on December 17.[99] There is no reason to believe that this formation would have been substantially stronger if it had arrived earlier. It would have had to travel the same distance under roughly the same conditions regardless of when it was released by *OKH*. In any case, the time lost in waiting for the LVII Panzer Corps to arrive from the Caucasus could not have been made up, nor could the time lost in forcing the Russians back from Verkhne Kumsky.

The delays here were caused both by the stubborn and determined resistance of the Russians, who were responsible for barring the German advance, and by the Germans themselves. The ten-hour battle by *Kampfgruppe* Huhnersdorff for Verkhne Kumsky on December 13, was ultimately decided in favor of the Germans. But, because of the unsecured supply route over the Aksay at Salivesky, the *Kampfgruppe* was forced to abandon the village it had just won. Once back on the Aksay, the Germans were delayed two days while they cleared the area of enemy forces and secured the bridgehead from further attack. By the time they were ready to advance again on December 16, the Russians had occupied the range of hills south of Verkhne Kumsky. Two days were needed to clear this ridge. By the time the Russians were forced from the hills north of Verkhne Kumsky on December 18, and the advance resumed, it was too late.

It was on December 18, that the Italians and *Armee Abteilung* Hollidt were struck by the first blows of the LITTLE SATURN offensive. Soon it would no longer be a question of rescuing the 6th Army, but the entire southern flank as well. Still, Manstein was determined that the 6th Army should be given an opportunity to escape, even after virtually all resistance along the Upper Chir had collapsed and the Russians threatened to isolate the front. From December 19–24, the LVII Panzer Corps remained exposed on the Myshkova waiting for the 6th Army to breakout. It was only when the situation on his western flank became completely untenable that Manstein was willing to accept failure. Even then, rather than order the LVII Panzer Corps to withdraw, he kept the 23rd Panzer and 17th Panzer Divisions on the Myshkova in the vain hope that Hitler would allow Paulus to break out.

Manstein's decision to leave the LVII Panzer Corps exposed on the Myshkova after the debacle along the Chir must be questioned. By that time there was little doubt that the Russians were trying to isolate the Chir Front and cut off the relief force, not to mention the threat to Rostov and the communications of the entire southern flank. In spite of this he persisted in keeping his most potent and mobile forces tied down east of the Don, exactly what he had warned Hitler against in his appraisal of December 9!

Notes

1. Quoted in Clark, p. 251.
2. Heeresgruppe Don Ia, Anlagenband 2 u. 3 z. KTB, November 27–December 14, 1942, Microcopy T 311, Roll 268, Frame 862. Cited henceforth as HG Don Anlg. 2/3 KTB with date, roll and frame number. Manstein, p. 295.
3. HG Don Anlg. 2/3 KTB, November 22, 1942, Roll 268, Frame 859. Manstein, p. 295.
4. HG Don Anlg. 2/3 KTB, November 24, 1942, Frame 838.
5. Ibid.
6. Manstein, p. 304.
7. Newton.
8. Kehrig, p. 570.
9. HG Don Anlg. 2/3 KTB, November 28, 1942, Roll 268, Frames 713–718.

10. Newton.

11. Quoted in Ibid.

12. Ibid.

13. Newton.

14. Ibid. HG Don Anlg. 2/3 KTB, November 29–30, 1942, Frames 621, 702, 809.

15. Newton.

16. Quoted in Mellenthin, *Panzer Battles*, p. 220.

17. Historical Division Headquarters, USA, Europe, Foreign Military Studies, Ms P060g part 3, *Small Unit Tactics: Unusual Situations, the Stalingrad Area,* by Erhard Rauss Gen. d.Pz. a.D., p. 2. Cited henceforth as Ms 060g. Ms P114c, p. 54. Manstein, p. 322.

18. HG Don Anlg. 2/3, November 21, 1942, Roll 268, Frame 771. Ms P114c, p. 544. Manstein, pp. 321–322.

19. This improvised battlegroup was composed of remnants of the Rumanian 3rd Army, the German liason staff to the Rumanian 3rd Army, as well as various German units.

20. HR Don Anlg. 2/3 KTB, December 1, 1942, Roll 268, Frame 558. Manstein, pp. 322–323.

21. HG Don Anlg. 2/3 KTB, December 1, 1942, Roll 268, Frame 558.

22. Ibid., Frames 553–555.

23. Newton.

24. Panzer Armeeoberkommando 4 Ia, Anlagenband C 2 z. KTB Nr. 5, Teil III, August 19–December 31, 1942, T 313, Roll 356, Frame 8,641,163. Cited henceforth as 4 Pz AOK Anlg. 2 KTB, with date, roll, and frame number.

25. HG Don Anlg. 2/3 KTB, December 4, 1942, Roll 268, Frame 353.

26. Hermann Balck, *Ordnung im Chaos, Erinnerungen 1893–1948* (Onsabruck: Bibilo Verlag, 1981), p. 399. XLVIII Panzer Corps Ia, Kriegstagebuch, December 1–31, 1942, Microcopy T 314, Roll 1160, Frames 691–692. Cited henceforth as XLVIII Pz Cp. KTB, with date, roll, and frame number.

27. Newton.

28. Balck, pp. 401–402. 11th Panzer Division Anlagenband 1–4 z. KTB 6, November 1–December 31, 1942, Microcopy T 315, Roll 595, Frames 105, 139–140. Cited henceforth as 11th Pz Div. Anlg. 1–4 KTB 6, with date, roll, and frame number. HG Don Anlg. 2/3 KTB, December 7–8, 1942, Roll 268, Frames 1394, 1448–1449, 1512.

29. HG Don Anlg. 2/3 KTB, December 8–10, 1942, Roll 268, Frames 1196–1198.

30. Ibid., December 11–12, 1942, Frames 1050, 1132–1133, 1135, 1138. 11th Pz Div. Anlg. 1–4 KTB 6, December 9–13, 1942, Roll 595, Frames 212–213, 286–287, 331, 414–415. December 15, 1942, Frames 537–538. Balck, pp. 403–407.

31. Ibid., December 11–12, 1942, Frames 1050, 1132–1133, 1135, 1138. 11th Pz Div. Anlg. 1–4 KTB 6, December 9–13, 1942, Roll 595, Frames 212–213, 286–287, 331, 414–415, 462–463. December 15, 1942, Frames 537–538. Balck, pp. 403–407.

32. Samuel W. Mitcham, *Hitler's Legions: The German Order of Battle in World War II* (New York: Stein and Day Publishers, 1985), pp. 78–79.

33. HG Don Anlr. 2/3 KTB, December 10–12, 1942, Roll 268, Frames 1050, 1111, 1135, 1181, 1184, 1192.

34. Ibid., Frame 1134.
35. Ibid., December 1, 1942, Frames 538, 564.
36. Ibid., December 2, 1942, Frames 514, 532.
37. Ms P060g, pp. 7–17.
38. HG Don Anlg. 2/3 KTB, December 7–10, 1942, Roll 268, Frames 1181, 1191, 1195, 1263, 1296, 1384, 1402, 1409, 1448.
39. Ibid., December 7, 1942, Frame 1448.
40. Ibid., December 9, 1942, Frame 1274.
41. Ibid., Frame 1275.
42. Ibid., Frames 1271–1275.
43. Ibid., Frames 1275–1276.
44. Manstein, p. 305.
45. Ibid.
46. Ibid., pp. 306–307.
47. LVII Panzer Corps Ia, Anlagen 4 u. 5 z. KTB, September 1–December 31, 1942, T 314, Roll 1482, Frames 200–202.
48. John Erickson, *The Road to Berlin: Continuing the History of Stalin's War With Germany* (Boulder, Colorado: Westview Press, 1983), p. 6.
49. Ibid., p. 7.
50. Ibid., pp. 8–9.
51. Ibid., pp. 9–10.
52. Ibid., p. 10.
53. Ibid., pp. 10–11.
54. Ibid., p. 11.
55. Ibid., p. 12.
56. Ibid., pp. 12–13.
57. Ibid., pp. 13–14, 17.
58. HG Don Anlg. 2/3 KTB, December 12, 1942, Roll 268, Frames 1055–1056.
59. This unit was substantially reinforced and included 143 tanks, the 2nd Battalion, 114th Infantry, the 1st Company, 6th Anti-tank Regiment, the 57th Engineers, and the 9th Heavy Battery, 76th Artillery Regiment. 4 Pz AOK Anlg. 2 KTB, December 13, 1942, Frames 8, 641, 134-8, 641, 135. Ms P060g, pp. 31-32. Retained in the *Reichswehr* after World War I, by 1938 Huhnersdorff held the post of operations officer at the 1st Panzer Division where he preceeded Wenck and worked with Kirchner who commanded the 1st Panzer Brigade. His superior ability as an operations officer of the II Corps during the campaign in the West was rewarded in 1941, when he was promoted to chief of staff of Hoth's *Panzergruppe* 3. Under Hoth, Huhnersdorff quickly learned that speed and maneuver were the keys to German success against superior Russian numbers. By 1942, Huhnersdorff enjoyed the personal confidence of not only the division but the corps and army commanders as well and was the logical choice to command the German relief drive. Later promoted to the rank of major general, he commanded the 6th Panzer Division at the battle of Kursk where he received a mortal head wound. Newton. Mitcham, pp. 355-356.
60. Ms P060g, pp. 32-33.
61. Ibid., pp. 33-34.

62. Ibid., pp. 34–35.
63. Ibid., p. 50.
64. Ibid., p. 36.
65. Ibid., pp. 36–37.
66. Ibid., pp. 37–38.
67. The actual number given by General Raus, the commander of the 6th Panzer Division, is closer to 120–125. This figure is probably too high, because he also claims that the 11th Panzer Regiment had 160 PzKw long barrel 75mm guns. Figures taken from the daily reports of the 4th Panzer Army for December 11, show that the 6th Panzer Division had only 143 tanks, of which only 23 were PzKw long barrel. Raus admits to 30 tanks lost, of which 22 were repaired by December 16.
68. HG Don Anlg. 2/3 KTB, December 13, 1942, Roll, 268, Frames 992, 1000.
69. Ms P060g, pp. 40–41.
70. Ibid., p. 41. HG Don Anlg. 2/3 KTB, December 14, 1942, Roll 268, Frames 892, 895, 900. Heeresgruppe Don Ia, Anlagenband 4 z. KTB, December 15–23, 1942, Microcopy T 313, Roll 269, Frames 264–266. Cited henceforth as HG Don Anlg. 4 KTB with date, roll, and frame number.
71. Ms P060g, p. 43.
72. Ibid., p. 44. HG Don Anlg. 4 KTB, December 16, 1942, Roll 269, Frame 625.
73. Ms P060g, p. 46. HG Don Anlg. 4 KTB, December 17, 1942, Roll 269, Frame 557.
74. Ms P060g, p. 47. HG Don Anlg. 4 KTB, December 17–18, 1942, Roll 269, Frames 506, 512, 553–554, 557–559.
75. HG Don Anlg. 2/3 KTB, December 12–13, 1942, Roll 268, Frames 991, 993, 997, 1000–1001, 1048, 1050, 1053.
76. Ibid., December 14, 1942, Frames 592, 895. The Russians had five corps on the Chir Front between Rytshov and Lobstsh (about 65 miles). From Rytshov to Verkhne Chirskaya was the 7th Tank Corps. Between the Chir railroad station and Ostrovsky was the 3rd Cavalry and 1st Tank Corps. Between Surovinkino and the Skretev railroad station was the 5th Motorized Corps and between Sekretev and Lobatsh was the 8th Cavalry Corps.
77. Ibid., December 11–12, 1942, Frames 1029–1030, 1044–1045, 1050, 1053–1054.
78. Ibid., December 12, 1942, Frame 1054.
79. Ibid., December 13, 1942, Frame 991.
80. Ibid., Frame 998.
81. Ibid., December 12, 1942, Frame 1068.
82. HG Don Anlg. 4 KTB, December 16–18, 1942, Roll 269, Frames 522, 560–561, 613, 630.
83. Ibid., December 18, 1942, Frames 507, 515.
84. Ibid., December 19, 1942, Frames 429–430, 434, 499–500.
85. Ibid., December 20–23, 1942, Frames, 73–74, 99, 116, 119, 137, 156–157, 163, 166, 178, 276–277, 282–284, 308–310, 365–366, 395–396, 427. Heeresgruppe Don Ia, Anlagenband 5 z. KTB, December 24, 1942–January 3, 1943, Microcopy T313, Roll 270, Frames 731, 735–736, 784. Cited henceforth as HG Don Anlg. 5 KTB, with date, roll, and frame number.
86. HG Don Anlg. 4 KTB, December 18, 1942, Roll 269, Frames 506–507, 512–513.

87. Ibid., December 19–20, 1942, Roll 269, Frames 308–309, 428, 736–737.
88. Ibid., December 19, 1942, Frame 469.
89. Ibid., Frames 469–470.
90. Ibid., Frame 470.
91. Ibid., December 21, 1942, Frames 202–203.
92. Ibid., December 19, 1942, Frames 463–464.
93. Ibid., December 21, 1942, Frames 205–206. Manstein, p. 337.
94. HG Don Anlg. 4 KTB, December 22–23, 1942, Roll 269, Frames 70, 100, 281. HG Don Anlg. 5 KTB, December 24, 1942, Roll 270, Frame 793.
95. Erickson, p. 23. HG Don Anlg. 5 KTB, December 24, 1942, Roll 270, Frame 738.
96. Manstein, p. 307.
97. Ibid., 303.
98. Clark, p. 273.
99. HG Don Anlg. 4 KTB, December, 18, 1942, Roll 269, Frame 513. Historical Division Headquarters, USA, Europe, Foreign Military Studies, Lecture by General Fridolin von Senger und Etterlin, *Failure of a Relief Mission*, pp. 2–3.

CHAPTER 3

Disaster on the Left, Decision on the Right

The Russian attacks against the LVII Panzer Corps on the Myshkova successfully blunted the 4th Panzer Army's relief drive and with it, the only real chance that the Germans had for freeing the 6th Army from Stalingrad. It was also clear that these attacks were intended to envelop the LVII Panzer Corps from the east and west. To prevent this, it was necessary for the corps to withdraw to Kotelnikovo and out of range of Stalingrad.

While Army Group Don had failed in its initial task—the relief of the 6th Army—it was still responsible for maintaining the southern wing of the Eastern Front. This included the forces not only of Army Group Don, but of Army Group A as well.

The successful execution of this mission would be difficult, at best, under any circumstances. Given the existing conditions of winter (the worst of which was yet to come), vastly superior enemy forces, troops that had been engaged in nearly continuous defensive fighting since mid-November, and with little prospect of receiving adequate replacements, to say nothing of reinforcements, the task now confronting Manstein and Army Group Don appeared nearly insurmountable.

Under normal circumstances, the 4th Panzer Army could have been expected to hold its own line of communications and that of Army Group A open through Rostov. It was, however, nearly impossible to expect it to do so when the northern flank of Army Group A was still nearly 200 miles from Rostov, and the bulk of the army was still engaged in the Caucasus with no immediate hope for its withdrawal. Moreover, the entire situation was complicated by the fact that superior Soviet forces threatened to outflank the 4th Panzer Army.

It was the task of covering the flank of the 1st Panzer Army that, more than any other responsibility, made the problem of maintaining the southern flank so extremely dangerous and difficult for Manstein and Army Group Don. As long as the 4th Panzer Army was forced to cover the 1st Panzer Army, the entire position of Army Group Don was compromised, because the remainder of its units were forced to defend either the large bend of the Don or the Donets, positions that themselves became increasingly vulnerable and in danger of being outflanked.

Manstein's situation could have been greatly alleviated had Hitler been willing to allow the 1st Panzer Army to retreat. As early as December 20, Manstein had alerted *OKH* to the fact that "There is no doubt that the enemy seeks his main decision against Army Group Don and the Caucasus Front."[1] At the same time, he pointed out that the Russians would next push on Army Group B and attempt to drive on Rostov.

This message should have alerted Hitler of the need at least to order preparations to be made for the withdrawal of Army Group A from the Caucasus. However, just as in the period immediately after the Russian breakthrough in November, Hitler's indecision limited the strategic options available to Manstein. Until Hitler allowed Army Group A to pull out of the Caucasus, Manstein was compelled to carry on the fight south of the Don, exposing the 4th Panzer Army to the danger of encirclement. As long as the 4th Panzer Army was forced to fight south of the Don, the remaining formations of Army Group Don were themselves forced to maintain positions that became increasingly untenable. The dangers that threatened Army Group Don, as well as the southern flank, were greatly complicated by the Russian offensives launched in mid-January.

According to Manstein, the ideal solution, once any hope of liberating the 6th Army was lost, was to abandon the territory gained in the summer campaign. To accomplish this, it was necessary to transfer forces of Army Group Don and Army Group A from the eastern extremities of the front, first behind the Lower Don or Donets, and then to the Lower Dnieper. Hitler, however, was opposed to any plan that called for the surrender of territory.[2]

Because *OKH* reserves were insufficient to secure the line of communications over the Lower Don and Dnieper, it was necessary for Army Group Don to retract its eastern flank and to shift the forces that were released to the western flank. Of course, this movement had to be timed and initiated in such a way that the forces being shifted from the east to west arrived one step ahead of the Russians, in time to intercept the outflanking movements as they gradually extended farther and farther west. However, this entire movement was made considerably more difficult because the right flank of Army Group B, and eventually the entire army group as well, was in the process of complete collapse. Moreover, sufficient forces could not be shifted to the west without relying on the forces of Army Group A, which were not under Manstein's command.[3]

On the Trans-Caucasus Front, General I. V. Tyulenev had already submitted his plan for the liberation of Maikop. However, on December 29, he was told to scrap his plan and to prepare a new operation designed to encircle Army Group A. The encirclement was to be carried out by two Russian drives, one by the Black Sea Group attacking through Krasnodar toward Tikhoretsk, and a second by the Southern Front (the newly designated Stalingrad Front, as of January 1), using the 51st and 28th Armies attacking through Salsk toward Tikhoretsk. The Trans-Caucasian Front was also to attack the right flank of the 17th Army and to seize the Taman Peninsula to keep the Germans from escaping to Crimea.[4]

Tyulenev proposed two operations: The first was intended to break the defenses of the 17th Army and to drive to the Kuban River and Krasnodon; the second attack would use the left flank of the 47th Army and an amphibious landing to clear the Germans from Novorossik. Stalin approved the plan, but stressed the fact that the 1st Panzer Army was beginning to pull out of the northern Caucasus and that it was necessary to reach the Tikhoretsk area to stop the enemy from moving west. The main assignment was formalized in a STAVKA directive on January 4, ordering the Black Sea Group to strike for Bataisk-Azov and to slip into Rostov from the east to cut off Army Group A.[5]

To trap the 1st Panzer Army, close cooperation was necessary between the Southern Front and the two groups of the Trans-Caucasus Front (Black Sea and Northern). While the Black Sea Group prepared to attack toward Krasnodon-Tikhoretsk, the Southern Front would attack in two directions; with its left flank (28th and 51st Armies) toward Salsk-Tikhoretsk, and with its right flank (5th Tank, 2nd Guards, and 5th Shock Armies) along the Lower Don toward Rostov.[6]

Already weakened from the fighting around Kotelnikovo in December, the Russian forces were now moving farther from their supply bases. The 51st and 28th Armies also ran into stubborn resistance at Zimovniky, which was not cleared until January 7. To close the open flank, the armor of the 2nd Guards Army was committed between the Don and Sal rivers. On the right flank, Popov's 5th Shock and part of the 2nd Guards and 51st Armies had reached the Manytsch River, between its mouth and the Proletarskaya railroad station. The 3rd Guards Corps (formerly the 7th Tank Corps) formed the core of a mechanized group composed of the 2nd and 6th Motorized Corps and the 98th Rifle Division, which the Soviets hoped to use to seize Rostov and Bataisk in a rapid drive.[7]

On December 24, the 2nd Guards Army attacked the LVII Panzer Corps on the Myshkova, pushing it back to the Aksay. On December 25, the 4th Panzer Army reported that the LVII Panzer Corps had sustained considerable losses in men and matériel. The same day, the Russians conducted aggressive reconnaissance thrusts against Shutov and Samchin, south of the Aksay, an indication that an attack by the 6th Motorized Corps of the 51st Army was imminent.[8]

On the morning of December 16, Hoth informed Manstein that the 3rd Guards Motorized Corps (51st Army) was concentrating against his east flank in the Mal Dberty-Tundutovo-Sadovoye area. Although elements of the 16th Motorized Division had arrived to the south at Saventoye, they were not strong enough to cover the east flank adequately. In addition, the winter conditions and bitter fighting of the past two weeks had reduced the LVII Panzer Corps to the point where it was capable of only limited offensive action (the 17th Panzer Division had only seventeen tanks). As a result, Hoth requested authorization to withdraw his army.[9]

By late afternoon, Hoth received Manstein's authorization for a limited withdrawal of the LVII Panzer Corps, which was to maintain contact with the enemy at all times. In the event of a frontal assault against the LVII Panzer Corps, Hoth was specifically instructed "not to make a premature withdrawal, but to frustrate the enemy's attempt with all available means to gain time for a thrust by mobile reserves on the flanks."[10] Meanwhile, it was essential to hold the line in front of Kotelnikovo.

Manstein had already sent a message to Zeitzler on Christmas Day in which he urged that it was at least necessary to move the III Panzer Corps up from the 1st Panzer Army.[11] Hitler's decision was relayed two days later. Manstein's request for the III Panzer Corps was dismissed as "impracticable" on the grounds that the two divisions (13th and 3rd Panzer) had only fifty-eight tanks between them, and that, in any case, without these units, the 1st Panzer Army would be unable to hold its positions and disengage from the enemy, an indication that a decision to withdraw Army Group A might soon be reached.

More encouraging was the news that badly needed reinforcements were being transported to Army Group Don. These reinforcements included the SS *Wiking* Division from the 1st Panzer Army, the 7th Panzer Division from France with 146 tanks and assault guns, and the 503rd Heavy Tank Detachment with twenty-nine of the new heavy Tiger Tanks and thirty-four PzKw III tanks equipped with the long barrel 50mm gun. Thirty more PzKw III and twenty PzKw IV tanks, both with long barrel guns, were promised by the first week in January 1943.[12] In addition, the 26th Infantry Division was to arrive in the Kupyansk area on December 31. The 320th Infantry Division was also scheduled to arrive in Kupyansk on January 8, and the 302nd Infantry Division was due north of Rostov on January 10. Both divisions were to remain available for use by OKH along with three other divisions from the west, which would arrive between the middle and end of January.[13]

This exchange marked the beginning of a month-long effort on the part of Manstein to get at least part of Army Group A out of the Caucasus. Hitler's indecision placed Manstein in the nearly impossible position of securing Army Group A's northern flank and his own line of communications through Rostov until a decision was made. The longer Hitler waited, the more difficult Manstein's task, and the greater the danger to the German southern flank became. Had Hitler made an immediate decision, even if it meant leaving all of Army Group A in the Caucasus, Manstein's position might not have been so desperate.

Despite the promise of much needed reinforcements, Manstein was still convinced that the situation would require the transfer of forces from Army Group A to Army Group Don. To Manstein, the transfer of forces was not only necessary, but entirely feasible, especially since Army Group A was fighting in terrain that favored the defense, while his own army group was being forced to fight in open country. He also warned Hitler that the already overextended forces of Army Group Don were not enough to hold the Chir Front.[14]

On December 28, Hitler issued Operations Order No. 2 which was designed to establish measures "to preserve the 6th Army in the fortress as a prerequisite to accomplishing its liberation."[15] More significantly, Army Group A was instructed to shorten its front gradually on several sectors, and the 13th and 3rd Panzer Divisions were authorized to shift to the northern flank, that is, toward the 4th Panzer Army. Even more welcome was the news that the "mobile formations of Army Group A and the 16th Motorized Division will be subordinated to Army Group Don."[16] Later the same day, specific orders were issued instructing the 1st Panzer Army to begin its withdrawal as quickly as possible to the general line of the Skola-Kuma River, about sixty-five miles from its present position south of Mozdok.[17]

While the withdrawal of the 1st Panzer Army was only a half measure, it nonetheless had to be encouraging to Manstein. There was now at least the prospect that the 3rd and 13th Panzer Divisions could be used to improve the situation. However, because of the lack of fuel, the 1st Panzer Army was unable to begin its movement until January 2, 1943.[18]

One possible solution to the situation south of the Don was to subordinate Army Group A to Manstein. OKH apparently had this under consideration for some time, and Manstein thought it was "advisable on technical grounds," since it would allow closer cooperation between the left flank of Army Group A and the right flank of the 4th Panzer Army once Army Group A had been withdrawn to the Kuma position. Manstein actually had little desire to accept the addi-

tional responsibility of Army Group A and the Caucasus Front. What
he really wanted was the authority to use Army Group A's mobile
formations. What he hoped to gain was absolute authority to carry out
his plans, which would probably include the evacuation of the
Caucasus. Hitler, of course, was unwilling to grant this, and, as a
result, Manstein was granted only the power to issue instructions to
Army Group A. The net result was practically nil as this arrangement
allowed Kleist to appeal to Hitler, who usually vetoed Manstein's
instructions.[19]

The crisis on the 4th Panzer Army's front south of the Don was not
the only one facing Manstein in the last week of December 1942. The
4th Panzer Army's left neighbor, *Armee Abteilung* Hollidt, was slowly
losing its grip on the Chir front. To the north of *Armee Abteilung*
Hollidt, the Italian 8th Army of Army Group B was in the process of
collapse in the face of the Soviet LITTLE SATURN offensive, unleashed on December 16.

Within seventy-two hours of their initial attacks, the 1st Guards and
6th Armies had opened a gap twenty miles deep and thirty miles wide
and the 3rd Guards Army had penetrated ten miles. By December 19,
the attacks were turned into a general pursuit, and the 17th, 18th, 24th,
and 25th Tank Corps and the 1st Guards Motorized Corps were turned
loose in a southwestern direction. The 24th Tank Corps had orders to
reach Tatsinkaya by December 23, while the 25th Tank Corps and the
1st Guards Motorized Corps were to reach Morosovskaya by December 22. Millerovo was to be taken by the 17th and 18th Tank Corps by
Christmas Eve.[20]

This was the prelude to a 125-mile drive deep into the German rear
by Major General V. M. Badanov's 24th Tank Corps, which became a
matter of concern for both the Russians and the Germans. By December 22, the 24th Tank Corps was fighting in the Bolshinka-Ilinka area
heading for Tatsinkaya, a major air base for supplying Stalingrad. The
24th Tank Corps was now over 150 miles from its supply base and was
running low on fuel and ammunition when its forward elements
bypassed Skassyrskaya to the north of Tatsinkaya. By the evening of
December 24, Badanov could report that he had accomplished his
mission, and the airfield at Tatsinkaya was littered with debris.[21]

On Christmas Day, the 24th Tank Corps had only fifty-eight tanks
left and was dangerously short of fuel and ammunition.[22] Meanwhile,
however, the Germans had managed to cut off Badanov's supply
route, and by December 26, the 24th Tank Corps had been effectively
bottled up by the 11th Panzer Division.[23]

For the next several days, German forces continued to close in on
Tatsinkaya. During the night of December 28–29, Badanov was given
permission for an independent breakout. Within thirty minutes, the

Russians were on the move, and throughout the next day, there was a long tank duel, until evening, when the Germans were able to retake the airfield. Nevertheless, the 24th Tank Corps managed to escape, and on December 30, made contact with the 25th Tank Corps and the 1st Guards Mechanized Corps. This incursion, while costly to the Russians, resulted in nearly 12,000 German casualties, 4,769 prisoners, the destruction of eighty-four tanks, 106 guns, and 431 aircraft.[24]

While the recapture of Tatsinkaya eliminated the most immediate threat to the position along the Chir, the collapse of the Italian 8th Army threatened to unhinge the left flank of Army Group Don and opened the way for a Russian drive toward Rostov.

Priority was given to reestablishing contact with the left flank of Army Group Don and preventing a breakthrough across the Morosovskaya-Foraschadt railroad. Both of these tasks were the responsibility of *Armee Abteilung* Fretter-Pico.[25] Meanwhile, the 304th Infantry Division, 19th Panzer Division, and Group Kreysing (remnants of the 3rd Mountain Division)[26] of Army Group B were to cooperate in an attack against the Soviet forces southeast and east of Millerovo and to drive them back across the Kalitva River.[27]

By the end of December, Manstein was facing a series of crises both north and south of the Don. North of the Don the XLVIII Panzer Corps (primarily the 11th and 6th Panzer Divisions) of *Armee Abteilung* Hollidt managed to stabilize the situation along the Bystraya River. From there, however, there was a gap adjacent to the left flank of the 304th Infantry Division of *Armee Abteilung* Fretter-Pico, which was holding blocking positions along the northern Donets and in front of Kamensk.[28] South of the Don, the 4th Panzer Army was fighting daily attempts to outflank it by the 6th Motorized Corps, the 13th Tank Corps, and the 3rd Guards Motorized Corps. At the same time, the 16th Motorized Division was being forced to abandon its positions around Elista, thus opening a gap between Army Group Don and the left flank of Army Group A.[29]

In attempt to salvage his position, Manstein made the following proposal to Zeitzler on December 31: because of the heavy pressure on the south flank of the 4th Panzer Army, it was doubtful that the SS *Wiking* Division could hold area between the Sal and Manytsch rivers. Therefore, the 4th Panzer Army had to be withdrawn. At the same time, the enemy was preparing to launch powerful attacks against the LVII Panzer Corps front. North of the Don a crisis was also developing.

Manstein told Zeitzler that it was not possible to hold all three positions, but that in his opinion the greatest danger was on the south flank of the 4th Panzer Army and north of the Don in the area between Army Group Don and Army Group B. To restore the situation, Manstein believed it was necessary to move the 11th Panzer Division south of the Don to support the 4th Panzer Army. The 7th Panzer Division, being held by *OKH* east of Rostov, was to be moved across the Donets to avert any crisis in the Don bend. Manstein also emphasized the need to move the panzer corps of the 1st Panzer Army as quickly as possible and the necessity of shifting a division from the 17th Army to cover Rostov.[30]

Armee Abteilung Hollidt was to establish contact with *Armee Abteilung* Fretter-Pico between the Bystraya and the Kalitva while gradually withdrawing its east and northeast flank to the Donets line Nikolayevskaya-Chrulevka-Novo Nikolaey. Its right flank was to be secured on the Don. One of its division was to concentrate in the area of Konstantinovskaya to strike the enemy advancing against the Donets along the Sal. In addition, it was also to hold open the bridge at Konstantinovskaya.[31]

Laboring under no illusions, recognizing that these measures could at best bring only a temporary respite, Manstein ordered all troops in Army Group Don's administrative area, in particular Rumanian and Italian stragglers, to be collected and organized for the defense of the Don and Donets crossing at Rostov.[32]

Even as he proposed these measures, Manstein knew that Hitler was not convinced of the urgency of the situation facing Army Group Don. Manstein had already been denied permission to move the 7th Panzer Division across the Donets on December 30. Hitler was concerned about the threat to Rostov and the connecting flank between Army Group Don and Army Group B. Undaunted, Manstein continued to press Zeitzler, but was again rebuffed, suffering the additional frustration of being denied authority to use the 11th Panzer Division south of the Don as well. He was also told that the infantry division requested from the 17th Army would not be forthcoming.[33]

Instead, Manstein was informed that II SS Panzer Corps (*Leibstandarte Adolf Hitler* [*LSAH*], *Das Reich*, and *Totenkopf* Divisions) was being moved to the Eastern Front and concentrated around Kharkov. From there it was to conduct a relief offensive against Stalingrad. However, because of the limited rail capacity in the Kharkov area, its assembly could not be completed until mid-February.[34]

During the first half of January 1943, Manstein's greatest concern was covering the withdrawal of the 1st Panzer Army from the Caucasus. To accomplish this, he was forced to keep the 4th Panzer Army exposed south of the Don and to maintain increasingly untenable positions with the remainder of his army group north of the Don. Army Group Don was directly engaged with six Soviet armies: the 3rd Guards, 5th Shock, and 5th Tank Armies north of the Don and the 2nd Guards, 51st, and 28th Armies south of the Don. In addition, the 1st Guards Army on the right flank of Army Group B also threatened Army Group Don.

There was no longer a "front," but a series of blocking positions and strong points to bar the Russian advance. Defenses were centered around key stretches of road or railroad junctions and major crossing points along the Don and Donets rivers. The fighting was characterized by rearguard actions, while the main body of troops took up new positions farther back. This routine was occasionally broken by sharp German counterattacks against the flanks of the advancing Soviet forces in order to gain valuable time while the 1st Panzer Army continued to withdraw.

To keep the Russians from turning their southern flank, the 4th Panzer Army took up a series of blocking positions between the Sal and Manytsch rivers. At the same time, powerful Russian forces were introduced between the Don and the Sal on the north flank of the 4th Panzer Army, threatening this flank as well. However, because it was still responsible for covering the withdrawal of the 1st Panzer Army, the 4th Panzer Army could not be retracted. In an effort to reduce the risks facing the 4th Panzer Army, Manstein sent daily urgent messages to *OKH* outlining his army's situation.

Faced with an extremely fluid situation, these daily appraisals and urgent pleas were designed to obtain freedom of action from *OKH*. Every new Soviet breakthrough or thrust had the potential of creating a major crisis. If Manstein was to avert these crises, it was essential that he be able to act quickly. Hitler was always slow to respond and was generally opposed to Manstein's ideas. However, when allowed to act, Manstein did so swiftly and decisively.

Because of the 4th Panzer Army's withdrawal from the Kotelnikovo area, the initial Russian attacks on the LVII Panzer Corps along the Mal Kuberle front were weak. However, movement across the Sal, southwest of Remontaya on the southeast flank of the 17th Panzer Division, was a clear indication that the Russians could soon be expected to pursue the 4th Panzer Army with stronger forces, with the main effort on the southern flank between the Sal and Manytsch. In addition, contact was lost with the 3rd Guards Motorized Corps, and it was still unclear whether the Soviet forces north of the Sal would attempt to outflank the 4th Panzer Army or advance on Konstantinovskaya near the junction of the Don and Donets.[35]

On January 4, German reconnaissance reported Russian forces advancing from Remontoye, as well as strong columns moving to the west and northwest between the Sal and the Don. This activity was an indication that there would soon be attacks against the north and south flanks of the 4th Panzer Army, as well as pinning attacks against the Mal Kuberle front. On the same day, Manstein reported that Army

Group Don was facing 189 Russian formations: eighty major formations and twelve independent tank regiments at Stalingrad, and 109
major formations and eleven independent tank regiments engaged
against *Armee Abteilung* Hollidt and the 4th Panzer Army. To oppose
these forces, Army Group Don, including *Armee Abteilung* Hollidt, had
only ten and one-third divisions, including some which were hastily
thrown together, ad hoc units from stragglers, remnants, and men on
leave.[36]

One day later, on January 5, the Russian 28th Army hit the south
flank of the 23rd Panzer Division north of the Manytsch, confirming
reports from the 16th Motorized Division that enemy forces on its
front were disengaging to the northwest. In a message to *OKH*,
Manstein urged the rapid movement of the 16th Motorized Division
and the concentration of the XL Panzer Corps (1st Panzer Army) in the
Salsk area as quickly as possible. In a second message, he expressed
concern over the ability of the 4th Panzer Army's three and one-half
divisions to hold the sixty-mile front between the Manytsch and the
right flank of *Armee Abteilung* Hollidt. While the Russian attempts to
outflank the 4th Panzer Army had thus far been thwarted, the Germans were unable to destroy the enemy. It was clear that Hoth could
not keep the Soviets from approaching the Don, maintain Salsk, and
cover the left flank of Army Group A. However, the timely arrival of
the XL Panzer Corps and the release of the 7th Panzer Division would
still make it possible to defeat the Russians south of the Don.[37]

Because the Soviet forces south of the Don were closer to Rostov and
threatened to wedge themselves between the 4th Panzer Army and
Army Group A, Manstein decided to deal with them first. The 4th
Panzer Army was incapable of preventing a Russian advance, but,
with additional forces, the XL Panzer Corps, and the 7th and 11th
Panzer Divisions, it might be possible to eliminate the Soviets as they
advanced between the Sal and the Don. The elimination of the Russian
threat to Rostov and the north flank of Army Group A would also
release German mobile formations which could then be used to deal
with the Russians opposite *Armee Abteilung* Hollidt.

On January 6, Manstein received Zeitzler's reply to his message of
January 5. Hitler had decided to use the 7th Panzer Division to support
an attack by the XLVIII Panzer Corps north of the Don. Hitler also
refused to release the 16th Motorized Division completely, despite the
fact that Manstein had earlier told him that an attack to restore the
situation could only be made with the 16th Motorized Division in
conjunction with the Tiger Tank Detachment.[38]

Hitler finally approved the release of the 16th Motorized Division
on January 7. The next day he also approved Manstein's request to
withdraw the 4th Panzer Army to the Bol Kuberle River, but authoriza-

tion for using the 7th Panzer Division south of the Don still rested with the Führer.[39]

By this time, elements of the 2nd Guards Army were across the Don north of Razdorskaya and Melichovskaya. This crisis was quickly cleared up, but the Russians were now attacking across the Don at and east of Konstantinovskaya, and were advancing across the Sal on the Betlayevskaya-Ilyinov sector. In addition, Russian reconnaissance units were advancing against the Manytsch crossing at Vesely about forty miles southeast of Rostov.[40]

Manstein again pleaded for the release of the XL Panzer Corps, which would enable the 4th Panzer Army to prevent the Russians from advancing on Rostov as well as cover the flank of Army Group A on the Manytsch. Since the XL Panzer Corps could not be released, it was necessary to decide which of the 4th Panzer Army's two tasks should take precedence.[41]

Once again, Hitler's reply failed to recognize the realities of the situation. While he acknowledged the threat to the south flank of the 4th Panzer Army, his authorization to allow it to retreat to the Manytsch on the line east of Salsk to Konstantinovskaya came too late. Furthermore, because of the long delays in moving the 16th Motorized Division, it was no longer possible to close the gap with *Armee Abteilung* Hollidt. Moreover, the 4th Panzer Army was in danger of being forced into the angle between the Don and the Manytsch. As a result, it was necessary to maintain the army in front of the Manytsch. In spite of this, there was, at least for the time being, an opportunity to launch an offensive to tie down the 3rd Guards Tank Corps, which was turning toward Proletarskaya from the north, and the 2nd Guards Motorized Corps advancing across the Sal. To accomplish this, it was necessary for the 4th Panzer Army to concentrate on the Lower Manytsch and subsequently to withdraw to the Proletarskaya bridgehead. It was also necessary to allow the 7th Panzer Division to operate in conjunction with the 4th Panzer Army.[42]

Instead, on January 12, Hitler ordered the 7th Panzer Division north of the Don to reestablish contact with *Armee Abteilung* Fretter-Pico. The same day, Hoth informed Manstein that his weakened divisions, especially the 23rd and 17th Panzer Division (together they totaled only fifty-four tanks and assault guns), could not hold Proletarskaya for any length of time unless the 23rd Panzer Division was supported by the still relatively strong infantry forces of the 16th Motorized Division.[43] In its present condition, the 23rd Panzer Division could at best only block the Manytsch at Sporny, or in an emergency, hold the area southwest of Proletarskaya. The 23rd Panzer Division was not in condition to conduct offensive operations.[44]

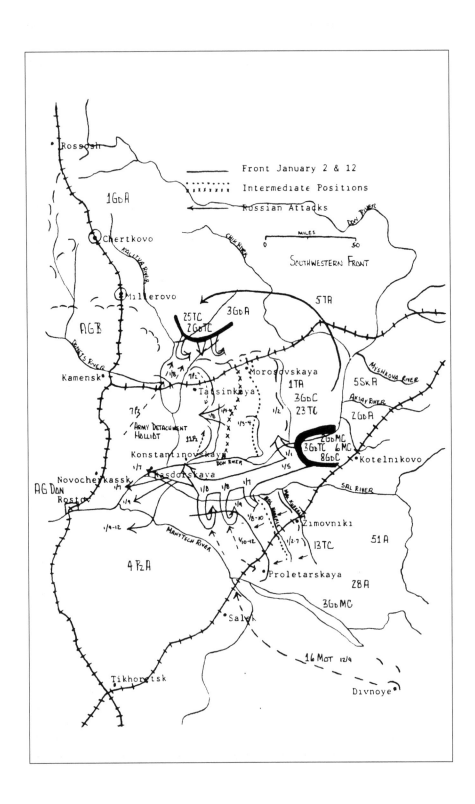

Rossosh

1GdA

Chertkovo

Millerovo

AGB

Kamensk

Front January 2 & 12
Intermediate Positions
Russian Attacks

MILES
0   50

SOUTHWESTERN FRONT

DON RIVER
CHIR RIVER
KALITVA RIVER
DONETS RIVER

57A

25TC   3GdA
2GdTC

Morosovskaya
Tatsinskaya   1TA
                     3GdC
                     23TC

7P3   1/3-4

ARMY DETACHMENT
HOLLIDT   1/3

Konstantinovskaya
1/7
Raadorskaya
Novocherkassk
Rostov
AG Don   1/8   1/8   1/7
                      1/9

1/9-12

MANYTSCH RIVER

4 PzA

MYSHKOVA RIVER
5SkA
AKSAY RIVER
2GdA

2GdMC
3GdTC   6MC
8GdC

Kotelnikovo

SAL RIVER

Zimovniki

1/2-7   13TC   51A

Proletarskaya   28A

3GdMC

Salsk

16 MOT 12/9

Tikhoretsk

Divnoye

Manstein, however, already knew that he could not expect help. As a result, he ordered the 4th Panzer Army to concentrate in the narrow bridgehead at Proletarskaya. If necessary, the 16th Motorized Division could conduct mobile operations to support the crossing of the Manytsch at Sherebkov and between the Manytsch and Sal at Vesely. The division was also to prevent the Russians from advancing on the Lower Don and Manytsch. Meanwhile, north of the Don, the Russians had again occupied Razdorskaya and strong columns were observed moving toward the Razdorskaya area.[45]

For the next several days, the Russians maintained pressure against the Lower Manytsch. On January 16, the Soviets made simultaneous attempts to advance strong forces across the Manytsch toward Salsk while attacking the north flank of the LVII Panzer Corps. Despite suffering heavy losses, Russian strength on the south flank remained intact because of the influx of reinforcements. By evening, however, they were disengaging from the LVII Panzer Corps front and moving to the northwest. These forces were apparently to be used across the Manytsch at and west of Sporny, where the 16th Motorized Division had temporarily eliminated the threat of a breakthrough.[46]

On January 17, the Russians renewed their attempts to outflank the LVII Panzer Corps by attacking Novy Yegorlyk and Bermiki and crossing the Lower Manytsch southwest of Budyennovskaya. German radio intercepts had earlier confirmed the shift of the 5th Guards Motorized Corps across Novo Sadovsky to the west, indicating that the Russians intended to attack either across the Don toward Novocherkassk or across the Lower Manytsch against the flank and rear of the 4th Panzer Army. By January 18, the Soviets had pushed the Germans from Svoboda, Tuslukov, Krasny Manytschskaya, Alitub, and Pustochkin, and were advancing on Rostov. At the same time, they were attempting to advance across the Don ice for a thrust on Aksayskaya.[47]

On January 20, the Russians were dangerously close to Rostov. The 28th Army was still attempting to break through east of Proletarskaya for an advance on Salsk. The 51st Army was trying to cross the Manytsch on a broad front northwest of Proletarskaya, and the 2nd Guards Army was attacking from a point northeast of Vesely to the mouth of the Manytsch to advance on Bataisk, which was itself attacked by fifteen Soviet tanks.[48]

While the 4th Panzer Army struggled to delay the Russians, the 1st Panzer Army was gradually moving back toward Rostov. By January 19, its left flank was on a general line running from Cherkask in the south, along the Klaus River through Divnoye thence to Priytunoye. There was still a gap of over ninety miles between the 1st and 4th Panzer Armies between Priytunoye and Proletarskaya, and it was temporarily necessary for the 1st Panzer Army to hold its positions for several days while its supplies were shifted. However, at least there was now some chance for cooperation between the two armies.[49]

Thus far, the 4th Panzer Army had managed to keep the Russians from crossing the Manytsch at Proletarskaya. However, the infantry formations of the 28th Army were being moved in as reinforcements. It was also becoming increasingly dangerous to have the mobile formations of Army Group Don tied down between the Sal, Don, and Manytsch rivers when, at any time, the Russians could advance their forces across the Lower Manytsch to the southeast and cut the 4th Panzer Army's link with Rostov or cross the Don. Moreover, the Soviets would soon be aided in their task by the expected frost period, which would facilitate the crossing of water obstacles.[50] Given the situation, Manstein advised Hitler to limit the movement of the 4th Panzer Army to enable it to maintain the supply route to Army Group A so that Army Group A could continue to withdrawal.[51]

The rapidly deteriorating situation on the left flank of *Armee Abteilung* Hollidt soon forced Manstein to modify his plans. Instead of leaving the 4th Panzer Army in front of Rostov, he now proposed to shift it rapidly to the left flank of *Armee Abteilung* Hollidt, leaving only one division to cover Rostov. He also suggested that the task of the 4th Panzer Army be limited to holding open the Rostov-Tikhoretsk railroad, making the 1st Panzer Army responsible for covering its own northern flank while the 4th Panzer Army continued to retreat.[52]

The commander of the 1st Panzer Army, General Eberhard von Mackensen, received his commission in 1910, as a lieutenant in the elite 1st Hussars Regiment. By 1933, he had risen to become Chief of Staff to the *Reichswehr's* cavalry corps. Mackensen's cavalry regiments subsequently provided the foundation for the first eight panzer regiments, and two of the first three motorized regiments.

During the Polish campaign, he served as Chief of Staff to the 14th Army. Serving in the same capacity in the 12th Army for the campaign in the West, Mackensen was responsible for overseeing the operations of *Panzergruppe* Kleist and *Panzergruppe* Guderian. In May 1941, Mackensen became one of only two men (the other was Manstein) to be promoted to command a panzer division without previous experience with armored troops.

He immediately proved his ability by spearheading Kleist's drive across the Ukraine in 1941, capturing Rostov in early winter. During the Soviet winter counteroffensive, Mackensen was given a second corps, "*Gruppe* Mackensen," and held the vulnerable flank between the 17th Army and 1st Panzer Army.

He displayed the best (or worst) traits of a Prussian cavalryman: apolitical, technically proficient, and unflinching in the face of danger.

These attributes led to his promotion in November to replace Kleist at the 1st Panzer Army when Kleist was appointed to command Army Group A.

Having captured Rostov once from the northwest, now, to save his beleaguered army, MacKensen faced the prospect of having to do so again, from the opposite direction.[53]

The Russian attack launched on January 20, by the 2nd Guards Army (3rd Guards Tank, 2nd Guards Motorized, 5th Guards Motorized, and 13th Guards Rifle Corps) threatened to cut off the 4th Panzer Army from Rostov. To counter this, Manstein proposed that the 11th Panzer Division be concentrated at Rostov so that, depending on the development of the situation, it could be used with either the 4th Panzer Army south of the Don or remain available in the Rostov area.[54]

The fluid combat on the southern front required that decisions be made quickly to allow decisive action to be taken. However, the situation could change so quickly that it was also necessary for Manstein to be flexible, to change his plans to meet new threats as they developed. While he was committed to securing Rostov, Manstein was not wedded to any single scheme to accomplish his goal. Once it became clear that the Soviets menaced Rostov from the north, through *Armee Abteilung* Hollidt, Manstein reacted quickly. Since there were no forces available to stop the Russians north of the Don, Manstein abandoned his original intention of using his panzers south of the Don and now proposed to do exactly the opposite. However, recognizing that the Soviets opposite the 4th Panzer Army still posed a danger, Manstein opted to keep the 11th Panzer Division at Rostov. From here, the 11th Panzer Division could intervene either north or south of the Don depending on where it was needed.

To the north, *Armee Abteilung* Hollidt was scrambling to keep its own left flank from being turned, and to close the gap with Army Group B. Its southern flank was now anchored on the Don at Tsim-lyanskaya and ran roughly northeast to Tormosin, where it curved northwest to Chernyshkov. From there it turned sharply west to a point just beyond Skassyrskaya on the Bystraya. However, between the Bystraya and the Kalitiva rivers, there was a gap to the left flank of Army Group B.[55]

While the LITTLE SATURN offensive had largely exhausted itself, the Russians were still able to maintain pressure against *Armee Abteilung* Hollidt, thereby forcing it to continue its withdrawal. On January 2, Soviet forces captured Chernyshkov and Skassyrskaya on the north flank. Additional Soviet units were spotted moving into the Gnilya Valley between the Bystraya and the Kalitva, where the Germans could, at best, hope to withstand only a weak reconnaissance thrust. On the eastern flank, Corps Meith (the 336th and 384th Infantry Divisions), except for Group Stahel (remnants of the 294th Infantry Division), which took heavy losses, managed to withdraw without difficulty to the Zimla sector.[56]

For the next several days, *Armee Abteilung* Hollidt continued to pull back under Russian pressure. Strong enemy groups were reported at Michaylovsky. In the meantime, the Soviets were directing their main effort against the area around Morosovskaya. By this time, the nearly continuous attacks and retreats of the past few weeks had taken their toll on the Germans who, without reserves, were unable to hold Morosovskaya. Moreover, the Russians were expected to advance to the south, west of the Bystraya, to tie down any remaining mobile units. The 3rd Guards Army was also expected to attack the XLVIII Panzer Corps between the Bystraya and the Kalitva. Subsequently, plans were made to shorten the front by retracting it an additional ten to fifteen miles. It was hoped that an armored group of the XLVIII Panzer Corps could be maintained to block possible Russian advances west of the Bystraya.[57]

The temporary loss of Group Stahel created a gap between Corps Meith and the XVII Corps that was screened only by weak forces. Manstein was advised by Hollidt that his troops were too weak to hold the wide bend around Morosovskaya. It was necessary to withdraw these forces before the Russians attacked from the northwest and the southeast. There were also reports of new forces advancing against the gap between Corps Meith and the XVII Corps. Furthermore, to preserve the troops and matériel necessary to close the breach with Corps Meith, it was necessary to abandon the Don. While these forces occupied an intermediate position, it was hoped that the 11th Panzer Division could be released as a mobile reserve behind the east front of Army Group Don.[58]

To the north, the 1st Motorized Corps and the 23rd Tank Corps were expected to push into the gap between the Bystraya and the Kalitva. The 6th Panzer Division and Group Peifer (miscellaneous units gathered around the 94th Infantry Division that had escaped from Stalingrad) were tied down east of the Bystraya and were unable to support the weak forces screening the gap. In Hollidt's opinion, only the speedy arrival of armored forces (7th Panzer Division) from Forschadt could eliminate the threat to the left flank.[59]

On January 5, Soviet motorized forces struck the 11th Panzer Division at Konstantinovskaya and turned a strong group to the west between the Sal and the Don. There were also signs that the Russians were preparing new attacks between the Bystraya and Kalitva rivers to break through the Belokalitvenskaya bridgehead position. The 6th Panzer Division had thus far managed to bring the Russian advance to a halt, but it was not powerful enough to eliminate the Russians. To restore the front, Hollidt requested the 7th Panzer Division.[60] The 7th Panzer Division was released by *OKH* and ordered to move the Forschadt area on January 4. Subsequently, Manstein ordered the division into the area between the Bystraya and the Kalitva to make a rapid thrust against the Soviet forces on the left flank of *Armee Abteilung* Hollidt. The attack was then to be exploited by advancing the left flank of *Armee Abteilung* Fretter-Pico. Manstein did not intend to have the division remain between the Bystraya and Kalitva beyond January 8.[61] Commanded by Major General Baron Hans von Funck the 7th Panzer Division was Rommel's old division. Funck might have had a career with the *Afrika Korps* were it not for his habit of reporting realistically, rather than tailoring his opinions to suit Hitler's prejudices. After leading the 5th Panzer Regiment in Poland and France, Funck's 3rd Panzer Brigade Headquarters was converted to the 5th Light Division and earmarked for deployment to Libya. Upon returning from North Africa, Funck reported to Hitler that the proposed reinforcements were inadequate and that the position of the Italians was hopeless. Hitler was so infuriated at what he believed was Funck's pessimism that he cashiered him on the spot. Nevertheless, Africa proved to be a boost to his career and when Rommel left the 7th Panzer Division Funck was selected to fill the vacancy.

Like Knoblesdorff, Funck had served with Hoth's *Panzergruppe 3*. His most outstanding characteristic, given the present circumstances, was that he could be counted upon to report exactly what he saw.[62]

At the same time that he authorized the release of the 7th Panzer Division, Hitler also approved the withdrawal of *Armee Abteilung* Hollidt's east front to the Kagalnik sector. This position had been barely secured when it was struck by heavy Soviet attacks. Several divisions broke through in the center and seriously threatened the entire position. The 336th Infantry Division was temporarily surrounded. Advancing through the breach to the southwest, the Russians quickly captured Kryukovsky, Trofimov, and Pletonov. Hollidt informed Manstein that his weak forces would tie down the enemy for as long as possible to enable a counterattack to be made on the left flank. However, because of the situation between the Bystraya and the Kalitva, the 7th Panzer Division was unable to intervene. Farther to the south, the 11th Panzer Division was tied down around Gapkin, where the Russians had also broken through.[63]

Without infantry to cover the front between the Bystraya and the Kalitva, Manstein had to rely on his panzer divisions to parry Russian thrusts until sufficient troops could be scraped together. While the 4th Panzer Army was engaged south of the Don, only the 6th, 7th, and 11th Panzer Divisions were available to deal with local crises. These divisions could not eliminate the Russian drive north of the Don, but they were strong enough to handle local breakthroughs and to halt the Soviet advance temporarily.

Immediately following the breakthrough in the Kagalnik sector, Manstein ordered the 7th Panzer Division to begin withdrawing from the area between the Bystraya and the Kalitva by removing its rear elements across the Donets at Belokalitvenskaya. He also ordered the left flank of *Armee Abteilung* Hollidt over to the defense. Leaving some of its forces to secure this flank against any further attacks, the mass of the 7th Panzer Division was used to restore the situation in the Corps Meith and XVII Corps sectors along Kagalnik.[64]

The Russian attacks were straining *Armee Abteilung* Hollidt to the breaking point. Nevertheless, the 7th Panzer Division's attack between the Bystraya and the Kalitva was beginning to show signs of success. However, German forces along the Kagalnik were too weak to prevent the Russians from breaking free. There were also heavy attacks north of Konstantinovskaya as well as another pressure point at Krylov, along the railroad to Tatsinkaya. The combination of these crises and the expected resumption of attacks on the eastern flank removed any hope that Manstein had for using the 7th Panzer Division south of the Don.[65]

The Russians continued to move reserves into the breach on the Kagalnik sector. Concentrations northwest of Krylov indicated preparations for a renewed attack from there. On the left flank, one hundred tanks struck the Bystraya-Kalitva sector. At Nadeshevka, Group Peifer was hit by about thirty tanks. To restore the situation, Hollidt intended to close the gap on the Kagalnik sector with simultaneous attacks by the 7th and 11th Panzer Divisions driving from the north and south, respectively. He also reported that it would be possible to delay the Soviet advance to the Donets only by using all of his armored forces. His infantry, however, was too weak to retake and hold the Kagalnik line. In any case, without adequate reinforcements, he would be forced to withdraw.[66]

Manstein responded quickly to Hollidt's plea for reinforcements, sending him approximately 900 men who had been on furlough. Manstein also sent an angry message to *OKH* complaining that two previously promised units, Battalion Bitsch and the 5th Flak Battalion, were being retained by Army Group B. Without notifying Army Group Don, Battalion Bitsch had been reassigned to Army Group B for ten days and the 5th Flak Battalion had been reallocated as well. Manstein had intended to use these troops (1,670 men) to replenish the heavily depleted units of *Armee Abteilung* Hollidt.[67]

Despite gaining some success at all three crisis points, it was evident that *Armee Abteilung* Hollidt could not hold its position. The Russians continued to move in reinforcements and were expected to intensify their attacks. In addition, one thousand trucks were seen moving southwest of Stalingrad, and there was heavy railroad traffic bringing in fresh forces against *Armee Abteilung* Hollidt. The Russians were also conducting aggressive attacks against Belokalitvenskaya in an effort to take the main supply road and railroad leading west. Manstein therefore requested permission to allow *Armee Abteilung* Hollidt to withdraw to the Donets-Kalitva line, while maintaining a bridgehead on the Donets. Surprisingly, Hitler authorized the move on January 13.[68]

To deal with the situation between the Bystraya and the Kalitva, *Armee Abteilung* Hollidt was preparing to attack to the northeast with the 7th Panzer Division, and with *Kampfgruppe* Huhnersdorff from the area west of Krutensky southward toward Dyadin.[69]

The attack by the 7th Panzer Division stalled against strong anti-tank defenses around Novocherkassk. *Kampfgruppe* Huhnersdorff came to within 800 yards of Dyadin before it also ran into stubborn defenses, losing eight tanks while destroying fifteen of the enemy's. Meanwhile, Soviet reinforcements were moving toward Dyadin. There were also Russian concentrations west of the Bystraya and on both sides of the Kalitva, confirming preparations for an attack against Tatsinkaya and Belokalitvenskaya.[70] To the south, in the 11th Panzer Division's sector, the Russians were moving in reinforcements along both sides of the Don. They also increased their patrol activity. In light of these developments, *Armee Abteilung* Hollidt continued its preparations to withdraw into an intermediate position.[71]

In an effort to stabilize the situation, Manstein ordered *Armee Abteilung* Hollidt to eliminate the Russians between the Bystraya and the Kalitva and to establish a link with *Armee Abteilung* Fretter-Pico west of the Kalitva. The 11th Panzer Division was instructed to conduct mobile operations to defend the Don between the mouth of the Sal and the mouth of the Stary Don.

To accomplish these tasks, the 7th Panzer Division was to throw the Russians across and occupy the line Masslov-Novocherkassk-Koursuny. After eliminating the enemy at Dyadin, *Kampfgruppe* Huhnersdorff was to thrust immediately to the north to establish contact with *Armee Abteilung* Fretter-Pico on the Kalitva. In addition, Fretter-Pico was to prepare to withdraw to the line Konstantinovskaya-Nishne Shuravsky along the course of the Donets to Maslov.[72]

Lieutenant General Maximillian Fretter-Pico was an infantryman cut in much the same mold as Hollidt. Although far more outspoken than Hollidt, the two men had similar careers. Fretter-Pico was Chief of Staff to the 1st Panzer Army (later XXIV Corps), which remained inactive during the Polish campaign and spent most of the French campaign holding positions opposite the Maginot Line. During the pre-*BARBAROSSA* expansion of the army he was given command of the 97th *Jager* Division and fought with Army Group South throughout the summer and fall of 1941. In December he was promoted to lead the XXX Corps in Manstein's 11th Army and designed the combined artillery and infantry assault that captured Sevastopol.[73]

On January 14, *Armee Abteilung* Hollidt was faced with yet another crisis. The Russian 2nd Tank Corps broke through the right flank of Army Group B and advanced toward the Donets. At the same time, Soviet tank and motorized forces in the Dyadin area pushed south and southeast toward Kamensk. As a result, *Armee Abteilung* Fretter-Pico was ordered to withdraw to the Donets-Durkel River line and to cover the left flank of the Army Group Don. *Armee Abteilung* Hollidt was ordered to withdraw its left flank behind the Donets at Krassny Yar. Shortly afterward, Manstein also took measures to secure the Donets crossings between Voroshilovgrad and Isyum.[74]

The increased Soviet activity opposite *Armee Abteilung* Hollidt and Fretter-Pico made it clear that strong Soviet motorized forces were attempting to break through the weak defenses of *Armee Abteilung* Fretter-Pico toward Kamensk to outflank *Armee Abteilung* Hollidt before it could occupy its new position behind the Donets. At least four mobile groups were involved, the 2nd Tank, the 2nd Guards Tank, the 1st Guards Motorized, and the 23rd Tank Corps. To the south it was not expected that the 16th Motorized Division would be able to tie down the 3rd Guards Tank and the 2nd Guards Motorized Corps, thus releasing these two formations for use against the right flank of *Armee Abteilung* Hollidt. Under these conditions, *Armee Abteilung* Hollidt could, at best, given the timely arrival of the 7th Panzer Division, secure the Donets between Kamensk and Forschadt, while the 11th Panzer Division conducted mobile operations along the Don. There were not enough forces to defend the Donets north of Kamensk.[75]

It was in response to this situation that Manstein wanted to shift the 4th Panzer Army across Rostov.[76] However, because the Russians were also pushing forces across the Manytsch and were trying to outflank the 4th Panzer Army, and because the 1st Panzer Army was still too distant, Manstein was forced to keep the 4th Panzer Army south of the Don.

On January 16, the 7th Panzer Division arrived in the area southwest of Kamensk and immediately threw back the Russian forces that had crossed the Donets to the west. In spite of this, more Soviet tank and motorized forces continued to move toward the Kamensk bridgehead. There were also numerous tank concentrations to the east and northeast of the city, indicating preparations for an attack. Subsequent prisoner interrogations confirmed that the main effort of the attack would be made by the 18th Tank Corps, which, after breaking through the Derkul sector, was to turn toward Voroshilovgrad.[77]

About this time, Manstein received a report from *Armee Abteilung* Fretter-Pico (subordinated to Army Group Don on January 19) that must have been disturbing. Fretter-Pico requested approval to withdraw his left flank from the Derkul to behind the Donets on the basis of decreasing strength and "completely inadequate weapons and equipment." This particular sector was mostly held by young troops with limited training. Moreover, these troops had never been in combat and were on the Eastern Front for the first time. "It is the feeling among its officers and NCOs that their equipment is completely inadequate (for example one company has only one machine gun). It has been inadequately provided with vehicles and sleds and the troops are nearly immobile. There is only a small field kitchen available. Winter clothing is lacking, one battalion has none at all. . . . As a result of inadequate mobile forces, it will be very difficult to conduct defensive battles against strong enemy tank and motorized forces."[78]

Manstein was all too familiar with the problems of having to fight a numerically superior foe without having to worry about the added burden of inadequately equipped troops. However, with more and more of his units reporting casualties from cold and frostbite, he felt compelled to alert *OKH* to the fact that replacements were arriving without suitable clothing, thereby keeping them from being used effectively. In addition, he also emphasized the need for more anti-tank weapons, especially as divisions arriving from the west, in particular the 302nd and 306th Infantry Divisions, were deficient in this area.[79]

Despite the plea from *Armee Abteilung* Fretter-Pico, Manstein refused to allow it to withdraw its left flank behind the Donets. Instead, he emphasized the need to bring the Russian advance to a halt. *Armee Abteilung* Fretter-Pico was to withdraw behind the Donets only if the Derkul sector could not be held.[80]

Confident that the German 6th Army was effectively sealed off from any possible relief, the Russians had already initiated plans to trap the three army groups in the south. On December 22, Lieutenant General F. I. Golikov, the commander of the Voronezh Front, attended a STAV-KA meeting that reviewed his plans for a second attack which would clear the enemy from the area between Kantemirovka and Voronezh in preparation for an attack toward Kursk and Kharkov. The Southwestern Front would make a simultaneous attack toward Voroshilovgrad. Golikov's offensive would bring his forces into the southwest sector of the Voronezh Front between the Don and the

Oskol rivers, the shortest route between Kursk and Kharkov. He would also attack on his left and center to eliminate the German forces between Voronezh and Kantemirovka and to seize the Liskaya-Kantemirovka railroad, which could then be used for future attacks against Kharkov and the Donets basin. The 6th Army of the Southwestern Front would cover the operation from the south and was to attack in the general direction of Pokrovskoye. The entire offensive was to be coordinated by Zhukov and Vasilevsky and was timed for mid-January.[81]

Manstein's position was made yet more untenable by Golikov's attack launched on January 12. A huge gap was ripped in the German front from south of Voronezh to Voroshilovgrad, threatening the German hold on the Donets basin by opening the way to the Donets and on to the Dnieper crossings or the Sea of Azov. The Voronezh Front had actually launched three simultaneous attacks. The "northern group" (Major General K. S. Mosalenko's 40th Army) was driving for Alekseyvka, where it was to link up with the "southern group" (Major General P. S. Rybalko's 3rd Tank Army), which was advancing from the area northwest of Kantemirovka. The "central group" (Major General P. M. Zykov's 18th Independent Rifle Corps) was moving west, southwest, and south.[82]

Because of delays in moving the 4th Tank Corps, the attack by the 40th Army was delayed until January 14. Two days earlier, however, the 40th Army conducted a reconnaissance in force that effectively caused the 7th Hungarian Division to flee. The 3rd Tank Army was committed on January 14, and by evening, it was twelve miles deep into the German positions. By the end of the month, 86,000 prisoners had been captured and the Hungarian 2nd Army, remnants of the Italian 8th Army, the Italian Alpine Corps, and the XXIV Panzer Corps were rubbed out of the German order of battle, leaving a 120- mile gap between Voronezh and Kantemirovka.[83]

Even before the Hungarians and the Italians had been completely eliminated, Vasilevsky presented Stalin with plans for a new attack. This new operation was to strike the German 2nd Army and destroy Army Group B. The liquidation of the 2nd Army (twelve divisions, totaling 125,000 men) would pave the way for an attack on Kursk. The Bryansk and Voronezh Fronts were responsible for encircling the 2nd Army. The 13th Army (Bryansk Front) would attack from the north to Krasnodon, and the 40th, 60th, and 38th Armies (Voronezh Front) would attack from the southeast (40th and 60th Armies) and the northwest (38th Army). The attack was launched on January 24, in the worst winter conditions: fog, a blizzard, and temperatures to −22°F. Despite this, the two fronts were able to link on January 28.[84]

In mid-January, the situation of Army Group Don was critical. With the collapse of the Hungarian and Italian forces, there was a gap between Voroshilovgrad and Voronezh in which the Russians had complete freedom of action. Manstein reported to Hitler that "Army Group Don must expect that the enemy will turn against its deep flank west of Voroshilovgrad. We cannot prevent this with our forces. These are at best adequate to maintain the Donets line Rostov-Voroshilovgrad, where the defense of the left flank of Voroshilovgrad is already in doubt due to the length of time that the 4th Panzer Army has been tied down covering the flank of Army Group A."[85]

Manstein saw two possibilities: one was to attempt to intercept the Russians as far to the east as possible between Voronezh and Voroshilovgrad while leaving the 2nd Army on the Donets. In this case, "the enemy will probably throw in the forces currently rolling up our flank and exhaust himself prematurely."[86] It was doubtful, however, whether forces would then be available in the spring to restore the situation.

The second option was to "concentrate two strong groups on the flanks of the breakthrough to attempt a later, decisive offensive. This is subject to the additional withdrawal of these groups for their concentration, before thrusting into the enemy to bring him to a standstill. Circumstances permitting, the enemy's rear will be cut."[87]

Either option required that Army Group Don be allowed to withdraw. However, if the first option was chosen, it was doubtful that II SS Panzer Corps could arrive in time to intercept the Russian flanking movement. In addition, it was necessary to make the final decision to bring the 1st Panzer Army through Rostov. Manstein further observed that "Army Group A cannot be supplied across the Strait of Kerch and operate from its bridgehead. Moreover, it will be limited to tying down enemy forces."[88]

Thus, as early as mid-January, Manstein had formulated a plan that he believed would enable the Germans to deliver an effective counterblow to blunt the Soviet drive. All the elements of the later offensive were present: a strategic retreat to draw the Russians forward; the concentration of two strong attack groups along the enemy's flanks; and the use of the II SS Panzer Corps and the successful passage of the 1st Panzer Army through Rostov. Although Manstein still had to deal with the immediate situation facing Army Group Don, his farsightedness allowed him to seek to accomplish the maximum that was possible with the means available.

At this time, no final decision had yet been made as to whether or not even the 1st Panzer Army should be brought through Rostov. Hitler was unwilling to abandon the Caucasus and insisted on maintaining the front south of the Don to safeguard the Maikop oilfields.[89]

While Manstein awaited Hitler's decision, the Russians continued to attack. In the 4th Panzer Army's sector, the Soviets were attempting to seize the Manytsch, using the 3rd Guards Motorized Corps (51st Army) to the north. At the same time, the 3rd Guards Tank, 2nd Guards Motorized, 5th Guards Motorized, and the 13th Guards Rifle Corps (2nd Guards Army) attacked across the Lower Manytsch between Sporny and the Donets.[90]

Along the Donets, the 5th Motorized and 8th Cavalry Corps were preparing thrusts on both sides of Belokalitvenskaya, and the 1st Guards Tank Corps was moving up to the front. Further up the river, the 23rd Tank and 2nd Tank Corps struck Kamensk, while the 2nd Guards Tank Corps prepared an assault west of the city. The 6th Guards Rifle and 18th Tank Corps were concentrated around Voroshilovgrad, and it was expected that the 25th Tank and 1st Guards Motorized Corps would also be shifted to the west.[91]

To alleviate the pressure along the Manytsch, Manstein ordered the 4th Panzer Army to make concentric attacks across the Lower Manytsch. The 17th Panzer Division was to strike from the Metshetinskaya area, and the 11th Panzer Division was to strike from the Rostov bridgehead, in cooperation with the 16th Motorized Division, to eliminate the Soviet forces that had crossed the Manytsch. The remainder of the 4th Panzer Army was to delay the advance of the 51st and 28th Armies. If this attack succeeded in dealing the enemy an effective blow, then there was at least a chance that the 1st Panzer Army could be brought through Rostov.[92]

Meanwhile, Soviet forces continued to concentrate against *Armee Abteilung* Fretter-Pico's left flank. There was some consolation in the fact that the 335th Infantry Division would soon arrive in the Voroshilovgrad area, but this division alone could not be expected to transform the situation.[93]

On January 21, Manstein alerted Hitler to the fact that the situation on his left flank would soon force him to shift two divisions from the 4th Panzer Army across Rostov to Voroshilovgrad to prevent the Russians from breaking through to the Sea of Azov. This move had to be made no later than January 24, since there was every indication that the Russians were shifting their main effort to Voroshilovgrad. Furthermore, it appeared that the 23rd Tank Corps to the north of Kamensk, on the right flank of Army Group B, was also working against Voroshilovgrad.[94]

In addition to transferring two divisions from the 4th Panzer Army to the west flank, Army Group Don would also have to move a division behind the Don to conduct mobile defense between the mouth of the Donets and Novocherkassk, where there were inadequate forces.[95]

A decision to bring at least part of the 1st Panzer Army out of the Caucasus was reached at last on January 23. Hitler ordered the 1st Panzer Army to move northward toward Tikhoretsk. From here it was to be decided if a further withdrawal to Rostov should be made. Meanwhile, Army Group Don was to hold Rostov open.[96]

This bit of encouraging news was tarnished, however, because, on the same day, Army Group Don inherited approximately forty miles of front from Army Group B between the Donets and Starobelsk. In addition, Manstein's request for using the II SS Panzer Corps to support *Armee Abteilung* Fretter-Pico was denied. Instead, the SS Panzer Corps was ordered to move to Kharkov, where it was to be available to Army Group B pending orders from *OKH*.[97]

To take pressure from the center, *Armee Abteilung* Hollidt was ordered to regroup some of its forces in the Novocherkassk area and to be prepared either to hold out against an attack in that sector, or to be able to thrust into the Russian flank in the event of an attack south of Novocherkassk.[98]

On January 24, Hitler finally decided to bring the entire 1st Panzer Army through Rostov, ordering the 3rd Panzer Division to "relieve the 4th Panzer Army by making an immediate thrust in a generally northward direction into the enemy flank."[99] However, because the south flank of the 1st Panzer Army was still at Armivar, the 4th Panzer Army was forced to hold Rostov open even longer, making it doubtful that the 4th Panzer Army could be thrown over to the west flank in time.[100]

The decision regarding Army Group A, however, was only a half measure. Instead of bringing all of Army Group A out of the Caucasus and through Rostov, only the 1st Panzer Army was being completely withdrawn. The 17th Army was to remain in the Kuban in hopes of mounting a future offensive to regain the Caucasus region. By the time the decision to withdraw Army Group A was reached, however, it was extremely doubtful that the 4th Panzer Army could hold Rostov open long enough for the 1st Panzer Army. Any attempt to hold the city any longer, given the situation north of the Don, would probably have been fatal to the 4th Panzer Army as well as the entire southern flank.

The following day, Manstein informed Zeitzler that with the continuing risk on the left flank, it was only possible to hold Rostov open for a few days. In order to preserve the value of Army Group A, Manstein suggested that the mass of the 3rd Panzer Division attack toward Metchetinskaya, to prevent the 4th Panzer Army from being outflanked from the south by the 4th Cavalry Corps, which was advancing south of the Salsk-Yegorlyskaya road. He also urged the withdrawal of the 1st Panzer Army through Rostov in a major move along the Armivar-Rostov railroad. This move would facilitate offensive action on the open east flank, in the gap between the 1st and 4th Panzer Armies.[101]

Later the same day, Manstein inquired about possible offensive action to relieve the threatened north flank of Army Group Don. Uncharacteristically, he received a reply within one hour: A relief attack was being prepared in the Kharkov area by *LSAH* and *Das Reich* Divisions. This attack, however, would not be ready until February 12.[102]

On January 27, the northern group of Army Group A (1st Panzer Army including Headquarters XL and III Panzer Corps, 3rd Panzer, 111th Infantry, 444th and 454th Security Divisions) was subordinated to Army Group Don and ordered to withdraw to Rostov. Manstein now had some measure of freedom to stabilize his situation. *OKH* also ordered the 13th Panzer Division to cover the north flank of Army Group A and, if necessary, to move also to Rostov.[103]

Once again, however, Hitler had chosen to take only half measures. Rather than bringing all the forces of Army Group A out of the Caucasus, Hitler insisted that the 17th Army withdraw into the Gothshead position in front of the Taman Peninsula. At the last moment, he also reallocated the 13th Panzer Division to Army Group A. As a result, valuable troops were bottled up in the Kuban and rendered virtually useless.[104]

The next day, Manstein ordered all forces of the 1st Panzer Army to withdraw to the Kuto Yeya River no later than January 31. The movement of the 1st Panzer Army was to be covered north of this line by the 4th Panzer Army. Once the organized retreat of all forces on the Don line was assured, the 1st Panzer Army was then to make the 3rd Panzer Division available for use in the Don-Donets bend. Until then, the 4th Panzer Army was to hold the Don defenses, including Rostov, using the LVII Panzer Corps, the XXIX Corps, and a headquarters formed for special use. Manstein also encouraged the 4th Panzer Army to conclude its battle on the Lower Manytsch as quickly as possible to enable it to move to Voroshilovgrad. At the same time, the 4th Panzer Army still had to delay the Soviet advance long enough for the 1st Panzer Army to pass through Rostov.[105]

At the end of January, the situation facing Manstein and Army Group Don seemed hopeless. Manstein had finally been given control of the 1st Panzer Army, but it was still necessary to hold a corridor through which it could pass through Rostov. To accomplish this, the 4th Panzer Army was faced with the Herculean task of not only holding open the way to Rostov, but in delaying the Russian advance south of the Don, while at the same time preparing for a major shift of its forces to the north. Maintaining the 4th Panzer Army south of

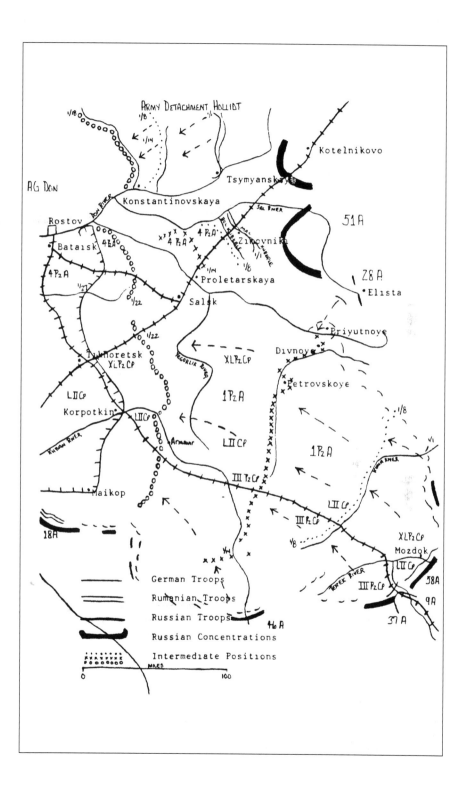

ARMY DETACHMENT HOLLIDT

Kotelnikovo

Tsymyanskaya

AG DON

Konstantinovskaya

Rostov

51 A

Bataisk

4 A

4 P₂ A

4 P₂ A

Zimovniki

28 A

Elista

Proletarskaya

Salsk

Priyutnoye

Tikhoretsk
YL P₂ CP

XL P₂ CP

Divnoye

Petrovskoye

LII CP

1 P₂ A

Korpotkin

LIII CP

LIII CP

Armavir

LII CP

1 P₂ A

III P₂ CP

LII CP

Maikop

III P₂ CP

18 A

XL P₂ CP

Mozdok

LII CP

58 A

III P₂ CP

9 A

37 A

German Troops

Rumanian Troops

Russian Troops

46 A

Russian Concentrations

Intermediate Positions

MILES

0   100

the Don would secure the movement of the 1st Panzer Army, but made it increasingly doubtful whether Hoth's valuable mobile forces could be shifted to the Donets in time to stop the Russians from advancing across the river.

Between the Donets bend north of Voroshilovgrad and the area just north of Starobelsk, the Russians had three tank corps (18th, 4th, and 10th Tank Corps) and three rifle corps (6th Guards, 4th Guards, and 15th Rifle Corps). It was still unclear whether the Russians intended to push toward Isyum-Slavyansk or, which seemed more likely, to turn against the Donets between Lisichansk and the area northwest of Voroshilovgrad.

On the Donets front there were four tank corps (23rd, 5th, 2nd Guards, and 1st Guards Tank Corps). Although these forces were engaged in only minor attacks, probably because of a lack of fuel and ammunition, they were expected to resume major attacks across the Donets between Voroshilovgrad and the area east of Kamensk.

On the front between the Donets bend north of Belokalitvenskaya to the Don, there were approximately ten rifle divisions and two cavalry corps. In addition, there were the 5th Motorized, 25th Tank, and 1st Tank Corps. These formations were expected to shift to the north to support the Russian attacks between Voroshilovgrad and Kamensk.

In the angle formed by the Don and Manytsch were the 3rd Guards Tank, 2nd Guards Motorized, 5th Guards Motorized, and the 1st Guards and 13th Rifle Corps. These formations were expected to make a thrust across the Don toward Rostov or to cross the Lower Manytsch to the south. Against this group the Germans had only nominal forces between Novocherkassk and Rostov (15th Luftwaffe Field Division and the staff of the 79th Infantry Division).

South of the Don, against the east flank of the 4th Panzer Army between the Manytsch and the Kugo Yeya, the Russians had seven rifle divisions, three rifle brigades, and one tank brigade (51st and 28th Armies). These forces were making heavy attacks against Met-shetinskaya. Behind the front, the 4th Guards and 3rd Guards Mechanized Corps were waiting to exploit any success.[106]

Recognizing his difficult situation, Manstein endeavored to release as many of his mobile divisions from the front as possible. Once disengaged, he used them to plug holes in the front by making immediate counterattacks against Soviet breakthroughs. This allowed time for the weary infantry divisions to regroup and retake the line once the panzers did their work. However, there were never enough mobile forces to deal with all the crises, and only the most dangerous penetrations could be dealt with. South of the Don, the 16th Motorized, 11th Panzer, 17th Panzer, 23rd Panzer, and SS *Wiking* Divisions were tied down, holding open the way to Rostov for the 1st Panzer Army. Along the Donets, the 6th and 7th Panzer Divisions were kept busy filling gaps around Belokalitvenskaya and between Voroshilovgrad and Lisichansk. The 19th and 22nd Panzer Divisions were also employed as mobile reserves, but their extremely weakened condition limited their use.[107]

Although the 6th and 7th Panzer Divisions had eliminated the danger of an immediate Soviet breakthrough between the Bystraya and the Kalitva, they were unable to do more than slow the Russian advance. As a result, both panzer divisions withdrew, together with the rest of *Armee Abteilung* Hollidt, to the Donets.

Armee Abteilung Hollidt had barely settled into its new position behind the Donets when it was threatened by Soviet penetrations at Belokalitvenskaya and Kamensk. By this time, German troops were fighting exhaustion and frostbite as well as the enemy. In early January the temperature had dipped below freezing, and since then the mercury had dropped steadily, accompanied by winter storms and icy winds.

Troop strength in the 6th and 7th Panzer Divisions was down to 2,000 and 2,400 respectively, although tank strength was relatively good: thirty in the 6th Panzer Divisions and forty-two in the 7th Panzer Division.[108] Once again, however, the 6th and 7th Panzer Divisions were called upon to counterattack enemy breakthroughs and reestablish the front. Manstein's use of these two divisions demonstrates how he was able to get the most out of his few available units north of the Don. Manstein's employment of the 6th and 7th Panzer Divisions also demonstrates the effectiveness of armored forces in a defensive role. Although he tried to maintain at least one division as a mobile reserve, Manstein was never able to achieve this ideal. The length of the front and continuous Soviet pressure made this impossible. As a result, the 6th and 7th Panzer Divisions were used in "hit-and-run" counterattacks. This method was used to forestall a Russian breakthrough between the Bystraya and the Kalitva and again to pinch off the penetration on the Kagalnik. Several factors dictated the hit-and-run tactics. Because the panzer division was the most potent and most mobile formation available, it was well suited to make strong, rapid counterattacks. In addition, Manstein knew that the Russians could penetrate the front at almost any time and place; therefore, it was important that the counterattacking force be able to reach the threatened area as quickly as possible. More importantly, the panzer divisions' mobility allowed them to disengage once they had completed their task. In either case, it was critical that the offensive power of the panzer divisions not be sapped by being tied down.

Once *Armee Abteilung* Hollidt reached the Donets, the 6th and 7th Panzer Divisions again resumed the familiar role of fire brigade. The 7th Panzer Division arrived in the Kamensk area on January 16, and was immediately pressed into the service to throw the advancing Russians back across the Donets. For the next four days, the 7th Panzer Division was counterattacking, pressing the Soviets into a narrower area until they were eliminated on January 23.[109]

Farther south, the 6th Panzer Division was attempting to keep the Russians from breaking across the Donets at Belokalitvenskaya. On January 21, the Soviets broke through west of the town, but were cut off by 6th Panzer Division counterattacks. The next day, however, Russian reinforcements arrived opposite the 6th Panzer Division. In fact, these reinforcements were only part of a much larger Soviet troop movement by the 3rd Guards and 5th Tank Armies of the Southwestern Front in preparation for a new offensive against Army Group Don at the end of January.[110]

The movement of Soviet troops and the Russian build-up did not go unnoticed by Manstein, who reported these developments daily to *OKH*. On January 22, Manstein informed *OKH* that the movement of enemy forces, across the front of *Armee Abteilung* Hollidt and *Armee Abteilung* Fretter-Pico, led him to believe that the Russians would attempt to envelop *Armee Abteilung* Hollidt with concentric attacks from the south flank toward Rostov, and on the northern flank from the Kamensk-Voroshilovgrad sector. Subsequent reports warned of an attack from the Starobelsk area toward Lisichansk.[111] These reports were an accurate reflection of Soviet plans for the upcoming offensive. To meet these attacks, Manstein, on January 31, worked out a timetable for releasing some of the armored formations of the 4th Panzer Army. By this time, most of the 1st Panzer Army had either passed through Rostov or was within easy reach of the city. To hold Rostov any longer than necessary would only have tied down troops that were needed elsewhere.

By February 4, it was planned that four divisions (3rd, 11th, 17th, and 23rd Panzer Divisions) would be concentrated in the area north and northeast of Rostov. In addition, the 1st Panzer Army would also take over the Donets sector held by *Armee Abteilung* Fretter-Pico.[112]

On February 1, Hoth informed Manstein that his army could not hold the narrow Rostov bridgehead with only the 444th and 454th Security Divisions and the 111th Infantry Division. The bridgehead was only weakly secured and it was possible for the Russians to break through at a number of points and penetrate Rostov. In order to stiffen the defenses, it was necessary to employ the SS *Wiking* Division and the 16th Motorized Division.

If the units could not be made available, Hoth suggested that the bridgehead be held for only one day and then to withdraw to the north bank to construct defenses there. Furthermore, the 3rd Panzer Division would not be able to hold the bridgehead around Bataisk, because the Russians would be able to slip through the gap to the north.[113]

Manstein passed this information along to Zeitzler, emphasizing the fact that infantry strength was very low and that there were only fifty-two artillery pieces available to support the bridgehead. Manstein could not, however, support Hoth's request for *Wiking* and the 16th Motorized Divisions, because these units were needed elsewhere. The area between the mouth of the Don and Novocherkassk was presently screened only by weak, ad hoc forces. The Russians were advancing against this sector, and it was decided to employ *Wiking* and the 16th Motorized Division to defend this area by means of mobile operations.[114]

Meanwhile, Army Group B issued its "Orders for the Conduct of Operations in the Army Group B Area and Transition to Counterattack." These measures were designed to "cover the flank and center of Army Group Don with mobile operations and to bring the enemy advance to a standstill on the general line Oskol-Seym sector."[115]

Armee Abteilung Lanz (including the SS Panzer Corps) had the task of preventing the outflanking of Army Group Don by screening the Kharkov-Belgorod area in mobile operations. In the event that the 304th Infantry Division (*Armee Abteilung* Fretter-Pico) was forced to withdraw behind the Donets, *Armee Abteilung* Lanz was to establish a link with *Armee Abteilung* Fretter-Pico at Mayako. *Armee Abteilung* Lanz was also responsible for securing movement between Oskol and the Donets rivers and between Oskol and Korotchka. Under no circumstances was the Oskol to be crossed to the east.

The 2nd Panzer Army was to cover the south flank of Army Group Center and to delay the Soviet advance from Kursk. At worst, it was to hold the general line Seyin-Kursk and to hold the Belgorod-Kursk-Orel railroad junction for as long as possible.[116]

East of Kursk, it was intended to assemble a strong group (four panzer divisions) to outflank and destroy the Soviet forces in cooperation with the VII and LV Corps. The SS Panzer Corps was to concentrate in the Kharkov area and be available to *OKH*.[117]

Army Group Don was also preparing counterattacks against the Russians. In late January, *Armee Abteilung* Fretter-Pico was struck by strong attacks by forces of the 2nd Guards and 6th Armies. The main effort of these attacks was on the left flank of *Armee Abteilung* Fretter-Pico with simultaneous attacks at and west of Krassny Liman. The enemy was also expected to thrust toward Artemovsk-Slavyansk. A weak Russian group was already across the Donets on the left flank of the 304th Infantry Division and was advancing toward Krasnodonksy. This advance was accompanied by pinning attacks on both sides of Lisichansk.[118]

Responsibility for stemming this latest Russian advance fell on the 1st Panzer Army, which took over command of *Armee Abteilung* Fretter-Pico's sector on February 3. In addition to the forces of *Armee Abteilung* Fretter-Pico (304th and 335th Infantry Divisions and 3rd Mountain Division), the 1st Panzer Army also commanded the III Panzer Corps, which included the 19th and 7th Panzer Divisions. To augment these forces, the 3rd Panzer Division was scheduled to arrive in the Tshernochino-Greko Timofeyevsky area on February 4, and the XL Panzer Corps with the 11th Panzer Division was scheduled to arrive in the Makeyevka-Illovaysky-Chartsky area on February 5. A motorized division was also due to arrive on February 6, in the same area as the 3rd Panzer Division.[119]

The 1st Panzer Army had orders "to intercept the enemy breakthrough on the right flank (304th Infantry Division), to hold the Donets line on both sides of Voroshilovgrad to the northwest of Lisichansk, and, depending on the development of the situation, to attack and to eliminate the enemy that has crossed the Donets to the west."[120]

While the combined strength of the 1st Panzer Army and the forces assembled by Army Group B were considerable, the intended attacks were too little too late. On January 29, *Armee Abteilung* Fretter-Pico was struck by the powerful forces of the 6th, 1st Guards, 3rd Guards, and 5th Tank Armies, and Group Popov, a front mobile group composed of four tank corps, three rifle divisions, and two tank brigades. On February 2, Army Group B was struck by the 3rd Tank, 40th, and 69th Armies. The objective of these combined offensives was nothing less that the liberation of the Ukraine and the destruction of Army Groups B and Don.[121] The same day, organized resistance in Stalingrad came to an end.

Notes

1. HG Don Anlg. 4 KTB, December 20, 1942, Roll 269, Frame 365. Manstein, p. 344.
2. Manstein, p. 372.
3. Ibid., pp. 373–374. HG Don Anlg. 5 KTB, December 27, 1942, Roll 270, Frames 563–564, 593.

4. Erickson, pp. 28–29.
5. Ibid.
6. Ibid., p. 31.
7. Ibid.
8. HG Don Anlg. 5 KTB, December, 25, 1942, Roll 270, Frames 600, 661, 669.
9. Ibid., December, 26, 1942, Frame 656.
10. Ibid., Frames 638–639.
11. Ibid., December 25, 1942, Frame 674.
12. Ibid., December 27, 1942, Frames 593–594.
13. Ibid., Frame 591.
14. Ibid., Frames 563–564. Manstein, pp. 348–349.
15. Ibid., December 28, 1942, Frame 467. There is some doubt that Hitler actually believed that the 6th Army could still be saved, or as is more likely, that he was not yet ready to accept its loss. Subsequent messages make few references to the 6th Army or its relief.
16. Ibid., Frames 467, 469.
17. Ibid., Frame 591.
18. Ibid., Frame 497.
19. Ibid., Frame 401. Manstein, p. 381. Historical Division Headquarters, USA, Europe, Foreign Military Studies, Ms T15 *Reverses on the Southern Wing, 1942–1943*, by Fredrich Schulz Gen. d. Inf., et al., pp. 54–55. Cited henceforth as Ms T15.
20. Erickson, p. 18.
21. Ibid., p. 19.
22. Ibid.
23. HG Don Anlg. 5 KTB, December 24–25, 1942, Roll 270, Frames 602, 731, 735.
24. Ibid., December 26–28, 1942, Frames 443, 448, 527–528, 602. Erickson, pp. 20, 22.
25. This improvised battlegroup was composed mostly of Italian remnants centered around the German 298th Infantry Division. It would later include the 304th and 335th Infantry Divisions. It was commanded by General Maximilian Fretter-Pico. HG Don Anlg. 4 KTB, December 23, 1942, Roll 269, Frames 707–709. HG Don Anlg. 5 KTB, December 28, 1942, Roll 270, Frame 469.
26. Kreysing participated in the abortive attack on Murmansk. As a veteran of campaigns in Norway and Finland, he was probably the only commanding general in southern Russia who thought the winter was mild. Newton.
27. HG Don Anlg. 5 KTB, December 27–28, 1942, Roll 270, Frames 469, 545–549.
28. Ibid., December 30–31, 1942, Frames 194–195, 286–287. Ms P114c, *skizzie 9* p. 9. Center for Land Warfare, US Army War College, *1894 Art of War Symposium, From the Don to the Dnepr: Soviet Offensive Operations, December 1942–August 1943*, transcript by Lt. Col. David Glanz, Map Set "Operation Little Saturn." Cited henceforth as Glanz.
29. HG Don Anlg. 5 KTB, December 29–30, 1942, Roll 270, Frames 282, 288–289, 366, 370.
30. Ibid., December 30–31, 1942, Frames 238, 261–262, 263–265, 320.
31. Ibid.

32. Ibid., Frames 226, 238, 247, 324.

33. Ibid., Frames 234, 295, 320.

34. Manstein, p. 349. The original Army Group Don copy of this message can be found in HG Don Anlg. 5 KTB, Roll 270, Frames 178–179. However, it is a handwritten copy that is only partially legible.

35. HG Don Anlg. 5 KTB, January 1–3, 1943, Roll 270, Frames 4, 10, 44, 47, 129–130, 134.

36. Heeresgruppe Don Ia, Anlagenband 6 z. KTB January 4–12, 1943, Microcopy T 313, Roll 270, Frames 1343, 1346. Cited henceforth as HG Don Anlg. 6 KTB, with date, roll, and frame number.

37. Ibid., January 5, 1943, Frames 1209, 1244, 1248, 1271.

38. Ibid., January 6, 1943, Frames 1263, 1267, 1270.

39. Ibid., January 7–8, 1943, Frames 1172, 1193.

40. Ibid., January 9, 1943, Frames 1054–1055.

41. Ibid., Frame 1055.

42. Ibid., January 10, 1943, Frames 964–965.

43. On January 12, 1943, the 17th and 23rd Panzer Divisions reported a combined total of forty-five tanks and nine assault guns operational. Ibid., January 12, 1943, Frame 803.

44. Ibid., Frames 813, 832.

45. Ibid., Frames 803, 815.

46. Heeresgruppe Don Ia, Anlagenband 7 z. KTB, January 13–20, 1943, Microcopy T 313, Roll 271, Frame 449. Cited henceforth as HG Don Anlg. 7 KTB, with date, roll, and frame number.

47. Ibid., January 16–18, 1943, Frames 165, 171, 381, 720.

48. Ibid., January 20, 1943, Frame 10.

49. Ibid., January 14, 1943, Frame 537. Manstein, pp. 387–388. Ms P114c, skizzie 15 p. 207.

50. Ice conditions along the Don and Donets for the second week of January ranged from approximately eight to twelve inches, or a capacity of from six to eighteen tons. While this was not enough to bear the weight of tanks, it was enough to suport the weight of infantry and light vehicles. HG Don Anlg. 7 KTB, January 15, 1943, Roll 271, Frame 498.

51. Ibid., January 14, 1943, Frame 537.

52. Ibid., January 15, 1943, Frame 484. January 18, 1943, Frame 169.

53. Newton.

54. January 20, 1943, Frames 55, 72, 74.

55. The three regiments of the 294th Infantry Division had a total strength of 1,920 men. No regiment had more than about 700 troops. Machine guns, mortars, anti-tank guns, and artillery were also greatly reduced. This division was one of the stronger units available to Armee Abteilung Hollidt. HG Don Anlg. 5 KTB, January 1–2, 1943, Roll 270, Frames 69– 74, 135.

56. Ibid., January 2, 1943, Frames 43, 49–50.

57. Ibid., January 3, 1943, Frames 4, 12–13, 25. HG Don Anlg. 6 KTB, January 4, 1943, Roll 270, Frame 1343.

58. HG Don Anlg. 6 KTB, January 4, 1942, Roll 270, Frames 1349–1350.

59. Ibid., Frame 1350.

60. Ibid., January 5, 1943, Frames 1272, 1275–1276.
61. Ibid., January 4–6, 1943, Frames 1243, 1267, 1379, 1403.
62. Newton.
63. Ibid., January 8, 1943, Frames 1071–1072, 1078–1079.
64. Ibid., Frames 1101, 1122.
65. Ibid., January 9, 1943, Frame 1054.
66. Ibid., Frames 996–997, 1002–1004.
67. Ibid., January 11, 1943, Frame 903.
68. Ibid., January 9–10, 1943, Frames 952, 930–933, 996–997. HG Don Anlg. 7 KTB, January 13, 1943, Roll 271, Frame 643.
69. HG Don Anlg. 7 KTB, January 13, 1943, Roll 271, Frame 656.
70. Ibid., Frame 570.
71. Ibid., Frames 570, 665.
72. Ibid., Frames 647, 665.
73. Newton.
74. Ibid., January 14–17, 1943, Frames 492, 518, 534.
75. Ibid., January 15, 1943, Frames 454, 484.
76. Ibid.
77. Ibid., January 16–17, 1943, Frames 165–166, 382, 387–389.
78. Ibid., Frames 350–351, 525.
79. Ibid., January 13, 1943, Frame 622. January 17, 1943, Frame 370.
80. Ibid., January 17–18, 1943, Frames 223, 226, 249.
81. Erickson, p. 28.
82. Ibid., pp. 32–33.
83. Ibid., pp. 33–34.
84. Ibid., pp. 34–35.
85. HG Don Anlg. 7 KTB, January 19, 1943, Roll 271, Frame 128.
86. Ibid., Frames 128–129.
87. Ibid., Frame 129.
88. Ibid.
89. Heeresgruppe Don Ia, Anlagenband 8 z. KTB, January 21–29, 1943, Microcopy T 313, Roll 271, Frames 1024–1025. Cited henceforth as HG Don Anlg. 8 KTB, with date, roll, and frame number.
90. Ibid., Frame 55.
91. Ibid.
92. Ibid., January 21, 1943, Frames 1204, 1212.
93. Ibid., January 22, 1943, Frame 1060.
94. Ibid., Frame 1204.
95. Ibid.
96. Ibid., January 23, 1943, Frame 1024.
97. Ibid., January 23–24, 1943, Frames 1060, 1081. At this time the SS Panzer Corps consisted of LSAH and Das Reich. It would later include the Totenkopf Division.
98. Ibid., January 24, 1943, Frame 1162.
99. Ibid., Frame 1064.
100. Manstein, p. 397.
101. HG Don Anlg. 8 KTB, January 25, 1943, Roll 271, Frame 987.

102. Ibid., Frames 958–986.
103. Ibid., January 27, 1943, Frame 845. January 29, 1943, Frame 705.
104. Ibid., Manstein, p. 398.
105. HG Don Anlg. 8 KTB, January 29, 1943, Roll 271, Frames 777–779.
106. Ibid., Frames 712–713.
107. The 6th Panzer Division, with sixty tanks and ten assault guns, and the 7th Panzer Division, with thirty tanks and eleven assault guns, were by far the strongest of the available armored formations. Of the remaining six mobile divisions, the 11th Panzer Division had twenty-eight tanks, *Wiking* had fifteen tanks, the 17th Panzer Division had eleven tanks, the 16th Motorized Division had ten tanks, the 19th Panzer Division had eight tanks and seven assault guns, and the 23rd Panzer Division had eight tanks. Ibid., January 17–19, 1943, Frames 753, 820. Heeresgruppe Don Ia, Anlagenband 9 KTB, January 31-February 6, 1943, Microcopy T 313, Roll 272, Frames 266, 343, 428. Cited henceforth as HG Don Anlg. 9 KTB, with date, roll, and frame number.
108. HG Don Anlg. 7 KTB, January 19, 1943, Roll 270, Frames 98, 121.
109. Ibid., January 16–20, 1943, Frames 8, 98, 173, 272, 387. HG Don Anlg. 8 KTB, January 21–23, 1943, Roll 271, Frames 1028, 1034, 1075, 1266.
110. HG Don Anlg. 8 KTB, January 21–22, 1943, Roll 271, Frames 1034, 1175.
111. Ibid., Frames 1030–1031, 1187. January, 26, 1943, Frame 884.
112. HG Don Anlg. 9 KTB, January 31, 1943, Roll 272, Frames 353–354.
113. Ibid., February 2, 1943, Frames 299.
114. Ibid., Frame 280.
115. Ibid., January 31, 1943, Frame 383.
116. Ibid., Frame 384.
117. Ibid., Frame 386.
118. Ibid., February 1, 1943, Frame 285.
119. Ibid., February 1–2, 1943, Frames 219–220, 285–286.
120. Ibid., February 1, 1943, Frame 285.
121. HG Don Anlg. 8 KTB, January 29, 1943, Roll 271, Frames 672, 680. Erickson, pp. 45–47.

A German winter supply column in the winter of 1942–43. German truck transport was unable to keep up with the insatiable demands for food, fuel, and ammunition constantly needed on the Eastern Front, and worse, it was ill-suited for the rugged conditions and inclement weather. Local solutions such as these Russian horses were employed. SCOTT PICK/SUMMIT PHOTOGRAPHICS

A Russian KV1 heavy tank with its turret blown off. The size, robustness, and quantity of Russian tanks surprised the Germans. SCOTT PICK/SUMMIT PHOTOGRAPHICS

German troops in a winter trench position wearing snow-camouflage suits. The bitter cold caught the Germans off guard and became an enemy just as challenging as the Russians. SCOTT PICK/SUMMIT PHOTOGRAPHICS

Battle-hardened German troops sitting outside their dugout in a winter frontline trench position. Note the captured Russian PPSH41 machine gun at right. SCOTT PICK/SUMMIT PHO-TOGRAPHICS

German troops take a moment to rest. Fighting in built-up areas such as Stalingrad took a massive toll on the infantry that had to clear out the Russians house-by-house. SCOTT PICK/SUMMIT PHOTOGRAPHICS

A long line of captured Russian soldiers. The Russians could afford far greater losses than the Germans. SCOTT PICK/SUMMIT PHOTOGRAPHICS

A German soldier wearing a captured Russian Ushanka fur hat. This soldier is decorated with the Iron Cross, 2nd Class; the Infantry Assault Badge; and the Wound Badge. SCOTT PICK/SUMMIT PHOTOGRAPHICS

German troops inspect a captured Russian T-34 that appears to be intact. The Germans were masters at reusing captured equipment on the battlefield. SCOTT PICK/SUMMIT PHOTOGRAPHICS

German troops pass through a southern Ukrainian village. Rivers were natural defensive lines and were used by both sides to slow down the enemy. SCOTT PICK/SUMMIT PHOTOGRAPHICS

A German soldier being awarded a medal. The fierce fighting on the Russian front created many heroes, though not all survived to collect their medals. SCOTT PICK/SUMMIT PHOTOGRAPHICS

A pair of knocked-out Russian tanks. The one in the foreground is a T-26, with a massive T-35 behind it in a ditch. SCOTT PICK/SUMMIT PHOTOGRAPHICS

German troops march past a knocked-out KV series Russian tank with its turret blown off by a massive internal explosion. SCOTT PICK/SUMMIT PHOTOGRAPHICS

A captured Russian soldier in the early stages of Operation Barbarossa in the summer of 1941. Note the early-war use of the traditional Russian hat with large star. SCOTT PICK/SUMMIT PHOTOGRAPHICS

German officers hold a conference in the field. Note the panzer soldier at right wearing the distinctive black uniform of the panzer corps. SCOTT PICK/SUMMIT PHOTOGRAPHICS

An early-model German Panzer VI Tiger tank moving through a Russian village. The Tiger's heavy armor and lethal 88-millimeter main gun made it a superb hunter on the vast Russian steppes, but there were never enough of these tanks to fend off the massive quantities of tanks the Russians were able to produce. SCOTT PICK/SUMMIT PHOTOGRAPHICS

A three-man German frontline machine-gun nest featuring the MG34 machine gun with antiaircraft sight. SCOTT PICK/SUMMIT PHOTOGRAPHICS

A German Luftwaffe bomber crew of KG 51 stands in front of their Ju 88 before embarking on a mission behind Russian lines. Hermann Goering had promised that the Luftwaffe would be able to bomb England into submission and keep Stalingrad supplied; neither promise was fulfilled, though the Luftwaffe crews tried valiantly. SCOTT PICK/SUMMIT PHOTOGRAPHICS

Two members of a German panzer crew stand beside their Panzer III armed with a 50-millimeter main gun. The armor of the Russian T-34 and KV series of tanks and their much larger caliber of guns meant that the Panzer III's usefulness on the battlefield was quickly limited. SCOTT PICK/SUMMIT PHOTOGRAPHICS

Russian children gather in a village. Too often, civilians became casualties in the fighting on the Eastern Front. SCOTT PICK/SUMMIT PHOTOGRAPHICS

CHAPTER 4

The Backhand Blow

By the beginning of February 1943, it seemed as if Manstein's worst fears were about to be realized. The Soviet offensives in mid-January against the Hungarian 2nd Army and the German 2nd Army shattered the German front, severing Army Group B from Army Group Don and eliminating it as an effective command. As a result, there was 150-mile gap from the Kursk-Kastrone railroad south to Kupyansk. With only five German divisions available to screen this chasm and only three divisions in reserve at Kharkov, Manstein's position appeared all but lost. Under the circumstances, the sooner the Russians advanced on Kursk the better for them, before the Germans could consolidate their defenses around Kharkov.

While the long months of arduous campaigning were straining Army Group Don to its limits, the strain of combat was also taking its toll on Manstein. His complexion, normally rosy, was now pale. There was also evidence of stress around his temples, which were now accented by numerous worry lines, making his eyes appear sunken. The most visible sign that Manstein was operating under great presure was his hair, which had turned snow white.

While Hitler entertained hopes of halting the Red Army with a relief attack mounted from the Kharkov area by one division of the newly assembled SS Panzer Corps, Manstein looked for a more realistic solution. Manstein sought to restore the situation by convincing Hitler of the need to withdraw German forces as a prerequisite for their concentration for a counterblow against the advancing Russians. In Manstein's opinion it was not possible to hold the Don-Donets salient for any length of time. Defending the Donets for the remainder of 1943 would require the commitment of all available forces on the southern flank. However, doing so would give the Soviets a free hand at any point along the rest of the front. Even if the Donets could be held, it was safe to assume that the Russians would still strive to encircle the entire southern wing of the Eastern Front on the Black Sea.[1]

If, on the other hand, Hitler wished to seek an offensive solution, he could do so only in the south, but not from the Don-Donets salient, because of the now familiar supply difficulties. Manstein believed that by first allowing the Russians to advance west toward the Lower Dnieper, a counterblow could be delivered from the Kharkov area to smash the connecting front, in order to turn south and surround the enemy on the Sea of Azov.[2]

This is exactly what Manstein had in mind when he advocated to Hitler a withdrawal to the Mius River line. Characteristically, Hitler was unwilling to accept any idea that would allow the Soviets to reoccupy the Donets coal region. Instead, he insisted on an attack by the SS Panzer Division *Das Reich* (the only division of the SS Panzer Corps then available) from the Kharkov area into the rear of the Soviet forces advancing on the Donets front. What Hitler failed to comprehend was that it was unrealistic to expect one division to achieve any major success. Moreover, the commitment of *Das Reich* would mean splitting up the only striking force (the SS Panzer Corps) that could join Army Group Don in the near future.[3]

Regardless of the significance of the Don-Donets region, Hitler ignored the military realities of the situation. By forcing Manstein to hold the Don-Donets salient, Hitler risked losing not only the coal region (which, in any case, had dubious economic value because of the low quality of the coal), but Army Group Don, which despite its battered condition was the only force standing between the Russians and the complete collapse of the southern flank and, consequently, the entire Eastern Front as well. Manstein's proposal at least offered the prospect of stabilizing the southern flank, not to mention the regaining of the initiative for the German side. Even if the coal region could not be held, it was a small price to pay for stabilizing a sector of the front that had been threatened with collapse for nearly four months.

While the Germans delayed, the Russians planned. That STAVKA was optimistic about winning a major victory in the south was demonstrated by the decision to enlarge the scope of the winter offensive to include the Voronezh Front (the Southwestern and Southern Fronts were already engaged against Army Group Don). Although still heavily engaged against the German 2nd Army in the Kastorne area, STAVKA planned to continue the offensive westward without stopping to regroup. This was a calculated risk that the Soviet high command was willing to take. Even though Russian forces were worn down by a month of fighting, a new offensive, in conjunction with pressure from adjacent fronts, could produce the final collapse of the German position on the southern flank of the Eastern Front. Thus, while the Southwestern and Southern Fronts planned to attack through the Donets basin to the Dnieper River, the Voronezh Front would advance on Kursk and Kharkov.[4]

With the destruction of the Hungarian 2nd Army and the German 2nd Army, it appeared as if the entire German position in southern Russia was about to cave in. STAVKA now sought means to accelerate its offensive and drive the Germans back to the Dnieper and beyond. Between January 20 and 23, STAVKA approved two plans that it hoped would produce the final collapse of the German southern flank. The first, Operation GALLOP, was designed to liberate the Donets basin and push the Germans across the Dnieper. The second, Operation STAR, was intended to capture Kharkov and drive the Germans as far west as possible. These two offensives, if successful, would liberate the Ukraine.[5]

The liberation of the Ukraine, the second largest political unit of the U.S.S.R. after the Russian Federal Republic, was assigned to three fronts, Voronezh (Operation STAR), Southwestern, and Southern (Operation GALLOP). The Voronezh Front was responsible for the northeast Ukraine, including Kharkov. Its left flank armies (north to south, 40th, 69th, and 3rd Tank) were directed at Kharkov; the right flank armies (60th and 38th) were directed against Kursk and Obyan, respectively. The Voronezh Front's final objective was a line running from Rylsk-Lebedin-Poltava. The eastern Ukraine, including the Donets basin, was the responsibility of the Southwestern and Southern Fronts. The Southwestern Front would be the primary attacking force, using the 1st Guards and 6th Armies and a mobile group to thrust from Starobelsk through Slavyansk and on to Mariupol, thus outflanking the German forces in the Donets basin from the west and pinning them against the Sea of Azov. The Southern Front would advance to the west along the coast to Mariupol.

The destruction of Army Group Center was also planned at the end of January, involving five more Soviet fronts in large scale offensive operations. The Bryansk Front and left flank of the Western Front were to destroy the 2nd Panzer Army around Orel. After the Central Front attacked (formed from divisions pulled from Stalingrad), fresh armies would drive through Bryansk and on to Smolensk, crashing into the German rear, at which time the Kalinin and Western Fronts would envelop and destroy the main force of Army Group Center. To the north, the Northwestern Front would eliminate the Germans in the Demyansk area, to secure the passage of mobile formations into the rear of German troops engaged against the Leningrad and Volkhov Fronts. By the beginning of February 1943, front commanders knew the main outline of this plan and had orders to begin operational preparations.[6]

Operations in the south were envisioned as pursuit, intended to bring the armies of the Voronezh, Southwestern, and Southern Fronts to the Dnieper on a sector running from Chernigov to Kherson by the time of the spring thaw. On February 6, STAVKA set the strategic objective of the Voronezh Front as the line Lgov-Glukhov-Chernigov-Poltava-Kremenchug, and ordered Vatutin "to prevent an enemy withdrawal on Dnepropetrovsk and Zaporozhye."[7] At the same time, the front should "drive the Donbas group of enemy forces into the Crimea, seal off the approaches at Prekop and the Savash, and isolate the [enemy] Donets forces from the remainder of the Ukraine."[8] After the Donets had been cleared, the Southwestern Front would drive to the Dnieper on a broad front running from Kremenchug to Nikopol, while the Southern Front would attack the Lower Dnieper.[9]

To exploit the weakness of the forces facing the Southwestern Front (*Armee Abteilung* Hollidt and Fretter-Pico), Vatutin planned to attack southward through Starobelsk to Mariupol deep into the rear of Army Group Don. The aim of the operation was to cut off the German withdrawal routes from the Donets basin and collapse the entire German position in southern Russia. STAVKA approved this plan, together with a follow-up operation in the north that would become Operation STAR.[10]

Vatutin's plan called for Soviet mobile formations to reach Mariupol, approximately 150 miles from the 1st Guards Army positions around Lisichansk, within seven days. These mobile forces were to capture the main Dnieper crossings at Zaporozhye and Dnepropetrovsk. The Southern Front would support the Southwestern Front by destroying the German forces in the Rostov area and driving along the northern coast of the Sea of Azov.[11]

Shortly after Vatutin's plan was adopted, STAVKA outlined a second offensive to liberate Belgorod and Kharkov simultaneously with the Southwestern Front's sweep through the Donets basin. Urged on by Zhukov, Kursk was added as an objective of the Voronezh Front.[12]

Despite its optimism, STAVKA was concerned about the durability of Soviet forces and their ability to sustain deep operations. Both the Voronezh and Southwestern Fronts would open their new offensives without rest. Consequently, their forces were weakened by previous operations and supplied by overextended supply lines running from increasingly distant logistic centers. The large attack sectors also dictated that both fronts commit all their forces up front with virtually no reserves on hand to reinforce these attacks. Moreover, unlike the situation at Stalingrad, STAVKA had no armies in reserve.[13]

The Southwestern Front was composed of the 6th, 1st Guards, 3rd Guards, and 5th Tank Armies, plus a front mobile group, Group Popov, deployed along a front of about 160 miles. By this time, the Southwestern Front's combat strength had been reduced to approximately 325,000 men and about 360 tanks. It would be joined later

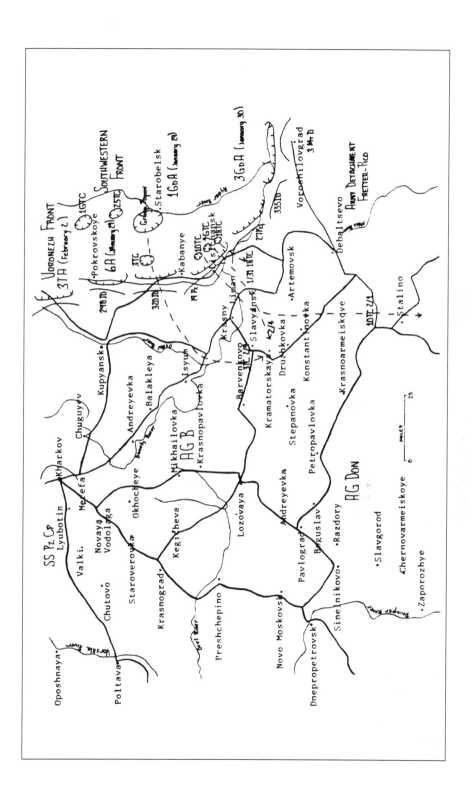

by the 1st Guards and 25th Tank Corps with an additional 300 tanks. Against this strength, *Armee Abteilung* Hollidt, the 1st Panzer Army (including *Armee Abteilung* Fretter-Pico), and the right flank of *Armee Abteilung* Lanz could muster only 160,000 men and about one hundred tanks, although these forces would be later augmented by two SS Panzer divisions with almost 200 tanks.[14]

The Southwestern Front was to strike westward across the Aydar and Oskol rivers, then swing to the southwest and south across the Donets, and through the Donets basin toward Dnieper. The terrain north and south of the Donets consisted of rolling hills with patches of sparse vegetation. The western bank of the Oskol and Aydar and the southern bank of the Donets were higher than the opposite banks, thus giving the Germans a tactical edge. Marshes and lakes along the river valleys, in particular along the Donets, hindered movement along or across the river. South of the towns of Slavyansk, Kramatorskaya, and Artemovsk, the hills became more pronounced.

All the roads were unpaved and followed the river valleys. Most of the larger towns and cities were also located in the valleys along these roads. The main road into the Donets basin from the northeast ran either through Voroshilovgrad or up the Katsney Torets River past Slavyansk and Kramatorskaya and up the Bachmuta River through Artemovsk. Because of the steep valley walls and the large built-up areas, the Germans considered the latter routes unsuitable for an advance by a large armored force. To the west, the more open terrain offered better cross-country movement for tanks through Barvenkovo or Lozovaya toward the southwest and the Dnieper River. However, even these open spaces were crisscrossed with gullies and dry washes, which impeded mechanized movement.[15]

The 6th Army of the Southwestern Front was to attack on January 29, on a forty-mile sector with all of its rifle forces committed forward. The 6th Army was assigned the mission of penetrating the German defenses and advancing toward Balakleya and Krasnograd, in order to cover the main attack to the south. Within seven days, the army was to drive seventy miles, to a line running from Mospanovo through Balakleya to Petrovskoye. The 3rd Tank Army of the Voronezh Front would attack on February 3, to cover the 6th Army's right flank.[16]

The main attack of the 6th Army would fall on a twelve-mile sector on its right flank. There, three rifle divisions would drive westward toward Kupyansk and push the German 298th Infantry Division back toward the Donets and away from Kharkov. Later, the 298th and, farther south, the 320th Infantry Divisions would both be surrounded and destroyed against the banks of the Donets. The 3rd Tank Corps of Group Popov would then be committed to exploit the 6th Army's attacks toward the southwest and west.[17]

On January 30, the 1st Guards Army would advance along a eighty-mile front. The 4th Guards Rifle Corps would attack on the right flank on a fifteen-mile sector to penetrate the German defenses and push toward Krasny Liman and across the Donets toward Barvenkovo. Following the commitment of Group Popov, the 4th Guards Rifle Corps would then turn southward to encircle the Germans defending in the Slavyansk-Artemovsk area. The 6th Guards Rifle Corps would thrust across the Donets opposite and south of Lisichansk to secure the city and support the 4th Guards Rifle Corps' wheeling movement. By the eighth day of the offensive, the 1st Guards Army would advance to a line running from Petrovskoye through Barvenkovo to Krasnoarmeisky Rudnik.[18]

Group Popov's mission was to attack with the advancing infantry of the 6th and 1st Guards Armies to Krasnoarmeiskoye and Mariupol to cut off the German withdrawal from the Donets basin. Popov's four tank corps were to advance up to 190 miles, disperse German defenses, and pin them into the towns and villages to be mopped up by the following infantry, and open the way for a decisive and rapid thrust by the main forces of the Southwestern Front.[19]

Advancing from the 6th Army's sector, the 3rd Tank Corps of Group Popov was to drive southwest to Slavyansk, which was to be captured by late February 4. The 3rd Tank Corps would then join the 4th Guards Tank Corps to secure crossings across the Donets, thrust on Kramatorskaya from the northeast, and occupy the town by February 4. A shortage of tanks forced all of the 4th Guards Tank Corps armor (forty tanks) to be concentrated in the 14th Guards Tank Brigade, which would spearhead the corps attack.[20]

Popov's 10th Tank Corps would advance against the center and cross the Donets on the first day. On the second day, the corps would occupy Artemovsk and Makeyevka and drive toward Stalino from the north. By the fifth day, the 10th Tank Corps was to reach the Volnovakha area deep in the rear of Army Group Don. Meanwhile, the last tank corps of Group Popov, the 18th, would cross the Donets opposite Lisichansk and seize the city. Subsequently, it was to turn southwest to join the other mobile formations. To support Popov, Vatutin held the 1st Guards and 25th Tank Corps in reserve.[21]

While the 1st Guards Army attacked on the Lisichansk sector, the 3rd Guards Army would attack from the north of Voroshilovgrad to a point east of Stalino on the Donets. These forces would penetrate the German defenses and advance through Stalino to link with the 1st Guards Army and surround all German troops in the Donets basin.[22]

On January 29, the 6th Army struck from the area northwest of Starobelsk, aiming for Balakleya. The following day, the 1st Guards Army struck from the southwest toward Krasny Liman, and within a few hours, Group Popov was inserted between the 1st Guards and 6th Armies to thrust southwest on an outward sweep through Krasnoarmeiskoye-Volnovakha to Mariupol to cut the German escape route from the Donets basin. On February 2, the 3rd Guards Army crossed the Donets east of Voroshilovgrad. On the same day, in the yawning gap between Voronezh and Voroshilovgrad, the 40th, 69th, and 3rd Tank Armies of the Voronezh Front struck the first blows of Operation STAR, aiming at Kursk-Belgorod-Kharkov.[23]

Thus, during the first week of February 1943, Army Group Don was faced with yet another crisis. Manstein found his situation deteriorating rapidly as a result of the new Soviet offensives against his left flank (*Armee Abteilung* Fretter-Pico) and the right flank of Army Group B (*Armee Abteilung* Lanz). The combined attacks by the Voronezh and Southwestern Fronts threatened to envelop Army Group Don and sever its line of communications across the Dnieper River. Together the two Soviet fronts totaled over twenty rifle divisions and eight tank corps. Although these forces had been worn down by a month's fighting, they were more than a match for the defending German troops.

To oppose this Russian wave, *Armee Abteilung* Fretter-Pico had only three battered infantry divisions (304th, 335th, and 3rd Mountain) and two woefully understrength armored divisions (19th and 27th Panzer). Most of the infantry divisions were down to battalion strength. The 3rd Mountain Division was composed mostly of walking wounded and men on leave whose parent units had been lost. Only the 335th Infantry Division displayed any real strength, but it too was reduced to about 3,500 troops. Combined, the 19th and 27th Panzer Divisions numbered only fifteen tanks and seven assault guns. There were virtually no reserves and little prospect of receiving fresh reinforcements.[24]

In Army Group B's sector, there were three infantry divisions (168th, remnants of the 298th, and 320th), one motorized division (*Grossdeutschland*), and a panzer grenadier regiment (from *Das Reich*) spread out along a front over 125 miles long. As a result of its weakened condition, Army Group B had earlier submitted a report informing Hitler that "The Army Group thus is no longer strong enough to secure the area assigned to it for its covering mission"[25] (i.e., the left flank of Army Group Don).

Elsewhere on Army Group Don's front, the 4th Panzer Army was still holding a small bridgehead at Rostov. Meanwhile, the 1st Panzer Army passed successfully through Rostov and was en route to the Middle Donets to take over the current sector of *Armee Abteilung* Fretter-Pico.

On February 3, *OKH* ordered Army Group Don to "engage and destroy the enemy forces that have advanced to the west and south-west across the line Lisichansk-Kupyansk and thereby eliminate the immediate threat to the deep flank of Army Group Don as well as the right flank of Army Group B."[26]

To accomplish this, the SS Panzer Division *Das Reich* of the SS Panzer Corps was ordered to concentrate around Kharkov. Characteristically, *OKH* (Hitler's) approval was necessary before the division could be employed.[27]

Once again, however, Hitler's tardy response to the developing situation was overtaken by events. Almost immediately, Manstein informed *OKH* that the order regarding *Das Reich* was out of date, as the division was already tied down. Moreover, to stem the attacks by the Southwestern Front against his left flank, Manstein would have to transfer nearly all of the mobile divisions of the 4th Panzer Army to the 1st Panzer Army. As a result, the 4th Panzer Army would be unable to hold the Don front. Stopgap measures using troops from *Armee Abteilung* Hollidt could not be counted on, because of the lack of forces. Finally, Manstein told Hitler that *Armee Abteilung* Hollidt must have freedom to move to the Novocherkassk-Kamensk line and, if necessary later, to the Mius River line.[28]

Meanwhile, Army Group B had already initiated measures to cover Army Group Don's flank by attempting to bring the Russian advance to a halt on the Oskol River. *Armee Abteilung* Lanz, composed of the SS Panzer Corps (SS Panzer Divisions *Leibstandarte Adolf Hitler* [*LSAH*], *Das Reich*, and *Totenkopf*) and Corps Cramer (168th Infantry Division and Panzer Grenadier Division *Grossdeutschland*), was to prevent Army Group Don from being outflanked, by employing mobile operations to screen the Kharkov-Belgorod region. To accomplish this task, *Armee Abteilung* Lanz was to eliminate the Soviet forces in the Kupyansk area. Elements of *LSAH* were to support the 298th Infantry Division on the east bank of the Donets, while on February 5, *Das Reich* launched its attack down the Volchansk-Kupyansk road. Provisions were also made to maintain contact with *Armee Abteilung* Fretter-Pico in the event that the 320th Infantry Division was forced to withdraw behind the Donets.[29]

Responsibility for restoring the situation on Army Group Don's left flank fell on the 1st Panzer Army. After taking over the sector held by *Armee Abteilung* Fretter-Pico (which was renamed the XXX Corps), the 1st Panzer Army was to intercept the Russian breakthrough on the left flank of the 304th Infantry Division in the Krasnodon area. It was also to hold the Donets line on both sides of Voroshilovgrad to the northwest of Lisichansk. Then, depending on the development of the situation, the 1st Panzer Army was to attack and eliminate the Soviet forces that crossed the Donets to the west. To accomplish this mission, the 3rd and 11th Panzer Divisions concentrated in the Artemovsk-Konstantinovsk-Gorlovka area. In addition, *OKH* supplied thirty PzKw III tanks which were being unloaded in Debaltsevo. Subsequently, the 1st Panzer Army also requested the 6th and 7th Panzer Divisions.[30]

On February 5, Manstein sent a report to Zeitzler in which he outlined measures that he believed should be taken to preserve the German southern flank. These measures included the immediate concentration of the 7th Anti-Aircraft Division to defend the Dnepropetrovsk-Stalino railroad and preparations for an extensive airlift for Army Group Don at the expense of Army Group B, whose units were practically worthless anyway, and Army Group A, which in any case was in much better shape than Army Group Don. Finally, he demanded that unless the attack by *Das Reich* was completely successful, which according to Manstein meant reaching Kupyansk by February 6, the entire SS Panzer Corps should be committed south of the Donets against Isyum. This message apparently prompted Hitler to dispatch an airplane to the front to bring Manstein back to General Headquarters.[31]

Manstein's meeting with Hitler focused on two issues: the future conduct of operations in the Army Group Don area, which depended on getting Hitler's immediate approval to abandon the eastern part of the Donets basin; and second, the question of supreme command.

Manstein wanted Hitler to appoint a single chief of staff with the requisite authority and responsibility to conduct the war. One cannot escape the conclusion that Manstein believed that he was the one best suited for the job. Unwilling to discuss the matter, Hitler declared that he could not put anyone above Göring, who would never subordinate himself to the guidance of a chief of staff. As a result, no progress was made on this subject.

In discussing the future conduct of operations, Manstein emphasized the fact that his forces were inadequate to hold the Don-Donets area. In his opinion the real issue was whether Hitler wanted to try to hold the entire Donets basin and lose it and Army Group Don, or to abandon part of the region to avert disaster.

Holding the Don-Donets balcony would give the Russians freedom to turn forces through Army Group B's area southward, toward the Lower Dnieper or the coast of the Sea of Azov, to cut off the entire southern flank. The outcome of events on the southern flank would determine the course of the war in the East. To ensure their success against the southern flank, the Russians could be expected to draw on reserves from around Stalingrad. Consequently, no counterthrust by the SS Panzer Corps could be adequate to intercept the wide flanking movement that the Soviets would surely make. Manstein argued that the Russians were strong enough to carry out their envelopment and screen it off to the west around Kharkov. Not even all the available German reinforcements could deflect the Soviet thrust. It was absolutely necessary that the 1st Panzer Army should be immediately followed to the Middle Donets by the 4th Panzer Army to intercept the danger of an envelopment between the Donets and Dnieper rivers. If this action were taken, it would then be possible, together with the approaching reinforcements, to restore the southern flank. This would only be possible if the 4th Panzer Army were pulled out of the Lower Don in time. It was already doubtful if *Armee Abteilung* Hollidt, defending the front from the coastline to the Middle Donets, could reach the Mius in time. It was imperative that Hitler grant permission that day to surrender the eastern part of the Donets area as far as the Mius.

Hitler once again avoided any real discussion of the matter at hand. He reiterated his reluctance to yield hard-won territory. Hitler also argued that shortening the front to release German forces would allow the Russians to free a proportionate number of their units. On this point Hitler was correct. However, Manstein pointed out that the decisive factor in shifting troops was which of the two sides gained the lead and thus the initiative. In this case, the length of the front and German weakness canceled out any defensive advantage by allowing the Russians to penetrate the overextended front when and where they wished. This was especially true since the Germans lacked reserves.

Unmoved, Hitler continued to debate by arguing that if every foot of ground were contested, the Russians would soon exhaust themselves. Furthermore, as the Soviets advanced they would experience increasing supply difficulties and this could be counted on to stall their outflanking movements.

Once again, Hitler was in large part correct. The Russians had in fact suffered fearful losses but, nonetheless, they were able to gain easy success in the sectors where the Germans had few troops. Casualties had also reduced the quality of Soviet forces, further contributing to the German ability to hold out. Nevertheless, the Russians had ample reinforcements, while the Germans did not. Manstein was unwilling to accept Hitler's contention concerning Soviet supply difficulties. In his opinion, the distances from the railheads to the Sea of Azov or the Lower Dnieper were not great enough to frustrate the enemy's drive to amputate the German southern flank.

Hitler's arguments concerning Soviet supply difficulties and the need to contest every foot of ground held some validity. However, Hitler held these views out of sheer obstinacy, without offering a realistic plan that would help Manstein stem the Russian tide. Hitler expected stubborn resistance and Soviet supply problems alone to halt the Red Army.

Manstein, however, took a more rational approach. It was unrealistic to count on supply difficulties to stop the Russian advance. Because of the months of continuous offensive operations, the Soviets were in fact experiencing some supply shortages. However, the shock and success of their initial attacks, and the offensive momentum thus gained, placed them within easy striking distance of the Dnieper crossings of Zaporozhye and Dnepropetrovsk and the vital lifeline of Army Group Don and the entire German southern flank. Even with supply difficulties, the Russians could be expected to continue their drive toward the Dnieper, unless the Germans were able to mount an effective threat to the Soviet rear. The possibility of severing the German southern flank from the rest of the front far outweighed the risk of the Germans mounting an effective attack of their own.

Army Group Don could not hope to contest every foot of ground, especially since the Germans lacked reserves and reinforcements to fill in the gaps in the front. It was Manstein who recognized that the only solution was to launch a counteroffensive against the increasingly strung out and vulnerable Russian flanks.

In this respect, Hitler's stubbornness was not without its value. By refusing to yield, Hitler helped to create conditions that were favorable for a counteroffensive. Every moment Hitler delayed carried the Russians deeper and deeper into the German trap. However, while Manstein was willing to allow the Russians to advance toward the Dnieper, it was not his intention to allow them to do so virtually unopposed. By continuing to refuse to permit Manstein to take action, Hitler unnecessarily risked losing Army Group Don and with it the entire German position in the east.

Hitler's most persuasive argument for not yielding the Donets area was political and economic. Politically, Hitler feared the repercussions on Turkey (there were in fact several Turkish battalions fighting with Army Group Don). Most of all, he stressed the importance of the Donets coal to the German economy and the effect on the Russian war economy if the Soviets continued to be deprived of its use. Hitler ignored the fact that even without the Donets coal, the Russians still produced large numbers of tanks and ammunition.

To these arguments Manstein replied that according to the president of the German Coal Cartel, Paul Pleiger, the coal in the area east of the Mius River was unsuitable for coking or locomotive combustion.

Still unwilling to concede, Hitler resorted to the weather. By chance, the last few days had seen an early thaw, and the roads across the ice of Taganrog Bay were not completely safe. Although the Don and

Donets were still frozen, it was possible that the ice would soon start to break up if the warmer weather continued. Hitler tried to convince Manstein to postpone the evacuation of the Don-Donets salient. Once the ice melted, the rivers would be impassable and the Russians would not attack until summer. At the same time, the 4th Panzer Army would get mired in the mud as it moved westward.

Manstein, however, refused to stake the fate of Army Group Don on the hope of an unseasonable change in the weather. At last Hitler relented and agreed to allow Manstein to withdraw his eastern front to the Mius River. In all, this conference, which resulted in only one major decision, had lasted four hours.[32]

This exchange between Hitler and Manstein typifies one of the many difficulties that German commanders had in dealing with their own high command. Throughout his tenure as head of Army Group Don, Manstein was forced, on an almost daily basis, to haggle with Hitler, either directly or through Zeitzler. Manstein's messages and requests were rarely answered on the day they were sent. More often, it was two to three days before Hitler sent his reply, by which time it was meaningless, because it had been outpaced by the course of events.

Hitler's decision to permit a retreat to the Mius was won only after a tiresome and lengthy debate. The fact that Manstein was successful in winning a decision from Hitler was probably due in large part to the fact that he was able to present his case face to face with the Führer. In a situation such as that confronting Army Group Don, swift action on messages from the front to general headquarters was essential. It was bad enough that the enemy had the initiative, worse that the army group commander could not take the proper action because he lacked sufficient authority.

The meeting of February 6, also demonstrates the moral courage and sheer physical strength needed when discussing operational matters with Hitler. Indeed, there were only a handful of generals who had the will to stand eye to eye with Hitler to argue their point to a favorable decision. During the meeting, Manstein sought only one decision on operational matters. After four long hours, Hitler gave in, but only after exhausting every argument against Manstein. It is not difficult to imagine how much longer this meeting might have lasted if Manstein had had more to discuss.

If Manstein is to be considered a great commander, then at least part of that evaluation must be based on his ability to deal effectively with Hitler. It is true that he had not yet fallen from favor with Hitler, but nonetheless, Manstein displayed considerable skill and determination in his arguments with the dictator. Many were those who tried to present their views only to be led astray by Hitler's talk of new weapons, moral superiority, or whatever other arguments that he could muster. Manstein refused to be distracted by side issues, returning again and again to the matter at hand despite Hitler's efforts to the contrary. The result was a timely decision to withdraw to the Mius River line, allowing the 4th Panzer Army to be shifted to the west.

Immediately upon his return to Army Group Don headquarters on February 7, Manstein issued orders to initiate the withdrawal of *Armee Abteilung* Hollidt from its position in the Donets bend to a new position along the Mius River. This new line, the *Maulwurf* position, ran from the coast of the Sea of Azov at Taganrog, northward along the course of the Muis River, through Krasny Lutsh, to the Donets River west of Voroshilovgrad. The timetable for *Armee Abteilung* Hollidt's withdrawal called for the occupation of five intermediate lines before reaching the final *Maulwurf* position on the night of February 18–19.[33]

Responsibility for covering the withdrawal fell on the 4th Panzer Army, which was to hold its position from the mouth of the Don to Novocherkassk. Its left flank was to be pulled back to conform with the movement of *Armee Abteilung* Hollidt. Upon reaching the first intermediate line on the night of February 12–13, *Armee Abteilung* Hollidt was to release the 6th Panzer Division to deal with the situation south of Voroshilovgrad. Once the final line was reached, three more divisions were to be released. The 1st Panzer Army was to fold back its right flank to correspond with the movement of *Armee Abteilung* Hollidt's left flank. It was also responsible for holding the Donets position as far as Orechovo and for elimination of the Russians between Orechovo and Slavyansk. In addition, once sufficient infantry forces were available, the army's mobile divisions were to be released for other employment.[34]

However, during *Armee Abteilung* Hollidt's withdrawal movement, the Russian 7th Cavalry Corps penetrated the front south of Voroshilovgrad and advanced on Debaltsevo, some thirty miles behind the northern flank of the *Maulwurf* position, and threatened to unhinge the new line before it was occupied. As a result, the 6th and 7th Panzer Divisions had to be diverted to deal with this danger. The 7th Panzer Division was employed to block the Russian advance at Debaltsevo, while the 6th Panzer Division was used to close the breach, thus isolating the 7th Cavalry Corps in the German rear. As a result, both of these divisions were tied down until February 20, and were unavailable for use elsewhere.[35]

By falling back to the *Maulwurf* position, Army Group Don shortened its front, thus making it easier to defend. The reduced front also allowed Manstein to disengage many of his precious armored units, either to use them as mobile fire brigades, or to assemble them for a concerted attack against the Soviet forces advancing toward the Dnieper.

Despite these measures, the situation grew worse at Rostov and Voroshilovgrad, where the Russians broke out of the bridgeheads they had gained earlier. The 1st Panzer Army found itself at once in a critical position as it was still unable to stop the Russian advance between Slavyansk and Lisichansk. Farther south, the Soviets had captured Bataisk, a suburb of Rostov, and were pushing troops into the city itself.[36]

By February 9, the Russians had seized Belgorod and Kursk to the north of Kharkov in Army Group B's sector. Soviet forces were also advancing to the west from the Donets bend around Isyum. Only *Armee Abteilung* Lanz, itself threatened by the Soviet breakthrough, and the badly battered 2nd Army barred the Russian advance in the gap between the Dnieper and the right flank of Army Group Center.

The Russians were now in a position to outflank Army Group Don upstream from Dnepropetrovsk. Under these circumstances, it appeared very doubtful that Army Group Don could continue to secure its own line of communications. On February 9, Manstein sent a teleprinter message to Zeitzler calling for a new army of at least six divisions to be deployed within two weeks, in the area north of Dnepropetrovsk, as well as an additional army behind the 2nd Army's front west of Kursk to make a thrust to the south.[37]

Zeitzler's reply held out the prospect of "really effective assistance." Zeitzler hoped that at least six divisions could be released from Army Groups Center and North and transported rapidly to Army Group Don. Manstein could count on one new division arriving every other day. Given the size of the hole in the German front, even these forces would be no more than a stopgap until the greatest danger passed and the muddy season arrived.[38]

The Russian threat to Army Group Don's deep flank was not the only matter that concerned Manstein. The 1st Panzer Army, which was trying to throw the Russians who had crossed the Donets back across the river, was actually dealing with two powerful Soviet groups. The first, the 3rd Guards Army, had crossed the Donets at Voroshilovgrad against Group Kreysing and was attempting to wedge itself between *Armee Abteilung* Hollidt, as it fell back to the Mius, and the 1st Panzer Army. The second Russian group, the 1st Guards Army, had crossed the Donets along the Lisichansk-Slavyansk line against the III Panzer Corps and was shifting its main efforts to the west along sides of the Krivoy Torets River.[39]

On February 3, the long and bitter fight for Slavyansk began. Unable to take the city quickly, a swarm of Russian reinforcements rolled into the area to take the key position. The 1st Panzer Army also shifted forces into this area. The III Panzer Corps, composed of the 19th and 17th Panzer Divisions, held a front from the north of Slavyansk to west of Voroshilovgrad. The 3rd Panzer Division was also scheduled to join the corps on February 4. In addition, the XL Panzer Corps, with the 11th Panzer Division, was moving toward Kramatorskaya south of Slavyansk. Later, the 333rd Infantry Division, arriving from France, and the SS *Wiking* Division would also join the 1st Panzer Army.[40]

For the Russians, Slavyansk was a major obstacle in the attainment of their objective. For the Germans, Slavyansk became the anchor of the 1st Panzer Army's defense line. As long as the Germans held Slavyansk, the Soviets were forced to extend their attacks farther westward. This extension, together with the thrust from Voroshilovgrad, threatened the 1st Panzer Army with double envelopment, but at the same time it offered an opportunity for a future German counterattack.

As the 1st Panzer Army moved more forces into the area, the German position at Slavyansk improved. On February 3, the III Panzer Corps was ordered to hold the Slavyansk-Lisichansk angle and to maintain contact with the 320th Infantry Division of Army Group B to its left. By February 4, the Russians had cut the link with the Slavyansk garrison and were advancing on Kramatorskaya with tanks and motorized infantry units. At the same time, the Soviets turned part of their forces to the west toward Barvenkovo.[41]

On February 5, the newly arrived XL Panzer Corps was given the task of holding Slavyansk, reestablishing contact with the garrison, and opening a crossing on the Suchoy Torets River in the Slavyansk-Snamenka sector for a later attack toward Isyum to reestablish contact with the 320th Infantry Division. Forces available to accomplish this mission included the 11th Panzer Division, which arrived in Konstantinovka the same day, and the 333rd Infantry Division, unloading in Lozovaya, Gavrilovka, and Konstantinovka.[42]

While it was doubtful whether these units could in fact hold Slavyansk, they were capable of maintaining a credible defense against the dwindling strength of the 4th Guards Corps and Group Popov. There were still no forces available to fill the void between the XL Panzer Corps and the SS Panzer Corps in the Kharkov area. The most immediate problem for the XL Panzer Corps, however, was to eliminate the threat to Slavyansk and the threat posed by the 4th Guards Tank and 3rd Tank Corps at Kramatorskaya. The 7th Panzer Division continued its defense of Slavyansk. The 11th Panzer Division, supported by elements of the 333rd Infantry Division, would secure Konstantinovka prepatory to moving north toward Kramatorskaya and Slavyansk. The 1st Panzer Army urged the XL Panzer Corps to take Kramatorskaya and reopen the routes to Slavyansk from the south and ordered those elements of the 333rd Infantry Division at Lozovaya and Barvenkovo to concentrate east of Barvenkovo. In accordance with these orders, on February 6, the 11th Panzer Division moved northward from Konstantinovka, but collided with the 4th Guards Tank Corps at Drushkova. Losing ten half tracks and all of its anti-tank guns, the division was forced to fall back on Konstantinovka. The next day, supported by its tank regiment, the 11th Panzer Division drove the 4th Guards Tank Corps north of Drushkovka.[43]

For the next several days, the 7th Panzer Division held off Russian attacks on Slavyansk. To the west, the main force of the 333rd Infantry Division managed to reach Barvenkovo, but was forced by Russian resistance to abandon its attacks and fall back toward Lozovaya. As a result, all immediate prospects for linking up with the left flank of the XL Panzer Corps was lost.[44]

By now the XL Panzer Corps was heavily engaged with the 4th Guards Tank and 3rd Tank Corps and the 4th Guards Rifle Corps. While the XL Panzer Corps was successful in holding onto Slavyansk, it was unable to throw Russians back across the Donets, although the 11th Panzer Division did manage to block a further advance to the south at Kramatorskaya. The longer the Russian offensive remained stalled in front of Slavyansk, the better the German position became, especially as the *Wiking* Division (moved up from the 4th Panzer Army on the Don) had arrived in the area.[45]

Unable to make any headway in the Slavyansk area, the Southwestern Front issued new orders in an effort to restore offensive momentum. The 1st Guards Army was ordered to smash German resistance and, in cooperation with Group Popov, to seize Slavyansk, Konstantinovka, and Artemovsk. To accomplish this, the 1st Guards Army, using the 4th Guards Tank and 3rd Tank Corps, was to eliminate the Germans in the Slavyansk and Konstantinovka area and at the same time move into the Krasnoarmeiskoye area. Meanwhile, the 10th Tank and 18th Tank Corps were to break through to Artemovsk. The 4th Guards Tank and 3rd Tank Corps would then thrust on Krasnoarmeiskoye and envelop Stalino from the west. Bogged down in fighting for Slavyansk and Kramatorskaya, the 1st Guards Army was unable to accomplish much before February 10.[46]

After February 10, a new STAVKA directive exhorted Vatutin to prevent a German withdrawal to Dnepropetrovsk and Zaporozhye, and demanded that all measures be taken to press the German Donets group into the Crimea and to isolate it from the rest of the German forces in the Ukraine. These directives underlined STAVKA's perception that German forces were preparing to retire to the west across the

Dnieper, and that heavy German resistance at Slavyansk was designed to cover that withdrawal.[47]

Urged on by STAVKA, Vatutin issued new orders. The 6th Army was to continue moving across the Kharkov-Lozovaya railroad toward Krasnograd. The 1st Guards Army was to shift its axis of attack westward, advance on Sinelnikovo (only twelve miles from the Dnieper), and seize Zaporozhye. At the same time, the 1st Guards Army would also capture Slavyansk and advance on Artemovsk.[48]

More specifically, the 4th Guards Rifle Corps would push toward Sinelnikovo while the 6th Guards Rifle Corps would reduce Slavyansk. Group Popov also received new orders. The 4th Guards Tank Corps was to turn over its defensive positions at Kramatorskaya to the 3rd Tank Corps. Then, after a forced march on the morning of February 11, the 4th Guards Tank Corps would seize the key rail junction of Krasnoarmeiskoye fifty miles to the south and well into the German rear.[49]

By 0900 hours on February 11, the main force of the 4th Guards Tank Corps had taken Krasnoarmeiskoye, along with a store of badly needed supplies. More importantly, the corps severed the main Dnepropetrovsk-Krasnoarmeiskoye rail line. This left only the rail-road through Zaporozhye, and its capacity was reduced by the fact that the big Dnieper bridge, destroyed in 1941, was still not open to traffic. As a result, all supplies had to be reloaded and tank wagons carrying fuel could not reach the front.[50]

Meanwhile, the 4th Panzer Army was still en route from the Lower Don to the west, its progress considerably hindered by poor road conditions. With the Russians still able to reinforce the 4th Guards Tank Corps in the Krasnoarmeiskoye area, the danger in the gap between the left flank of the 1st Panzer Army and the Kharkov area, where the Soviets enjoyed complete freedom of action, remained as acute as ever.[51]

Once again, Army Group Don faced an impending disaster. The Russians were now in a position that would allow them to screen off Kharkov and advance southward on Pavlograd with the forces push-ing west of Isyum (the 6th Army). Once at Pavlograd, the Soviets were within easy striking distance of the Dnieper crossings of Dnepropetrovsk and Zaporozhye and Army Group Don's line of communications. The Russians could also attempt to overrun *Armee Abteilung* Lanz, which was not fully assembled. If this attempt were successful, there would be nothing to bar the crossing of the Dnieper on either side of Kremenchug, enabling the Soviets to block the ap-proaches to the Crimea and the Dnieper crossings at Kherson. These moves would effectively sever the entire German southern flank from the rest of the front.

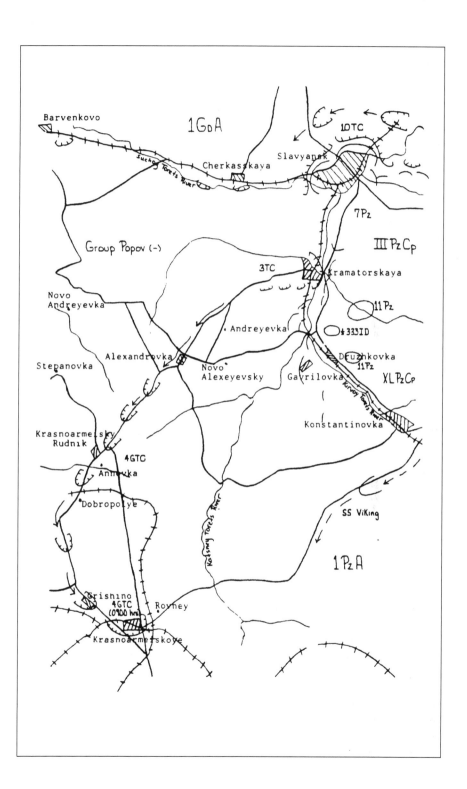

With these considerations in mind, Manstein sent a fresh appraisal
of the situation to *OKH* on February 12. Despite the fact that the
Russians had been engaged in offensive operations for nearly three
months, they were still able to maintain a force ratio of eight to one
against Army Groups B and Don, while against Army Groups North
and Center the ratio was only four to one. The latter two army groups
were fighting from entrenched positions, while the former fought in
the open. The critical factor, however, was that the Russians were not
seeking a major decision against the northern or central sectors, but
rather in the south. Even if Army Group Don managed to hold on to
the Dnieper crossings, the Soviets could still be expected to pursue
their aim of encircling the southern flank against the coast. To prevent
this it was necessary that sacrifices be made elsewhere to improve the
balance of forces.[52]

Later that day, Manstein received Hitler's reply to his proposals of
February 9. Army Group Don was renamed Army Group South. A new
army, *Angriffsarmee Sud*, was to be deployed on the Poltava-Pavlograd
line. A second army, designated *Angriffsarmee Nord*, was to be
deployed in the area southwest and south of Orel, behind the south
flank of the 2nd Army. Both of these armies were to be in place by the
end of February. In fact, however, neither army materialized. The 2nd
Army was reinforced, but at the expense of troops promised to Army
Group South. The army that was to take the Polatav-Pavlograd line
turned out to be *Armee Abteilung* Lanz, which was already engaged at
Kharkov. *Armee Abteilung* Lanz was subsequently subordinated to
Army Group South, giving Manstein control of the forces on Army
Group B's right flank as far north as Belgorod.[53] Headquarters Army
Group B was then removed from the German order of battle in the East
and placed in reserve.[54]

Having been just given command of *Armee Abteilung* Lanz,
Manstein nearly lost it. The Voronezh Front launched Operation STAR
on February 2, and within ten days was approaching Kharkov. On
February 13, Hitler ordered that "Kharkov is to be held at all cost."[55]
Moreover, to relieve pressure on Army Group South's left flank, the
SS Panzer Corps was to thrust toward Lozovaya with the two SS
Panzer divisions that were available.[56]

Manstein knew of course that with such limited forces at its disposal
that *Armee Abteilung* Lanz could not possibly fulfill both tasks. *Armee
Abteilung* Lanz could either defend Kharkov or support Army Group
South's left flank. Manstein suggested to Hitler that Kharkov be
abandoned, in an effort to eliminate the Russian forces south of the
city (the 6th Army). If successful, the danger of Army Group South's
being enveloped across the Dnieper, on either side of Kremenchug,
would be temporarily eliminated. The 4th Panzer Army would be

used to deal with the 25th Tank and 1st Guards Tank Corps advancing on the Dnieper crossings at Zaporozhye and Dnepropetrovsk. Once the Soviet forces south of Kharkov had been eliminated, Lanz could then turn his attention to recapturing the city.[57]

Luckily for Manstein, circumstances proved stronger than Hitler's will. Threatened with encirclement, the SS Panzer Corps abandoned Kharkov on February 15, against the orders of Lanz. The order to abandon the city was issued by the commander of the SS Panzer Corps, SS Lieutenant General Paul Hausser, late in the afternoon of February 14. Lanz quickly reminded Hausser, that "In accordance with the Führer's order, the SS Panzer Corps is to hold its present positions on the east front of Kharkov to the last man."[58] Hausser then rescinded his order, but it was too late, as elements of *Das Reich* had already begun to abandon their positions. In any event, Kharkov was abandoned and the SS Panzer Corps was saved.[59]

By February 16, advanced elements of the Russian 6th Army were approaching Pavlograd and Dnepropetrovsk. Manstein had been expecting this move for some time. If the Soviets reached the Lozovaya rail junction or Pavlograd or the Sinelnikovo Station, they could cut the rail link through Poltava.

With events taking such a critical turn, Hitler decided to visit Manstein's headquarters at Zaporozhye on February 17. Once again, Manstein tried to impress Hitler with the urgency of the situation. *Armee Abteilung* Hollidt managed to reach the Mius on the same day, closely pursued by the Russians. The 1st Panzer Army had managed to stop Group Popov in the Krasnoarmeiskoye-Grishino area, but had not yet eliminated it. Meanwhile, *Armee Abteilung* Lanz had withdrawn southwest to the Mosh River.[60]

Manstein then informed Hitler of his intention to take the SS Panzer Corps out of the Kharkov area. The SS Panzer Corps was then to thrust to the southwest from the Krasnograd area, toward Pavlograd, coming together with the 4th Panzer Army as it also moved up from the south. These forces would crush the Russians advancing in the gap between the 1st Panzer Army and *Armee Abteilung* Lanz. Once this aim was accomplished and the danger to *Armee Abteilung* Hollidt and the 1st Panzer Army eliminated, Kharkov could be attacked.[61]

As usual, Hitler refused to discuss Manstein's proposal, advancing the by now familiar argument of operations getting bogged down in the mud. What Hitler wanted was the immediate recapture of Kharkov once all three divisions of the SS Panzer Corps were available. What Hitler failed to recognize was that as a prerequisite for any thrust against Kharkov, the threat to the Dnieper crossings had to be eliminated. The recapture of Kharkov was meaningless unless a line of communications could be maintained. Furthermore, since it was certain that the spring thaw would put an end to operations, it was reasonable to expect the thaw to do so in the south, between the Donets and Dnieper, before it affected the region around Kharkov. This being the case, there was every prospect that there would still be enough time to attack Kharkov after those Russians who were advancing between the 1st Panzer Army and *Armee Abteilung* Lanz had been eliminated.[62]

Hitler's obstinacy resulted in yet another protracted discussion. Manstein finally succeeded in "winning" his point by telling Hitler that it was necessary, in any case, for the SS Panzer Corps to assemble first on the Kharkov-Krasnograd road. Since this deployment could not be completed until February 19, the final decision on whether to go north or south could wait until then. While he preferred an immediate settlement in his favor, Manstein knew that the 4th Panzer Army would not be available before February 19, either. As a result, he was willing to bide his time, assuming that the course of events would dictate a favorable decision.[63]

On February 18, Manstein saw Hitler again. The Russians had attacked and penetrated *Armee Abteilung* Hollidt's front along the Mius at several places. Although the 7th Cavalry Corps, encircled at Debaltsevo, was still offering resistance, Manstein proposed to Hitler to shift motorized units from this area to the western flank, where Group Popov was still tying down German forces committed in the Krasnoarmeiskoye-Grishino area.[64]

By now there was no mistaking the Soviet intention to advance in force to the gap between the 1st Panzer Army and *Armee Abteilung* Lanz. The 267th Rifle Division was spotted south of Krasnograd, and the 35th Guards Rifle Division had taken Pavlograd.[65]

Armee Abteilung Lanz reported that the mobile elements of SS Panzer Division *Totenkopf* were bogged down between Kiev and Poltava, a development obviating the northward strike to retake Kharkov that Hitler hoped for. Manstein argued that the only course of action to take now was to strike southeastwards to eliminate the enemy advancing south of Kharkov. Hitler relented and agreed to commit *Das Reich* in the direction of Pavlograd. The 1st SS Panzer Division would cover the 4th Panzer Army against Soviet forces driving southward from Kharkov.[66]

Manstein next endeavored to discuss the overall situation of the German southern flank with Hitler. He began by pointing out that as commander of Army Group South, it was his responsibility to think ahead. Even if Army Group South managed to survive until the spring thaw, the muddy season would give only a few weeks' respite. To hold a 430-mile front, Army Group South, including *Armee Abteilung* Lanz, had thirty-two divisions. Once the ground began to firm up, the

Russians could be expected to direct their main effort against the German southern flank to encircle it on the Black Sea. Army Group South could not hope to defend such a long front with so few, weak divisions. Nor could it remain static until the Russians broke through or outflanked it to the north. It could stay where it was only if *OKH* launched a well-timed offensive to relieve pressure on the front that still projected to the east. Hitler, however, refused to be drawn into discussion, preferring instead to put his faith in new weapons to restore the situation in the coming summer offensive.[67]

On February 19, Russian troops reached Sinelnikovo. Later the same day, the 25th Tank Corps arrived in the same area. Meanwhile, thirty miles to the south, Manstein was trying to convince Hitler of the need to use all of Army Group South's available panzer formations to deliver a blow against the Russians on the western flank, thus securing his line of communications. As the day wore on, the sounds of the battle to the north grew louder, indicating that the Russians were advancing steadily toward Zaporozhye. Hitler spent the day conferencing with Manstein and studying the situation maps.

Hitler's visits to front headquarters, even one as far from the fighting as an army group, were rare. His visit to Manstein's headquarters at Zaporozhye was occasioned by his desire to end the winter's long string of defeats. Once at Manstein's headquarters, Hitler quickly found himself engrossed in planning and began to appreciate more fully the critical situation facing Army Group South.[68] Hitler was now more inclined to accept that the only way to salvage the southern flank was to allow Manstein to carry out his bold counterstroke.

Finally, after two days of discussion, Hitler agreed with Manstein. The same day, the 4th Panzer Army was ordered to deploy for a counterattack against the Russian forces that crossed the line Pereshchepino-Pavlograd-Grishino.[69]

Meanwhile, the appearance of the 4th Guards Tank Corps so deep in the German rear at Grishino and Krasnoarmeiskoye had a dramatic effect on the German plans to hold Slavyansk and capture Kramatorskaya. After crossing what the Germans believed was impassable terrain west of the Krivoy Torets River, the 4th Guards Tank Corps was now on the XL Panzer Corps flank. More significantly, Soviet interdiction of the railroad threatened Army Group South, as well as the entire southern flank of the Eastern Front. The XL Panzer Corps immediately shifted *Wiking* westward from Artemovsk to Krasnoarmeiskoye to drive out the Russian forces and reopen the rail line. The 1st Panzer Army also abandoned its planned attack on Kramatorskaya, and in its place ordered a concentric attack on Krasnoarmeiskoye by *Wiking* and the available elements of the 333rd

Infantry Division. However, *Wiking* and the 333rd Division, whose two regiments were retreating toward Krasnoarmeiskoye, were inadequate for the task.[70]

To gather enough forces to deal with the 4th Guards Tank Corps around Krasnoarmeiskoye, without also being forced to abandon Slavyansk, the 1st Panzer Army decided to sortie westward from Slavyansk with elements of the 7th Panzer Division and the 11th Panzer Division. These forces would then turn southward into the rear of the Soviet units at Krasnoarmeiskoye. This attack was designed to force the Russians to evacuate Kramatorskaya and to cut the 4th Guards Tank Corps' line of supply, thus keeping it from being reinforced. Overall command of the attack rested with the 7th Panzer Division, while Balck, commander of the 11th Panzer Division, would lead the armored thrust westward (*Kampfgruppe* Balck).[71]

On February 12, *Kampfgruppe* Balck broke through the Russian positions west of Slavyansk, advancing as far as Cherkaskaya, where it was engaged in heavy fighting with the 10th Tank Corps, which itself had been shifted from east of Slavyansk. Attacking from Rovney, elements of *Wiking* gained a foothold in the northeastern part of Krasnoarmeiskoye. Other elements, thrusting from the south, pushed to within two and a half miles of the town. A third group swung to the west and blocked the Slavyansk-Grishino road to cut the 4th Guards Tank Corps line of communications. Meanwhile, the 333rd Infantry Division advanced from the northeast in an attempt to break into the Krasnoarmeiskoye area.[72]

On February 13, *Kampfgruppe* Balck made good progress, driving the 10th Tank Corps out of Cherkaskaya and advancing on Kramatorskaya, destroying twenty-three tanks and six anti-tank guns along the way. By evening, small detachments of its supporting infantry forces had occupied the northern edge of Kramatorskaya. However, the next day Balck made only minor headway against stubborn resistance. With its advance grinding to a halt and having lost surprise, the 1st Panzer Army ordered Balck to pull back to the Slavyansk area to regroup for a new thrust on Kramatorskaya with one regiment of the 333rd Infantry Division. At the same time, *Wiking* and the two regiments of the 333rd Infantry Division, and elements of the 7th Panzer Division (which began moving south on February 15) were to open the Stalino-Dnepropetrovsk railroad. Measures were taken to isolate both Krasnoarmeiskoye and Kramatorskaya and to cut the Russian supply lines until other plans could be made.[73]

Despite the unsuccessful attempt to seize Kramatorskaya, the German thrust did disrupt the Southwestern Front's renewed offensive. Most of the 4th Guards Rifle Corps was tied down around Slavyansk, leaving only one division to advance on Sinelnikovo. In the III Panzer

Corps sector, the 6th Guards Rifle Corps also failed to take Artemovsk. The only substantial progress was made by the 6th Army, which cut the Kharkov-Lozovaya railroad and seized Zmiyev.[74]

On February 9, Army Group B ordered *Armee Abteilung* Lanz to prevent a further Russian advance against the north flank of Army Group Don. By February 15, however, the Voronezh Front had pushed back the weak German defenses and captured Kharkov. Subsequently, *Armee Abteilung* Lanz was instructed to tie down the Soviet armies using mobile operations. In particular, it was to keep the 6th Army from turning the left flank of the 1st Panzer Army. Pursuant to these orders, elements of *Das Reich* moved into positions against the right flank of the 6th Army. As a result, the 6th Army's advance was deflected into the gap between Lozovaya and Krasnograd.[75]

To aid the hard-pressed 4th Guards Tank corps at Krasnoarmeiskoye, Popov ordered the 10th Tank corps to regroup and then move south to Krasnoarmeisky Rudnik (fifteen miles to the north of Krasnoarmeiskoye) to establish contact with the 4th Guards Tank corps. On February 12, the 10th Tank Corps began moving southward, but made extremely slow progress because of deep snow. By February 15, however, contact had been made with the 4th Guards Tank Corps.[76]

With new orders and reinforcements, Southwestern Front rifle units and Group Popov continued their offensive. The 6th Army, opposed only by *Das Reich* on its right flank, consolidated its bridgehead across the Donets west of Zmiyev, and was able to advance against *Das Reich* to within nine miles of Krasnograd. On the 6th Army's left flank, the important regional center of Pereshchepino on the Orel River, midway between Krasnograd and Dnepropetrovsk, was occupied. By the morning of February 20, Russian forces reached Novo Moskovsk, fifteen miles from the Dnieper River and Dnepropetrovsk. Pavlograd was taken on February 17, and the following day the railroad to Dnepropetrovsk was cut. Meanwhile, the 1st Guards Cavalry Corps was able to drive the newly arrived 15th Infantry Division from Sinelnikovo. Early on February 19, the Southwestern Front released the 25th Tank Corps to the 6th Army, and lead elements of the armored corps reached Sinelnikovo the same day.[77]

While the 6th Army rushed toward the Dnieper, the rest of the 1st Guards Army endeavored to break the stalemate at Slavyansk. Renewed Russian attempts to take Slavyansk coincided with a German decision to abandon the city to release the 7th Panzer Division, which was needed around Krasnoarmeiskoye.[78]

As the 7th Panzer Division moved south on February 17, the 11th Panzer Division moved to Drushkovka (twenty miles northeast of Krasnoarmeiskoye) in preparation for a westward attack into the rear of Group Popov. The III Panzer Corps took over the XL Panzer Corps' defensive sector south of Slavyansk. Meanwhile, *Wiking* continued to attack the southern part of Krasnoarmeiskoye, while the 333rd Infantry Division struck Soviet forces at Krasnoarmeiskoye and Grishino.[79]

After the initial attacks by *Wiking* on February 12–13, the 4th Guards Tank Corps clung to its positions in Krasnoarmeiskoye until it was reinforced by the 10th Tank Corps on February 16th. Under constant German pressure, by February 18, the 4th Guards Tank Corps was down to seventeen tanks and was low on fuel and ammunition. The 10th Tank Corps had only a few more tanks than the 4th Guards Tank Corps and had established an all-around defense of Krasnoarmeisky Rudnik.[80]

Under cover of bad weather and poor visibility on the morning of February 18, the 7th Panzer Division moved off from the Rovney area to outflank the 4th Guards Tank Corps positions from the west. The division penetrated the western part of the town and broke through to the southern edge, destroying eleven T-34s in the process. At the same time, a regimental *Kampfgruppe* struck from the east, but gained only little ground against stubborn resistance. Throughout the entire day there was difficult street fighting against increasing enemy resistance. *Wiking*'s attacks in the western part of Krasnoarmeiskoye were also stalled in heavy street fighting, although the division repulsed a Soviet relief thrust from Grishino. The 333rd Infantry Division fared no better, having been stopped by the Russians about three miles from the town.[81]

During the fighting, Popov ordered reinforcements to assist the beleaguered 4th Guards Tank Corps. On the evening of February 18, the 18th Tank Corps was instructed to make a forced march toward Krasnoarmeiskoye and to strike the German rear at Grishino in cooperation with the 10th Tank Corps. The 3rd Tank Corps was also ordered to move from Kramatorskaya to Krasnoarmeiskoye on February 20.[82]

Meanwhile, the 4th Guards Tank Corps attempted to affect its own fate. On the evening of February 18, a special group containing most of the corps' remaining tanks was ordered to retake the center of the town. Early on February 19, this group attacked and regained some ground. However, by then the 7th Panzer Division and *Wiking* had decided to bypass the town and left the Soviet garrison to be mopped up by the 333rd Infantry Division. Ironically, on February 19, the 4th Guard Tank Corps received an order from the Front Military Council that read: "I order the envelopment and destruction of the enemy at Krasnoarmeiskoye. Fully restore the situation. Do not, in any case, permit an enemy withdrawal."[83] This order exemplified the air of unreality prevalent at STAVKA and front headquarters.

The German attack on Krasnoarmeiskoye marked a change in the direction of the winter campaign of 1942–1943, but as evident by the Front Military Council order to the 4th Guards Tank Corps, Soviet headquarters was unaware of that change. Optimism and overconfidence had infected the high command for weeks and colored every facet of Russian planning. It was a mood that was fatal for the Soviet offensive.

The positive feeling of STAVKA and the General Staff was founded on the Soviet perception of the tremendous damage inflicted upon German and allied forces since November 19. After all, three major armies, the German 6th, Italian 8th, and Hungarian 2nd, had been wiped out of the German order of battle. The 4th Panzer Army and 2nd Army had been badly mauled, and the remainder of German forces suffered heavy losses. The Russian high command reasoned, as Hitler had at Stalingrad, that reinforcements from the west could not make up for the losses.[84]

As the Russian forces advanced in February 1943, STAVKA failed to heed the warnings of commanders who sensed impending setbacks. STAVKA's optimism also tainted the evaluation of intelligence, which was thus misinterpreted. Both the Southwestern and Voronezh Front commanders were convinced that the Germans were retreating toward the Dnieper and safety. The Southwestern Front erroneously interpreted the large-scale German regrouping that it detected as preparations for a German withdrawal. So convinced was Vatutin that he ignored repeated warnings from his army commanders on the condition of their troops and growing German strength. Instead, he insisted on carrying out his mission of encircling and destroying the German Donbas group before the spring thaw.[85]

The movement of German tanks did not go unnoticed. Soviet air reconnaissance spotted large German armored columns near Krasnograd, noted the forward movement of equipment from Dnepropetrovsk, and detected the shifting of tank forces from the east toward Krasnoarmeiskoye. However, the Russians were not alarmed by these developments. The conclusion drawn from these reports in an intelligence estimate of February 20, was that these concentrations were an attempt to clear the German lines for a "withdrawal of troops from the Donbas to the Dnieper." Vatutin used this interpretation to justify further extending offensive operations, ordering the 6th Army to continue its advance, and demanding that the front mobile groups "fulfill their assigned missions at any cost."[86]

During the first half of February 1943, the 4th Panzer Army continued to cover the withdrawal of *Armee Abteilung* Hollidt to the Mius River. By mid-February, the new position had been secured and enough forces were released to allow Manstein some operational freedom. On February 19, Manstein issued new orders that reviewed the overall situation and outlined the basic tasks of Army Group South. North of Isyum the Russians had captured Belgorod and Kharkov and were pressing *Armee Abteilung* Lanz steadily to the southwest. In the gap between the 1st Panzer Army and *Armee Abteilung* Lanz, lead units of the Soviet 6th Army were approaching the Dnieper with virtually no German forces to bar the way. The only positive development was that the 4th Guards Tank Corps was bottled up at Krasnoarmeiskoye.[87]

In spite of this unpromising situation, Manstein sought to reverse the trend of events by offensive action to deliver to the Russians a crushing blow that would not only restore the German front, but regain the initiative. The Soviet perception of the situation fit perfectly into the plans being developed by Manstein, designed to arrest the Russian advance and restore operational freedom to German forces. Manstein's order of February 19, laid the foundation of such an offensive. "Army Group South is to defend the *Maulwurf* position and the connecting north front up to Slavyansk, and, with the newly organized 4th Panzer Army, to eliminate the enemy in the gap between *Armee Abteilung* Lanz and the 1st Panzer Army."[88]

To accomplish this, it was critical that *Armee Abteilung* Hollidt hold its position along the Mius River and prevent a Russian breakthrough.[89]

The 4th Panzer Army would take over the gap between *Armee Abteilung* Lanz and the 1st Panzer Army on February 21. In addition, it would take command of *Das Reich* and *Totenkopf* Divisions of the SS Panzer Corps.[90] Meanwhile the German armored divisions concentrated for the attack. The three panzer divisions of the XL Panzer Corps, the 7th, 11th, and *Wiking*, would continue their attacks against Group Popov in the Krasnoarmeiskoye area, then thrust northward toward Barvenkovo, where they would come into line with the advance of the XLVIII Panzer and SS Panzer Corps.[91]

The XLVIII Panzer Corps of the 4th Panzer Army (6th and 17th Panzer Divisions) and the two divisions of the SS Panzer Corps would strike the Russian units in the gap between Krasnograd and Krasnoarmeiskoye. *Totenkopf* and *Das Reich* would deploy near Krasnograd and push southeastward against the Soviet forces driving to the Dnieper River. The SS Panzer Division *Leibstandarte Adolf Hitler* remained under the command of *Armee Abteilung* Lanz to cover the north flank between Krasnograd and Merefa. The XLVIII Panzer Corps would position its two divisions on the rail line between Boguslav and Petropavlovka and thrust into the 6th Army from the south. The SS Panzer and XLVIII Panzer Corps would converge on Lozovaya in the

Soviet rear. Subsequently, all three corps would continue northward against the Russians in the Kharkov region.[92]

The objective of the planned offensive was simple, to attack from the south (XLVIII Panzer Corps), east (XL Panzer Corps), and the northwest (SS Panzer Corps) to crush the units of the 6th Army and Group Popov that were driving toward the Dnieper River. What made Manstein's task difficult was that his plan was formulated as the Russian offensive developed, requiring him to anticipate Soviet movements. Manstein's plan was not without its dangers. While the XL Panzer Corps and XLVIII Panzer Corps were thrusting northward, it was essential that *Armee Abteilung* Hollidt keep the Russians from breaking through the Mius position. If it could not, the Soviets would then have a virtually free path from the Mius to the Dnieper, cutting not only the rear of both panzer corps, but encircling Army Group South as well.

To achieve his aim, Manstein put all of his eggs into one basket. The initial attacks were to be carried out by almost all of Army Group South's panzer divisions (6th, 7th, 11th, 17th, SS *Wiking*, SS *Das Reich*, and SS *Totenkopf* Divisions, with approximately 225 tanks and assault guns), with very little infantry support.[93] It was not so much the overwhelming strength of his panzer divisions that Manstein was counting on, but their shock effect and mobility when used in concert. In true "Blitzkrieg" fashion, the panzer divisions were to advance together, relying on shock and mobility both to overcome Russian resistance and to secure their flanks. In fact, only two infantry divisions were provided for direct support of the armored assault, the 15th and 333rd. The initial task of both divisions was to block further Russian advances in key areas, the 15th Infantry Division at Sinelnikovo and Novo Moskovsk, and the 333rd Infantry Division around Slavyansk. Later, both divisions would follow in the wake of the panzers to clean out bypassed pockets of resistance and to mop up cutoff Russian forces.[94]

In its final form, Manstein's plan involved the use of three shock groups to attack the 6th Army and Group Popov in the flank and rear. The SS Panzer Corps would thrust from Krasnograd and the XLVIII Panzer Corps from the Chaplino area. Both corps would converge on the Pavlograd region to cut off and isolate advanced elements of the 6th Army. The two corps would then converge on Lozovaya and drive to the Donets to complete the elimination of Soviet forces in the area. The XL Panzer Corps would continue its attacks from the Krasnoarmeiskoye area and drive toward Barvenkovo to crush Group Popov and the right flank of the 1st Guards Army.[95]

The attack by the SS Panzer Corps would be carried out with two divisions. On February 20, *Das Reich* would thrust southward from

Krasnograd via Pereshchepino to Novo Moskovsk, where it would
link up with two regiments of the 15th Infantry Division. The next day,
Das Reich was to thrust toward Pavlograd, while *Totenkopf* would also
drive eastward from Pereshchepino. On February 22, *Das Reich* would
advance on Lozovaya from the southwest, while *Totenkopf* moved in
from the northwest. Both divisions would then attack northward
along the railroad toward Merefa. The 15th Infantry Division would
support the SS Panzer Corps advance and mop up bypassed Russian
forces. The corps left flank would be covered by *LSAH* under the
command of *Armee Abteilung* Lanz.[96]

The two divisions of the XLVIII Panzer Corps would launch their
northward thrust from the Chaplino area on February 23. The 6th
Panzer Division would drive northward to the rail line east of
Lozovaya and the 17th Panzer Division would attack toward the rail
line midway between Lozovaya and Barvenkovo. The XL Panzer
Corps would continue its attacks launched February 19. *Wiking* would
attack northward toward Barvenkovo. The 7th Panzer Division would
thrust east of Krasnoarmeiskoye toward Barvenkovo, while the 11th
Panzer Division continued its westward assault from the Gavrilovka
area to Andreyevka, where it would turn to the north. All three
divisions would then strike at Barvenkovo. Two regiments of the
333rd Infantry Division would finish clearing out Krasnoarmeiskoye
and mop up bypassed Russian resistance. The third regiment would
hem in the Soviet forces in Kramatorskaya.[97]

On February 19, the Germans renewed their attacks on Krasnoarmeiskoye. While the 7th Panzer Division bypassed the town to the
north, the 333rd Infantry Division and *Wiking* pressed into the town
itself. Simultaneously in the north, the 11th Panzer Division drove
westward from Gavrilovka and captured Novo Alexeyevskaya and
Alexandrovka, shooting up in the process a 3rd Tank Corps column
(destroying five T-34s and twenty-eight trucks), moving to succor the
4th Guards Tank Corps. As a result, the 4th Guards Tank Corps found
itself surrounded without any prospect for immediate relief. *Wiking*
then joined the 7th Panzer Division in a northward thrust toward
Dobropolye (fifteen miles to the northwest of Krasnoarmeiskoye),
leaving the 333rd Infantry Division to mop up Krasnoarmeiskoye. The
4th Guards Tank Corps held out with its remaining twelve tanks until
February 20, when it ran out of supplies. That night, Russian survivors
began to filter out of the area toward Barvenkovo, where they
gathered around the 13th Guards Tank Brigade (thirty-two T-34
tanks). Remnants of the 4th Guards Tank Corps reached Barvenkovo
on February 24, just in time to join the 1st Guards Army's withdrawal
to the Donets.[98]

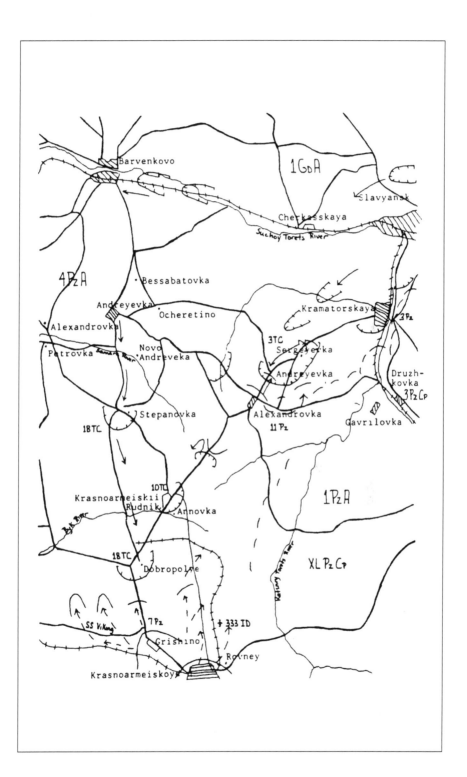

While Manstein's panzer divisions completed their deployments, the Russians continued to advance blindly westward, all the while being urged on by STAVKA and front headquarters. Soviet exhilaration was only slightly dampened by the sudden attack of *Das Reich* on February 20.[99]

Attacking before dawn on February 19, *Das Reich* began its southward drive from the Krasnograd area pushing through the 6th Rifle Division. By noon, the SS troopers were engaged against heavy resistance eight miles south of Krasnograd. A Russian counterattack was repulsed and the battalion destroyed, but it was nearly evening before Soviet resistance was cleared enough to allow the advance to resume. During the night, the *Deutschland* Regiment moved toward Pereshchepino, while the *Führer* Regiment advanced toward Novo Moskovsk.

Pereshchepino was taken shortly after midnight on February 20, and by 0230, the division was again moving south. By 1400, contact was established with the 15th Infantry Division in Novo Moskovsk. After the Russians abandoned their positions around the city, a *Kampfgruppe* of *Das Reich* drove south through Pereshchepino and joined the main force of the division.[100]

Throughout February 21, *Das Reich* and the 15th Infantry Division consolidated their positions around Novo Moskovsk and prepared to advance on Pavlograd. Meanwhile, *Totenkopf* completed its movement into the Krasnograd area and elements of the division marched south to Pereshchepino in preparation for an advance on Pavlograd on the morning of February 22.[101]

Ignoring the threat posed to the 6th Army by the German attacks, front headquarters still insisted that the 6th Army fulfill its mission. To assist the 6th Army, a front mobile group, composed of the 25th Tank and the 1st Guards Tank Corps, was dispatched to the Lozovaya-Pavlograd area. The 6th Army was also ordered to force a crossing of the Dnieper on the night of February 21–22, and to take and hold a bridgehead on the right bank of the river. At the same time, elements of the mobile group were to seize Zaporozhye and to prepare to advance on Melitopol. The right flank of the army was to capture Poltava by the evening of February 23.[102]

Already severed from its right flank, on February 21, the 6th Army continued its offensive. The 25th Tank Corps bypassed Sinelnikovo and advanced ten to twenty miles southeast of the city toward Slavgorod. Lead elements pushed to Chernoarmeiskoye, fifteen miles from Zaporozhye. Meanwhile, repeated attempts were made to open a passage to the main forces of the 6th Army through the SS Panzer Corps positions north of Novo Moskovsk and north of Pereshchepino.[103]

In the predawn hours of February 22, *Das Reich* crossed the Samara River and pushed on to Pavlograd, breaking the resistance of the 35th Guards Rifle Division. By midmorning, the division had reached Pavlograd. By afternoon, it had cleared a path through the 35th Guards Rifle Division, linked up with the 15th Infantry Division at Sinelnikovo and was ready to resume its advance from Pavlograd. Meanwhile, *Totenkopf* pushed southwest of Pereshchepino to broaden the gap between the main forces of the 6th Army and the now isolated 267th Infantry Division and the 106th Rifle Brigade.[104]

The 6th Army's position deteriorated further on February 23. *Das Reich* solidified its position at Pavlograd while the 15th Infantry Division mopped up the area northeast of Sinelnikovo, pushed the Russians out of Razdory, and established contact with the 6th Panzer Division, which had just initiated its attacks from the southeast. *Totenkopf* also attacked on February 23, and by nightfall a *Kampfgruppe* reached Vyazovok northeast of Pavlograd. By this time, in the area south of the Samara River, the Russians had already lost the 175th Tank Brigade, the 60th Motorized Brigade, and the 35th and 41st Guards and Rifle Divisions.[105]

While the SS Panzer Corps tightened its grip on Pavlograd, the XLVIII Panzer Corps launched its attacks from the southeast. Driving twenty miles on the first day, the 6th Panzer Division seized a bridgehead across the Samara at Bogdanovka, although the Russians retained possession of the village itself. The next day the division took Bogdanovka and advanced to the northeast. The 17th Panzer Division also made good progress on February 23, reaching Petropavlovka. The next day, it too continued to push northward. By February 25, both divisions had reached the area of Starye Blisnetsy, about midway between Lozovaya and Barvenkovo.[106]

Still unaware of the magnitude of the disaster it faced, Southwestern Front headquarters sent new orders to the 6th Army on February 22. With its right flank cut off and its center crumpling in, the 6th Army was now ordered to push its mobile group (25th Tank and 1st Guards Tank Corps) forward aggressively to cut off the German withdrawal from the Donbas and to step up its attacks on Krasnograd. Sixty miles in front of the 6th Army's lines, the 25th Tank Corps was running low on fuel and ammunition. Any hope that the armored corps might escape vanished on February 23, when the XLVIII Panzer Corps launched its offensive. Caught between the German forces at Zaporozhye, *Das Reich*, and the 6th Panzer Division, the 25th Tank Corps was doomed. Finally, given the order to break out by the 6th Army, the 25th Tank Crops personnel abandoned their equipment and scattered to the northeast, joining the legion of Russian troops fleeing the German armored thrust.[107]

By February 24, Vatutin could no longer ignore the true situation and asked for help from the Voronezh Front in the form of a southward drive by the 3rd Tank and 69th Armies. Neither attack substantially affected the 6th Army's position.[108]

Without reserves, the best that Vatutin could do was to shift the 6th Guards Corps from the left flank of the 1st Guards Army to its right flank, to bolster the collapsing center and right flanks. Two rifle divisions, supported by mobile forces, were to occupy defenses on a broad front south of the Lozovaya-Barvenkovo-Slavyansk rail line. There was still no order instructing the right flank to go over to the defense.[109]

Meanwhile, the 4th Panzer Army continued its advance against the Southwestern Front's already shattered right flank. On February 24, *Totenkopf* took Orelka (ten miles to the northwest of Lozovaya), enveloped Vyazovok, and pushed Russian forces back toward Pavlograd. To the north of Pavlograd, *Das Reich* captured Verbilk and established contact with *Totenkopf*. To the rear, the 15th Infantry Division was mopping up isolated Russian pockets in the Pavlograd-Novo Moskovsk-Sinelnikovo area. By the end of the day, the 4th Panzer Army could report that "The enemy in front of the SS Panzer Corps north of Pavlograd can be considered destroyed."[110]

While the SS Panzer and XLVIII Panzer Corps ripped into the 6th Army and 1st Guards Army, the XL Panzer Corps, having destroyed the 4th Guards Tank Corps, now turned its attention to the rest of Group Popov as it drove northward toward Barvenkovo. Popov's situation was desperate. Holding positions around Krasnoarmeisky Rudnik, the seventeen tanks of the 10th Tank Corps tried to deflect the thrust of the 7th Panzer Division and *Wiking* from the south. In the Andreyevka area, twelve remaining tanks of the 3rd Tank Corps braced themselves against the 11th Panzer Division driving from Alexandrovka and Novo Alexeyevsky. Further south, the 18th Tank Corps, with only eight tanks, defended Dobropolye.[111]

By February 20, the 7th Panzer Division had pushed northward to the Dobropolye area while a reconnaissance group advancing farther to the north reported only weak enemy forces in the area. Meanwhile, elements of the 11th Panzer Division held off repeated attacks against Alexandrovka, inflicting heavy Russian casualties. Two divisional assault groups then captured Sergeyevka and drove several miles to the southwest. By nightfall there were over 800 enemy dead.[112]

On the night of February 20–21, Popov asked Vatutin for permission to pull back his armored forces northward to the Stepanovka area, roughly twenty miles. Incredibly, Popov was reprimanded and told by Vatutin that such a move would allow the Germans to withdraw to Dnepropetrovsk and would also uncover the flank and rear of the 6th Army. Popov was also reminded that his proposal contradicted the group's mission. As a result, Popov was told to carry out his mission and forbidden to withdraw. Instead, he was instructed to cut all routes from Dobropolye and Krasnoarmeiskoye and to launch a pursuit of German forces parallel to Dobropolye and Pokrovskoye.[113]

The XL Panzer Corps continued its advance on February 21. The 7th Panzer Division blasted its way through the 18th and 10th Tank Corps at Dobropolye and reached the south bank of the Byk River, about half way between Krasnoarmeiskoye and Stepanovka. Meanwhile, elements of *Wiking* swung west and north through Krivorzhye to Petrovka where they slammed into the 3rd Tank Corps. The next day, the 7th Panzer Division secured the villages along the north bank of the Byk and established contact with *Kampfgruppe* Balck advancing from the east. By the twenty-fourth of February the 7th Panzer Division also had troops in Stepanovka while Balck, after screening off the town to the north and east, attacked Besabotovka to the north.[114]

Trapped between the advancing columns, the 18th Tank Corps retreated toward new Russian lines south of Barvenkovo. Here, two rifle divisions, the remnants of the 3rd, 10th, 18th, and 4th Guards Tank Corps and the 13th Guards Tank Brigade (a total of thirty-five T-34 and T-70 tanks) put up stubborn resistance against the XL Panzer Corps advance.[115] As the Germans had done in November and December 1942, the Russians were now using small ad hoc forces, formed from the wreckage of destroyed or retreating units, to construct makeshift defenses.

By the evening of February 24, the three German armored groups had established a nearly continuous front, with the SS Panzer Corps in the Pavlograd area, the XLVIII Panzer Corps southeast of Lozovaya, and the XL Panzer Corps south of Barvenkovo. The armored counteroffensive effectively isolated the 6th Army and eliminated the threat of both Russian mobile groups (Group Popov and the 25th Tank and 1st Guards Tank Corps). Between February 3 and 24, the 1st Panzer Army reported 300 enemy tanks captured or destroyed, 6,000 enemy dead, and nearly 1,700 prisoners. Manstein now moved to exploit the momentum already achieved and crush the remainder of the 6th and 1st Guards Armies.[116]

On February 25, Manstein issued new orders to Army Group South. German air reconnaissance had spotted fresh Soviet forces moving from the Lisichansk area across Isyum to support the 6th Army's front. Manstein intended, therefore, to "attack enemy forces still south of the Donets and to destroy them to create operational freedom for a thrust into the south flank of the enemy's Kharkov group."[117] The rapid elimination of the Russian forces still south of the Donets would also allow Manstein to turn his armored formations to the north.

After breaking out of Barvenkovo, the 1st Panzer Army would cover its right flank with a rapid thrust against Slavyansk. At the same time, it was necessary to drive northward to the line Pertovskaya-Isyum to prevent the Russians from retreating across the Donets. Meanwhile, the 4th Panzer Army would attack to the northeast to the general line Metshebilovka-Krasnopavlovka, then turn northward toward Kharkov.[118]

Although it was too late, Vatutin finally recognized the dangerous position of his forces. On February 24, the long overdue order for the 6th Army to go over to the defense was issued. His evening report to STAVKA finally reflected conditions as they actually were and requested that STAVKA order adjacent fronts to launch supporting attacks. The Germans, however, acted too quickly for Vatutin's measures to be effective.[119]

On February 25, the SS Panzer Corps pushed north from Pavlograd with its two panzer divisions abreast. *Das Reich*, advancing along the main rail line, was met by increasingly stubborn resistance as it neared Lozovaya. For the next two days, a bitter battle raged around the town, with the Russians clinging tenaciously to the hills to the northeast of the city. Meanwhile, *Totenkopf* advanced as far north as Alexandrovka, and by February 26, had reached Krasnopavlovka.[120]

The XLVIII Panzer Corps rolled inexorably forward as well. The 6th Panzer Division broke through stubborn defenses and occupied the hills west of Starye Blisnetsy. By now the Russians were fighting to the bitter end. On February 25, the 6th Panzer Division reported over a thousand enemy dead in a single day's action; there was no mention of prisoners. The 17th Panzer Division also overcame tenacious resistance and took the high ground around Starye Blisnetsy, and secured Dobrovolye on the Lozovaya-Barvenkovo rail line. The pace of the 17th Panzer Division's advance disrupted organized Russian defense, allowing the division to approach the Burbulatovo Station, east of Starye Blisnetsy in the 6th Panzer Division's sector of advance. The 6th Panzer Division was still eight to twelve miles behind.[121]

By the evening of February 25, the 17th Panzer Division was still far ahead of the 6th Panzer Division, and the XL Panzer Corps, to its right, was still tied down in heavy fighting in front of Barvenkovo. There, three rifle divisions, the 3rd, 10th, 18th, and the 4th Guards Tank Corps under the 1st Guards Army's control, occupied defensive positions. The 1st Guards Army stripped its left flank in an effort to hold Barvenkovo at all costs. Tank strength, which had risen to fifty, enabled the 1st Guards Army to stiffen its resistance against the XL Panzer Corps, although most of the Russian tanks were dug in because they were out of fuel. To crush the Soviet defenses at Barvenkovo, the 1st Panzer Army ordered the XL Panzer Corps and 333rd Infantry Division to attack past Barvenkovo, toward the Donets River. The III Panzer Corps would then join the XL Panzer Corps assault with an attack on Kramatorskaya and Slavyansk.[122]

The intention of the 1st Panzer Army, using the XL and III Panzer Corps, was to retake the south bank of the Donets, block the Donets crossing at Isyum, and to establish a bridgehead at Petrovskaya. On February 26, the XL Panzer Division began its sweep around the city to the northeast and reached Krasnorevka as it thrust toward Isyum. The Russians held out at Barvenkovo until threatened with encirclement on February 28, when they fell back toward Isyum.[123]

On February 27, STAVKA and Southwestern Front headquarters, sobered by the prospects of defeat, ordered those elements of the 1st Guards and 6th Armies that were still capable, to withdraw to the Donets River. To cover the retreat of the 6th Army, STAVKA ordered the Voronezh Front to turn the 3rd Tank Army sharply south into the flank of the advancing SS Panzer Corps. Its strength already sapped in battles with *LSAH* from Merefa to Krasnograd, the 3rd Tank Army was reinforced with infantry divisions pulled from other sectors. In a desperate, hopeless attack, the 3rd Tank Army was to hurl its last tanks southward into the gap between *LSAH* and the two SS Panzer Divisions driving north from Lozovaya.[124]

Meanwhile, the SS Panzer Corps continued its northward advance from Lozovaya, along either side of the Krasnopavlovka-Milhailovka railroad. The 15th Infantry Division supported the corps by warding off the endless stream of Russian troops fleeing northward west of Lozovaya.[125]

By this time, the German counteroffensive was turning into an all-out pursuit, with most of the fighting taking place in the rear areas where small detachments were engaged in running battles with bypassed Russian forces. Soviet defenses were in disarray everywhere the Germans attacked. Even local counterattacks met with disaster, in particular on February 27, when the divisional staff of the 17th Panzer Division held off a Soviet attack and took 300 prisoners, twelve artillery pieces, 200 horses, and eighty vehicles.[126]

On February 28, the 6th and 17th Panzer Divisions continued their drive toward the Donets west of Isyum, opposed by the 1st Guards Cavalry Corps. To the east, the 11th Panzer Division finally cleared Barvenkovo, while *Wiking* the 6th and 7th Panzer Divisions pushed to the south bank of the Donets, although the Russians retained a bridgehead on the high ground south of Isyum. At the same time, the 3rd Panzer Division (III Panzer Corps) and 333rd Infantry Division attacked Slavyansk, driving the Russians back across the Donets River.[127]

On March 2, the III Panzer Corps and the XXX Corps launched their attacks on Russian positions from the Bachmuta River Valley to Voroshilovgrad. Both corps made good progress and forced the Russians back across the Donets. Meanwhile, on the right flank of the Southwestern Front, the 3rd Tank Army met its doom. On March 1, the 12th Tank and 15th Tank Corps, reduced to approximately battalion strength each, and the 6th Guards Cavalry Corps (all now subordinated to the Southwestern Front) began their ill-fated southward advance toward Lozovaya and immediately clashed with forward elements of *Totenkopf* and *Das Reich*. By March 2, what little offensive power the 3rd Tank Army had left was exhausted. Moreover, the SS Panzer Corps launched an attack of its own. *Leibstandarte Adolf Hitler* drove eastward toward Kegichevka and Okhocheye. Only the 6th Guards Cavalry Corps managed to escape to the north. The rest of the 3rd Tank Army was encircled and destroyed, although some personnel fought their way out over the next two days.[128]

The destruction of the 3rd Tank Army marked a grim and costly end to Operation GALLOP. In less than two weeks' time, Manstein's counterstroke successfully recovered what the Soviets had fought for nearly three months to gain. On February 28, the 4th Panzer Army reported that, in the eight days between February 21 and 28, it had recovered an area of territory seventy-five miles wide and ninety-five miles deep. In addition, its forces captured or destroyed 156 tanks, 178 guns, and 284 anti-tank guns, took 4,643 prisoners, and were responsible for 11,000 enemy dead.[129] Combined with the losses inflicted by the 1st Panzer Army between February 3 and 24, the total Russian losses for this period was in excess of 500 tanks, 6,343 prisoners, and 17,000 dead. The Russian 6th Army, including the 25th Tank and 1st Guards Tank Corps, Group Popov (3rd, 10th, 18th, and 4th Guards Tank Corps), and the 4th Guards Rifle Corps were wiped out. In addition, considerable elements of the 1st Guards Army were rendered useless. Finally, the 12th Tank and 15th Tank Corps of the 3rd Tank Army were eliminated, while the 6th Guards Cavalry Corps and the remaining rifle divisions also suffered severe losses. Not content to rest on his laurels, Manstein next turned his attention northward to the Soviet salient west of Kharkov. With a few adjustments to his deployments, the panzer divisions were ordered to the north to repeat in the Kharkov area what they had accomplished south of the Donets River.

Notes

1. Manstein, p. 403.
2. Ibid., pp. 403–404.
3. Ibid., 403.
4. Glanz, p. 230. Erickson, pp. 34–35.
5. Glanz, p. 122. Erickson, p. 35.
6. Erickson, p. 45.
7. Ibid.
8. Ibid., p. 46.
9. Glanz, p. 123.
10. Glanz, p. 123.
11. Ibid., p. 126.
12. Ibid.
13. Ibid., pp. 126–127.
14. Glanz, pp. 128–129. HG Don Anlg. 9 KTB, February 3, 1943, Roll 272, Frame 156. Panzer Armeeoberkommando 4 Ia, Anlagenband C 3 z. KTB Nr. I u. II February 1–July 31, 1943, Microcopy T 313, Roll 367, Frame 8,653,025. Cited henceforth as 4 Pz AOK Anlg. 3 KTB, with date, roll, and frame number. Panzer Armeeoberkommando 1 Ia, Anlagen zum KTB Nr. 10, February 1–28, 1943, Microcopy T 313, Roll 42, Frame 7,280,719. Cited henceforth as 1 Pz AOK 10, with date, roll, and frame number.
15. Glanz, pp. 130, 132.
16. Ibid., p. 133. Erickson, p. 46.
17. Glanz, p. 133. HG Don Anlg. 10 KTB, February 2, 1942, Roll 272, situation map Frames 714–715.
18. Glanz, pp. 133–134. Erickson, p. 46.
19. Glanz, p. 134. Erickson, p. 46.
20. Glanz, p. 134.
21. Ibid., pp. 134–135.
22. Ibid., p. 135.
23. Erickson, p. 46.
24. Glanz, pp. 136–137. Map sets **Operation GALLOP** and **Operation STAR**. 1 Pz AOK KTB 10, February 6, 1943, Frame 7,280,832. HG Don Anlg. 8 KTB, January 28, 1943, Roll 271, Frame 753. HG Don Anlg. 9 KTB, situation map February 2, 1943, Frames 714–715.
25. Glanz, pp. 136–137, map sets **Operation GALLOP** and **Operation STAR**. Ms T15, p. 72.
26. HG Don Anlg. 9 KTB, February 3, 1943, Roll 272, Frame 199.
27. Ibid., Frames 188, 199, 201.
28. Ibid., Frame 109.
29. Ibid., January 31, 1943, Frames 383–384. February 4, 1943, Frames 108–109. Ms T15, p. 73. II SS Panzer Corps Ia, Anlagenband A II, Teil zum KTB 4, January 3–March 27, 1943, Microcopy T 354, Roll 118, Frame 3,751,525. Cited henceforth as II SS Pz Cp. Anlg. A II KTB 4, with date, roll, and frame number.

30. HG Don Anlg. 9 KTB, January 30–31, 1943, Roll 272, Frames 491, 285–286. February 2, 1943, Frame 219.
31. Ibid., February 5, 1943, Frames 91–92. Manstein, pp. 405–406. Schwarz, p. 69.
32. Manstein, pp. 406–413. Schwarz, pp. 69–73.
33. 1 Pz AOK KTB 10, February 7, 1943, Roll 42, Frames 7,280,799–7,280,800. Panzer Armeeoberkommando 4 Ia, Anlagenband C 1 z. KTB Nr. I u. II, February 1–July 31, 1943, Microcopy T 313, Roll 365, Frames 8,650,820–8,650,822. Cited henceforth as 4 Pz AOK Anlg. 1 KTB, with date, roll, and frame number.
34. 4 Pz AOK Anlg. 1 KTB, February 9, 1943, Roll 365, Frames 8,650,821–8,650,822. 1 Pz AOK KTB 10, February 10, 1943, Roll 42, Frames 7,280,883–7,280,885.
35. 1 Pz AOK KTB 10, *passim* February 11–20, 1943, Roll 42.
36. Ibid., February 5–7, 1943, Frames 7,280,735–7,280,736, 7,280,743, 7,280,769–7,280,770, 7,280,827. 4 Pz AOK Anlg. 3 KTB, February 7–8, 1943, Roll 367, Frames 8,652,892, 2,852,901. HG Don Anlg. 9 KTB, February 6, 1943, Roll 272, Frames 6–7.
37. Manstein, p. 415.
38. Ibid., pp. 414–415.
39. 1 Pz AOK KTB 10, February 9–10, 1943, Roll 42, Frames 7,280,849, 7,280,852, 7,280,873, 7,280,888, 7,280,891–7,280,892.
40. Glanz, p. 141. HG Don Anlg. 9 KTB. February 2, 1943, Roll 272, Frame 2,190,220. February 5, 1943, Frames 129–130.
41. 1 Pz AOK KTB 10, February 4, 1943, Roll 42, Frame 7,280,808. HG Don Anlg. 9, February 4, 1943, Roll 272, Frame 98.
42. 1 Pz AOK KTB 10, February 5, 1943, Roll 42, Frames 7,280,735–7,280,736, 7,280,743.
43. Ibid., February 6–7, 1943, Frames 7,280,770, 7,280,784–7,280,785, 7,280,791. Glanz, pp. 146–147.
44. 1 Pz AOK KTB 10, February 8–10, Roll 42, Frames 7,280,827, 7,280,852, 7,280,891–7,280,892.
45. Ibid., February 10, Frames 7,280,873, 7,280,888. February 12, 1943, Frame 7,280,968.
46. Glanz, pp. 148–149.
47. Ibid., p. 149.
48. Ibid.
49. Ibid., p. 150.
50. Ibid. Manstein, p. 417. 1 Pz AOK KTB 10, February 11, 1943, Roll 42, Frame 7,280,935.
51. Manstein, p. 418.
52. Ibid., pp. 419–420.
53. Ibid., p. 421.
54. *Oberkommando des Heeres*, General Stab des Heeres, Operationen Abteilung I/N Band Nord, Microcopy T 78, Roll 337, Frame 6,293,747.
55. II SS Pz Cp. Anlg. A II KTB 4, February 14, 1943, Roll 118, Frame 3,751,635.
56. Ibid., February 17, 1943, Frame 3,751,689. Manstein, p. 421.
57. Manstein, p. 422.

58. II SS Pz Cp. Anlg. A II KTB 4, February 14, 1943, Roll 118, Frame 3,751,657.
59. Ibid., Frames 3,751,657, 3,751,678. Glanz, p. 257.
60. Manstein, pp. 423–424.
61. Ibid., p. 424.
62. Ibid., pp. 424–425.
63. Ibid., p. 425.
64. Ibid., 1 Pz AOK KTB 10, February 10, 1943, Roll 42, Frame 7,281,250. Schwarz, p. 254.
65. Manstein, p. 425.
66. Ibid., pp. 425–426. Schwarz, p. 254.
67. Manstein, p. 426. Schwarz, p. 255.
68. Earl F. Ziemkie, *Stalingrad to Berlin: The German Defeat in the East,* (Washington, D.C.: U.S. Army Center of Military History, 1968), p. 92.
69. Manstein, p. 427. Schwarz, pp. 257–258.
70. Manstein, pp. 428–429. 4 Pz AOK Anlg. 1 KTB, February 19, 1943, Roll 365, Frames 8,650,900–8,650,902.
71. 1 Pz AOK KTB 10, February 10–11, 1942, Roll 41, Frames 7,280,891, 7,280,921, 7,280,835, 7,280,942, 7,280,944. Glanz, pp. 150, 152.
72. 1 Pz AOK KTB 10, February 11, 1943, Roll 41, Frames 7,280,921, 7,280,944. Glanz, p. 152.
73. 1 Pz AOK KTB 10, February 12, 1943, Roll 42, Frame 7,280,968. Glanz, p. 152.
74. 1 Pz AOK KTB 10, February 13–15, 1943, Roll 42, Frames 7,281,028, 7,281,038–7,281,039, 7,281,148.
75. II SS Pz Cp. Anlg. A II KTB 4, February 14, 1943, Roll 118, Frame 3,752,015. 1 Pz AOK KTB 10, February 15, 1953, Roll 42, Frame 7,281,134. Glanz, pp. 153–154.
76. Glanz, p. 154.
77. Ibid., p. 155. 4 Pz AOK Anlg. 3 KTB, February 21, 1943, Roll 367, Frame 8,652,999.
78. 1 Pz AOK KTB 10, February 15, 1943, Roll 42, Frame 7,281,148. Glanz, p. 155.
79. 1 Pz AOK KTB 10, February 16–17, 1943, Roll 42, Frames 7,281,175, 7,281,214–7,281,215, 7,281,217.
80. Glanz, pp. 156–157.
81. 1 Pz AOK KTB 10, February 18, 1943, Roll 42, Frame 7,281,251.
82. Glanz, p. 157.
83. Ibid., p. 159.
84. Ibid., p. 160.
85. Ibid., pp. 160–161.
86. Ibid., p. 161. Erickson, p. 50.
87. Glanz, p. 161. Erickson, p. 50.
88. 1 Pz AOK KTB 10, February 19, 1943, Roll 42, Frames 7,281,287–7,281,288.
89. Ibid., Frame 7,281,288.
90. Ibid., Frames 7,281,288–7,281,289.
91. Ibid., Frames 7,281,289–7,281,291. February 24, 1943, Frame 7,281,434.
92. Ibid., February 19, 1943, Frames 7,281,290–7,281,291. II SS Pz Cp. Anlg. A II KTB 4, February 20, 1943, Roll 118, Frame 3,751,722.

93. 1 Pz AOK KTB 10, February 21, 1943, Roll 42, Frame 7,281,290. 4 Pz AOK Anlg. 3 KTB, February 23, 1943, Roll 367, Frame 8,653,025.
94. 1 Pz AOK KTB 10, February 19, 1943, Roll 42, Frame 7,281,290. February 22, 1943, Frame 7,281,374.
95. II SS Pz Cp.Anlg. A II KTB 4, February 20, 1943, Roll 118, Frame 3,751,722. February 22, 1943, Frame 3,751,751. 1 Pz AOK KTB 10, February 23, 1943, Roll 42, Frames 7,281,394–7,281,396.
96. II SS Pz Cp. A II KTB 4, February 20, 1943, Roll 118, Frame 3,751,751. 4 Pz AOK Anlg. 1 KTB, February 23, 1943, Roll 365, Frame 8,650,995.
97. 4 Pz AOK Anlg. 1 KTB, February 22, 1943, Roll 365, Frame 8,650,950. 1 Pz AOK KTB 10, February 19, 1943, Roll 42, Frames 7,281,282, 7,281,316–7,281,317. February 24–25, 1943, Frames 7,281,433–7,281,434, 7,281,462.
98. 1 Pz AOK KTB 10, February 19–20, 1943, Roll 42, Frames 7,281,282, 7,281,285–7,281,286, 7,281,316, 7,281,321. Glanz, pp. 159–160.
99. Glanz, p. 166.
100. II SS Pz Cp. Anlg. A II KTB 4, February 19, 1943, Roll 118, Frame 3,731,712. Glanz, p. 166.
101. II SS Pz Cp. Anlg. A II KTB 4, February 20–21, 1943, Roll 118, Frames 3,751,722, 3,751,744. 4 Pz AOK Anlg. 3 KTB, February 21–22, 1943, Roll 367, Frames 8,652,999, 8,653,008–8,653,009.
102. Glanz, p. 167.
103. Ibid., pp. 167–168. 4 Pz AOK Anlg. 3 KTB, February 22, 1943, Roll 367, Frame 8,653,008.
104. 4 Pz AOK Anlg. 3 KTB, February 22–23, 1943, Roll 367, Frames 8,653,008–8,653,009, 8,653,024. Glanz, p. 168.
105. 4 Pz AOK Anlg. 3 KTB, February 22, 1943, Roll 367, Frames 8,650,323–8,650,324. II SS Pz Cp. Anlg. A II KTB 4, February 24, 1943, Roll 118, Frame 3,751,793.
106. 4 Pz AOK Anlg. 3 KTB, February 23–25, 1943, Roll 367, Frames 8,650,323–8,650,324, 8,560,342–8,650,343, 8,650,365–8,650,366. II SS Pz Cp. Anlg. A II KTB 4, February 24, 1943, Roll 118, Frame 3,751,793.
107. Glanz, pp. 168–169.
108. Ibid., p. 170.
109. Ibid.
110. 4 Pz AOK Anlg. 3 KTB, February 24, 1943, Roll 367, Frames 8,650,342–8,650,343. II SS Pz Cp. Anlg. A II KTB 4, February 24, 1943, Roll 118, Frame 3,751,793.
111. Glanz, pp. 172–173.
112. 1 Pz AOK KTB 10, February 20–21, 1943, Roll 42, Frames 7,281,315, 7,281,321, 7,281,346–7,281,347, 7,281,351.
113. Glanz, p. 173.
114. 1 Pz AOK KTB 10, February 24, 1943, Roll 42, Frame 7,281,440.
115. Glanz, p. 173.
116. 1 Pz AOK KTB 10, February 24, 1943, Roll 42, Frame 7,281,440.
117. Ibid., February, 25, 1942, Frame 7,281,460.
118. Ibid., Frames 7,281,460–7,281,461.
119. Glanz, p. 174.

120. 4 Pz AOK Anlg. 3 KTB, February 25–26, 1943, Roll 367, Frames 8,650,365–8,650,366, 8,650,386. II SS Pz Cp. Anlg. A II KTB 4, February 26, 1943, Roll 118, Frame 3,751,861.
121. 4 Pz AOK Anlg. 3 KTB, February 25, 1943, Roll 367, Frame 8,650,365. II SS Pz Cp. Anlg. A II KTB 4, February 26, 1943, Roll 118, Frame 3,751,861.
122. 1 Pz AOK KTB 10, February 25, 1943, Roll 42, Frames 7,281,462, 7,281,466. Glanz, pp. 175–176.
123. 1 Pz AOK KTB 10, February 25–27, 1943, Roll 42, Frames 7,281,462, 7,281,498, 7,281,500, 7,281,526–7,281,527.
124. Glanz, pp. 177–178.
125. II SS Pz Cp. Anlg. A II KTB 4, February 26, 1943, Roll 118, Frame 3,751,882. February, 28, 1943, Frame 3,752,006. 4 Pz AOK Anlg. 3 KTB, February 27, 1943, Roll 367, Frame 8,653,095.
126. 4 Pz AOK Anlg. 3 KTB, February 27, 1943, Roll 367, Frame 8,653,085.
127. Ibid., February 28, 1943, Frames 8,653,111–8,653,112. 1 Pz AOK KTB 10, February 28, 1943, Roll 42, Frames 7,281,543–7,281,544. II SS Pz Cp. Anlg. A II KTB 4, February 28, 1943, Roll 118, Frames 3,752,009–3,752,010.
128. 1 Pz AOK KTB 10, February 28, 1943, Roll 42, Frames 7,281,534, 7,281,543–7,281,544. March 1–2, 1943, Frames 7,281,576, 7,281,582. II SS Pz Cp. Anlg. A II KTB 4, March 3, 1943, Roll 118, Frame 3,752,084. 4 Pz AOK Anlg. 3 KTB, March 3, 1943, Roll 367, Frame 8,653,226. Glanz, p. 179.
129. 4 Pz AOK Anlg. 3 KTB, February 28, 1943, Roll 367, Frame 8,653,111.

CHAPTER 5

Recovery

The Southwestern Front's attack through the Donets basin, Operation GALLOP, was only part of a much larger Soviet offensive designed to liberate the entire Ukraine and amputate the German southern flank from the rest of the Eastern Front. In particular, the attacks by the 6th Army and the 25th Tank and 1st Guards Tank Corps posed a mortal danger to Army Group South. Simultaneously with the attack by the Southwestern Front, the Voronezh Front struck *Armee Abteilung* Lanz and threatened Kharkov.

The combined Soviet offensives against the German southern wing presented Manstein with a unique problem. By the end of the first week of February, the Russians were experiencing considerable success. The 6th Army of the Southwestern Front, advancing to the west from around Isyum, was driving steadily toward Pavlograd. Once at Pavlograd, the Soviets were within easy striking distance of the Dnieper crossings of Dnepropetrovsk and Zaporozhye (about thirty-five and fifty miles, respectively), and could cut Army Group South's line of communications. Meanwhile, if the Voronezh Front were successful in overrunning *Armee Abteilung* Lanz, the Russians could cross the Dnieper upriver on either side of Kremenchug and block the approaches to the Crimea and the Dnieper crossing at Kherson, thus cutting off the entire German southern flank.

The problem for Manstein was how to deal with both Soviet offensives. Army Group South was already overextended and could not possibly blunt both Russian threats simultaneously. Under these circumstances, Manstein was faced with the choice of defending Kharkov or eliminating the threat to the deep flank of Army Group South. Hitler, however, insisted that Kharkov be held.

The outline for Operation STAR, to be conducted by the Voronezh Front, was laid out on January 23, shortly after STAVKA approved Operation GALLOP. In the larger scheme of Soviet operations, the Voronezh Front was responsible for the northeastern Ukraine, including Kharkov.

The Voronezh Front consisted of five armies, the 38th and 60th, which would drive on Kursk, and the 40th, 69th, and 3rd Tank, which would attack Kharkov. The 40th Army was the strongest of the five armies, although all Voronezh Front formations were a bit worn by a month of action. The 3rd Tank Army provided the armored punch with the 12th Tank and 15th Tank Corps and the 6th Guards Cavalry Corps. The combined strength of the three armies earmarked for the assault on Kharkov was just under 200,000 men and 300 tanks.[1]

The German divisions of *Armee Abteilung* Lanz, opposite the Voronezh Front, held a sector along the northern bank of the Oskol River from the north of Chernyk to Kupyansk. Considerably reduced by their earlier defeats, these forces were capable, at most, of screening the front for a short period of time. Composed of the 168th, 298th, and 320th Infantry Divisions, Panzer Grenadier Division *Grossdeutschland*, and the *Deutschland* Regiment of *Das Reich*, *Armee Abteilung* Lanz was expected to hold a sector of nearly one hundred miles with an over-extended force of about 50,000 men.[2]

The Voronezh Front was to eliminate the German forces opposing it, and to advance and seize Kursk, Belgorod, and Kharkov. The main attack would be carried out by the 40th, 69th, and 3rd Tank Armies. These forces would advance southwestward to converge on Kharkov, enveloping it from the west and south, trapping the Germans in the city. Ultimately, Operation STAR was to achieve a depth of 130 to 160 miles to reach the line Ratitnoye-Graivoron-Bogoduhkov-Lyubotin-Merefa. The advance would take place in two stages: After breaking German resistance along the Oskol River, the Voronezh Front would advance to the Donets on a broad front from Belgorod, through Volchansk, to Pechenegi. In the second stage, Russian forces would seize Kharkov and advance to the final line.[3]

Manstein's first reaction to the attacks launched by the Voronezh Front against *Armee Abteilung* Lanz on February 2, 1943, was not to overreact. As the Russian offensives against Army Group South and *Armee Abteilung* Lanz developed, it became evident that both Soviet fronts threatened Army Group South (formerly Don). Manstein, however, determined that the most immediate danger was that posed by the 6th Army of the Southwestern Front advancing in the gap between the 1st Panzer Army and *Armee Abteilung* Lanz. As far as Manstein was concerned, the attacks by the Voronezh Front were an unwelcome distraction.

Hitler was unable to grasp these facts. For a second time, the situation opposite *Armee Abteilung* Lanz precipitated an argument between Hitler and Manstein. Hitler's reaction was the opposite of Manstein's. Once it became obvious that the Voronezh Front's objective was Kharkov, Hitler stubbornly insisted that the German effort

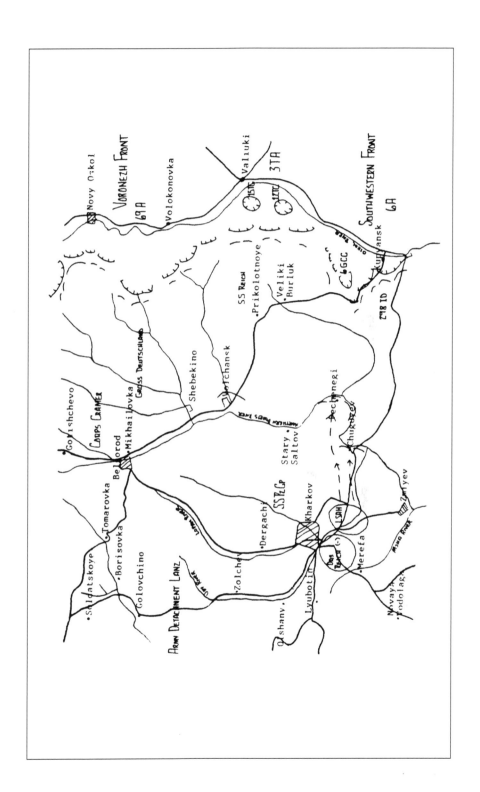

should be focused in the north, rather than in the area south of Kharkov in the gap between the 1st Panzer Army and *Armee Abteilung* Lanz. Hitler immediately ordered an attack by one division (*Das Reich*) against the Voronezh Front, an attack that at best could be only a minor irritation to the Russian advance. This fundamental difference in priorities between Hitler and Manstein was nearly ruinous to the German cause.

Manstein's meeting with Hitler on February 6, and again between February 17–19, resulted in two extremely important decisions. Although these decisions directly affected Army Group South to a greater degree than *Armee Abteilung* Lanz, both meetings arose out of the difference of opinion between Manstein and Hitler over where the Germans should make their main effort. Manstein, on the basis of sound military reasoning, advocated that the Germans exert themselves against the Southwestern Front, which posed the most immediate danger to Army Group South's line of communications. Hitler, however, was hypnotized by Kharkov, the second city of the Ukraine and the fourth largest in the Soviet Union. Holding Kharkov would not improve Army Group South's positions. As he had only four months earlier, Hitler elevated a prestige objective above all else and nearly repeated at Kharkov the disaster of Stalingrad.

The northward advance of Army Group South and the subsequent recapture of Kharkov was not a separate operation. Having shattered the 6th Army and disrupted organized Russian resistance along the front, Manstein merely took advantage of the momentum already gained to pursue the Soviets, who were desperately trying to establish a solid defensive front. In fact, the initial order for the attack to the north did not even mention Kharkov as an objective. Army Group South was to "attack enemy forces still south of the Donets to destroy them, in order to create operational freedom for a sharp thrust into the southern flank of the enemy Kharkov group."[4]

A subsequent order on February 28, still failed to designate Kharkov as an objective, but identified the aim of the attack as "the enemy southwest of Kharkov facing *Armee Abteilung* Kempf on its southern flank."[5]

In other words, despite the spectacular success he had just achieved, Manstein, unlike Hitler, was not dazzled by the prospects of retaking Kharkov. Rather, Manstein realized that by maintaining pressure on the already depleted Russian forces and turning his panzers southward into the flank of the Soviet units attacking *Armee Abteilung* Kempf, he could further disrupt the Russian offensive and possibly take Kharkov by *coup de main*.

During the first half of February, *Armee Abteilung* Lanz acquitted itself surprisingly well, despite being outmatched. This was due primarily to the stubborn resistance of the German 168th, 298th, and 320th Infantry Divisions, which conducted skillful delaying actions and managed, on more than one occasion, to escape Russian encirclement and fight their way out to German lines. *Grossdeutschland* Division and *Deutschland* Regiment also delayed the Soviet advance in fighting withdrawals. Interrogation of Russian prisoners revealed that the Soviets had suffered fifty percent losses in their attacks against *Deutschland* Regiment at Velki Burluk. The fighting there was so fierce that in two days, SS Corporal Haider singlehandedly destroyed seven enemy tanks. Also notable was the defense of the Donets crossings at Chuguyev and Pechenegi by *LSAH*, which frustrated the 3rd Tank Army's attempts to cross the Donets off the march. As a result, the 3rd Tank Army spent three days preparing deliberate assaults to take the vital crossings. The 69th Army also met stubborn resistance.[6]

However, the 40th Army advanced against only weak resistance and by February 9, captured Belgorod. The loss of Belgorod threatened the left flank of *Armee Abteilung* Lanz and compromised the German forces still fighting east of the Donets. This situation precipitated a general withdrawal of German troops to the west and southwest across the Donets to new positions covering Kharkov.[7]

On February 10, the 3rd Tank Army launched its prepared attack across the Donets. The 15th Tank Corps advanced from Pechenegi against the withdrawing forces of *LSAH*. The 12th Tank Corps also drove across the Donets near Chuguyev. However, the Russians were soon forced to a grinding halt east of Kharkov, where the Germans occupied prepared positions. As a result, a new Soviet plan was adopted on the evening of February 10. On February 12, the 15th Tank Corps would hit the Germans east of Kharkov, while the 12th Tank Corps attacked the city from the south. Simultaneously, the 6th Guards Cavalry Corps would strike from the south to occupy Lyubotin, where it was to make contact with the 40th Army advancing from the north.[8]

The SS Panzer Corps also received new orders on February 10. The mass of *Das Reich* and *LSAH* were to concentrate for an attack to the southeast. Elements of both divisions began disengaging from the 3rd Tank Army and were replaced by *Grossdeutschland* and the 168th Infantry Division. By shifting the bulk of the SS Panzer Corps to the south, the Germans anticipated the new Russian plan. As a result, the Soviets encountered immediate difficulty.[9]

Thus far, all attempts by the 3rd Tank Army to envelop Kharkov had been frustrated. Attacks against the eastern and southeastern approaches to the city also proved fruitless and served only to reduce further the diminishing strength of the 3rd Tank Army. However, the

3rd Tank Army's attacks diverted the SS Panzer Corps to the east and southeast where it was now tied down, leaving only weak German forces north and west of Kharkov.

The only substantial progress being made by the Voronezh Front was on the 40th Army's sector north of Kharkov. After securing Belgorod, the 40th Army began its southward drive on February 10. On February 12, the 5th Guards Tank Corps was committed at Zolchev, about fifteen miles northeast of Kharkov. By nightfall on the thirteenth, the Russians were approaching Kharkov's inner defenses, and lead elements of the 5th Guards Tank Corps reached the city's northernmost defenses.

On February 14, *Armee Abteilung* Lanz was subordinated to Army Group South. Manstein immediately issued orders instructing *Armee Abteilung* Lanz to make a thrust across the Donets south of Kharkov toward Lozovaya to "roll up and eliminate the enemy forces there."[10] Kharkov was to be "held as long as possible, although our forces are not to be enveloped."[11]

Manstein's orders were contrary to those of Hitler's, who, on February 13, ordered the SS Panzer Corps to hold Kharkov at all cost. Hitler's orders notwithstanding, the SS Panzer Corps abandoned Kharkov, saving themselves from encirclement.

Despite capturing Kharkov, the Russians failed to trap substantial German forces. Moreover, German defenses remained intact, and there was still a line of communications westward to Poltava and south to Krasnograd. However, while fighting still raged for Kharkov, new orders were issued to the Voronezh Front to continue its offensive to the west and southwest to reach Lebedin and Poltava by February 20.[12]

Before these orders could be implemented, the Russian forces within Kharkov had to be unraveled. While the 3rd Tank Army covered the regrouping, the 40th and 69th Army units hurried west and northwest to occupy their new positions. It took nearly three days to complete realignment. By this time, 40th Army rifle divisions were down to 3,500–4,000 men, while some 69th Army rifle divisions were down to 1,000–1,500 men.[13]

By February 20, the 40th Army was on a line, running from Krasnopolye to Akhtyrka, and was ready to resume its advance toward Lebedin and the Psel River. At this point, however, events in the 3rd Tank Army's sector farther south in the Southwestern Front's area transformed the situation on the 40th and 69th Army fronts. Immediately after occupying covering positions around Kharkov, the 3rd Tank Army resumed its offensive. Across its entire front, the 3rd Tank Army's advance slowed as Corps Raus (formerly Cramer) and *LSAH* executed skillful delaying actions to buy time for Manstein to launch his planned counteroffensive farther south. By February 18, the 3rd Tank Army was down to 110 tanks (out of 165). German defenses were firmed up with the arrival of the 167th Infantry Division south of Kotelva. The 40th Army's overextended front, stretching from Sumy to Akhtyrka, was also facing increasingly stronger resistance.[14]

As a result of stiffening German resistance and its deployment along a broad front, the Voronezh Front was overextended and unable to offer any assistance to the Southwestern Front to the south precisely at the moment when Manstein was seeking to crush the Southwestern Front with a converging thrust by the 4th Panzer Army.

On February 19, Manstein unleashed his mailed fist against the strung-out 6th Army. It took over one week for Vatutin and STAVKA to appreciate the scope of the disaster. The 3rd Tank Army was engaged around Lyubotin and could do little to assist the 6th Army except to pressure the German front south of Kharkov. Meanwhile, three German armored groups, the SS Panzer Corps, XLVIII Panzer Corps, and the XL Panzer Corps crushed the 6th Army and Group Popov.

By the evening of February 22, STAVKA was concerned enough over the situation of the Southwestern Front to shift the attack of the 3rd Tank and 69th Armies southward against the Germans in the Krasnograd area. The 69th and 3rd Tank Armies, however, made only slow progress.[15]

The slow Russian progress was due to the tenacious resistance of *Armee Abteilung* Kempf south of Kharkov, which was ordered by Manstein to "hold out against the enemy and conduct the battle in its present positions as long as possible."[16] It was especially important that "Under no circumstances is the *Armee Abteilung* to be forced away from the Kharkov-Krasnograd road on the south flank."[17] After February 13, *Armee Abteilung* Kempf was slowly pushed back, but neither the 3rd Tank nor 69th Armies could muster enough strength to crack the German defenses.

Incredibly, the 40th Army continued to receive orders to accelerate its advance on an even broader sector. On February 28, STAVKA issued yet new orders to the Voronezh Front. By this time, the Southwestern Front was in full collapse. The 1st Guards Army was retreating toward the Donets, while the 6th Army struggled to avoid encirclement. In a desperate effort to salvage the remains of the 6th Army, the 3rd Tank Army was subordinated to the Southwestern Front. The 3rd Tank Army was then to wheel and attack southward toward Lozovaya to blunt the German advance by destroying the SS Panzer Corps and rescue the 6th Army. While the 3rd Tank Army concentrated for its attack, the 40th Army was to continue its advance to the west.[18]

The 3rd Tank Army's relief drive was doomed before it ever started. On the same day that STAVKA issued new orders to the Voronezh Front, Manstein issued new orders to the 4th Panzer Army. After mopping up the south bank of the Donets and blocking the Donets crossings south of Kharkov, the 4th Panzer Army was "to turn with strong forces to attack Tarnovka-Paraskovka.... The objective of these attacks is chiefly to destroy the enemy forces south of Berestovaya."[19] The 3rd Tank Army's concentration area for its southward drive was located almost in the center of the 4th Panzer Army's new attack sector.

Early on March 3, the 3rd Tank Army launched its desperate attack into the armored jaws of *Totenkopf* and *Das Reich*. The initial collision forced the 15th Tank Corps and its supporting infantry to be immediately on the defensive. While *Totenkopf* struck the 15th Tank Corps from the east, *LSAH* delivered crushing blows from north and south of Krasnograd, linking with *Totenkopf* at Paraskovaya and Yefremovka and sealing the fate of the doomed 15th Tank Corps.[20]

To the north, the 12th Tank Corps met a similar fate. It, too, ran headlong into lead elements of *Totenkopf* and *Das Reich*. More significantly, the capture of Okocheye and Yefremovka by *Das Reich* forced the 6th Guards Cavalry Corps from its defense position and cut the 3rd Tank Army's line of supply.[21]

By nightfall on March 3, the commander of the 3rd Tank Army, Major General P. S. Rybalko, realized that further resistance was useless and ordered a breakout to the north and northeast. The 15th Tank Corps was unable to organize a coordinated effort, but the 12th Tank Corps managed to disengage and escape to the northwest. Resistance continued for several days, during which individual Russian groups made their way north toward Soviet lines.[22]

By March 5, the 3rd Tank Army was a total wreck. Its two tank corps were virtually wiped out, along with three rifle divisions. Rybalko had scrambled to establish a solid front anchored on Okhocheye and Novaya Vodolaga. He had received several units from front reserve, but had only the brief period from March 3, to construct new lines, while the SS Panzer Corps subdued the 12th Tank and 15th Tank Corps. It would not be long before Manstein struck the Voronezh Front on its southern flank.[23]

The 3rd Tank Army's disaster south of Kharkov and signs of German preparations against its own front prompted the 69th Army to draw back to positions south of the Merla River from north of Chutovo and south to Valki. The 40th Army was also finally ordered to go over to the defense, but was to maintain its forward positions west of the Psel River. After withdrawing three rifle divisions into reserve, the 40th

Army had only three rifle divisions and a tank corps to cover a seventy-mile front from Sumy to Oposhnya.[24]

German pressure was already disrupting the Russian defensive adjustments. In the 3rd Tank Army's sector, the 6th Panzer Division was engaged against stubborn resistance around Tarnovka, while *Das Reich* threw the 6th Guards Cavalry Corps from Okhocheye. *Leibstandarte Adolf Hitler* also pushed the Russians back from Staeoverka and Novaya Vodolaga. Shifting its axis of attack to the west, the 4th Panzer Army's sector now included the area south of Kharkov. Once the remaining elements of *LSAH*, *Totenkopf*, and the 11th Panzer Division (now subordinated to the XLVIII Panzer Corps) were released from their present engagements, the 4th Panzer Army would strike northward.[25]

With the SS and XLVIII Panzer Corps in the van, Manstein's plan called for the 4th Panzer Army to continue driving northward against the Voronezh Front forces in the Kharkov area "to destroy the enemy still south of the Msha sector and take the south bank of the sector east of Merefa-Valki."[26] More specifically, the 6th and 11th Panzer Divisions would attack northward from the area south of Tarnovka. Meanwhile, the SS Panzer Corps, now with all three of its component divisions, was to drive through Novaya Vodolaga toward Merefa. *Armee Abteilung* Kempf would support the 4th Panzer Army by expanding the attack to the west.[27]

On March 6, the SS Panzer Corps struck Russian defenses east and west of Novaya Vodolaga. Advancing northward along the railroad to Novaya Vodolaga, Das Reich succeeded in enveloping the town from the east. LSAH moved north in two columns toward Valki and the area west of Novaya Vodolaga. By evening, the Soviets were falling back to new positions along the Msha River south of Lyubotin. By then, the mass of Totenkopf, previously engaged in mopping up the encircled 3rd Tank Army units, was concentrated north of Krasnograd and was ready to join the advance on Valki.[28]

While the SS Panzer Corps pushed back the Russians west and southwest of Kharkov, the XLVIII Panzer Corps (6th and 11th Panzer Divisions) attacked from the south with orders to take the south bank of the Msha east of Merefa. The 6th Panzer Division continued to be tied around Tarnovka until March 8, although elements of the division, in cooperation with the 11th Panzer Division, took Borki to the north. During the next two days, the 6th Panzer Division broke Russian resistance around Tarnovka, while the 11th Panzer Division pushed to the Msha opposite Merefa.[29]

The Germans continued to press their attacks on March 7. Driving northward, *Das Reich* took Starya Vodolaga. *LSAH* seized Valki, followed on its left rear by *Totenkopf*. Meanwhile, to the left of the SS

Panzer Corps, Corps Raus added its weight to the attack, forcing the
69th Army to give ground south of the Merla River. The German
advance now threatened to split the 69th Army from the remnants of
the 3rd Tank Army.[30]

The German onslaught continued on March 8. After breaking Soviet
resistance at Tarnovka, the 6th Panzer Division advanced to the Msha
River. The same day, *Das Reich* reached Odrynka, midway between
Novaya Vodolaga and Lyubotin. *LSAH* advanced against only weak
defenses, seized Ogultsy south of Lyubotin, and cut the Lyubotin-
Kharkov road. After mopping up the area northeast of Valki, *Totenkopf*,
together with elements of *Grossdeutschland*, advanced to Stary Merchik, west of Lyubotin.[31]

The next day, the SS Panzer Corps sped northward to finish the job
of splitting the 69th from the 40th Army and simultaneously swung
eastward to isolate Kharkov. *Das Reich* approached the western out-
skirts of Kharkov. After taking Lyubotin, *LSAH* pushed across the Udy
River at Pereschaya and reached Polevaya west of Dergachi, enveloping Kharkov from the north. After seizing Olshany, *Totenkopf* crossed
the Udy to the east, chasing elements of the 6th Guards Cavalry Corps,
the only organized force covering the gap between the 69th and 3rd
Tank Armies, before it.[32]

Corps Raus also stepped up it attacks on the 69th Army.
Grossdeutschland continued pushing up the Merla River in cooperation
with *Totenkopf*'s drive on Stary Merchik. With the SS Panzer Corps
firmly   wedged   between   the   69th   and   3rd   Tank   Armies,
Grossdeutschland now turned northward toward Bogodukhov against
the left flank of the 69th Army.[33]

On March 10, the Soviets launched a futile counterattack near
Bogodukhov.   However,   this   attack   had   little   effect,   and
Grossdeutschland continued to roll forward, hardly noticing the Soviet
assault. The next day, *Grossdeutschland* secured the southern part of
Bogodukhov and by late on March 11, captured the rest of the town.
the   167th   Infantry   Division   also   moved   toward   Kotelva   and
Akhtyrka.[34]

Meanwhile, the XLVIII Panzer Corps pushed against Kharkov. After
driving the Russians out of Korotisch, *Das Reich* forced its way into
the western suburbs of Kharkov. After heavy street fighting, *LSAH*
took Dergachi, thus blocking Kharkov from the north. Elements of the
division then turned south and penetrated Kharkov from the north
and northeast.[35]

On March 11, Manstein ordered the 4th Panzer Army to complete
the encirclement of Kharkov by using the mass of the SS Panzer Corps
to cut the Kharkov-Chuguyev road to the east. *Armee Abteilung* Kempf
was charged with covering the movement of the SS Panzer Corps

against Russian attacks from the Belgorod and Borisovka-Graivoron area.[36]

The next day, Hoth ordered the SS Panzer Corps to advance west of Kharkov to block Chuguyev. At the same time, *Das Reich* was ordered to disengage most of its troops for a southward thrust against the Udy sector at Vodyanoye. *LSAH* was to continue compressing the Russians still in the Kharkov area.[37]

To complete the envelopment from the south, the XLVIII Panzer Corps was to clear Merefa. After being relieved by infantry, the XLVIII Panzer Corps was to assemble for a thrust from either the Zmiyev area or from between the Merefa and the Udy, to the southeast.[38]

By March 12, the SS Panzer Corps blocked the Kharkov-Chuguyev road at Loseva, as *Totenkopf* prepared for a thrust on Chuguyev. By then it was decided that the XLVIII Panzer Corps should advance on March 14, from the area north of Merefa to roll up the Russian position on the Merefa and the Msha from the northwest.[39]

On March 13, Voronezh Front's situation took a turn for the worse when the 4th Panzer Army and *Armee Abteilung* Kempf made a major thrust to disrupt Soviet efforts to restore the front. In Kharkov, *LSAH* was still engaged against stubborn resistance in the eastern part of the city. Meanwhile, *Totenkopf*'s advance made good progress despite heavy resistance at Rogan. By early evening, elements of the division cut the main line of communications of the 3rd Tank Army at Rogan. The next day, *Totenkopf* cut the remaining line of communications of the 3rd Tank Army.[40]

In an effort to restore the deteriorating situation, the Voronezh Front released the 3rd Guards Tank Corps to defend Boriskova and Tomarovka. Threatened by the XLVIII Panzer Corps and the SS Panzer Corps from the north and east, the remnants of the 3rd Tank Army withdrew from the Msha River to the east of Kharkov. On March 14, the 2nd Guards Tank Corps was spotted in the area west of Belgorod.[41]

Meanwhile, *LSAH* and *Das Reich* cleared Kharkov and pushed through the city to the east. The 11th Panzer Division, thrusting from east of Lyubotin, advanced to the south of Kharkov and established a bridgehead across the Udy River. The 6th Panzer Division was equally successful in its drive from the Msha to the Udy to complete the encirclement of the 3rd Tank Army.[42]

The 3rd Tank Army's position was hopeless. Fuel and ammunition supplies were low and only a narrow supply line remained southeast of the Donets. Unable to establish contact with the 3rd Tank Army, on the evening of March 14, the Voronezh Front granted permission to abandon Kharkov and withdraw to the Donets River.[43]

On March 12, Manstein ordered *Armee Abteilung* Kempf "To prevent
the enemy from escaping from Kharkov area to the north . . . across
the Donets."[44] To accomplish this task, *Grossdeutschland* was to pursue
the Russians from Graivoron to Belgorod. *Grossdeutschland*'s advance
would also allow the 4th Panzer Army to encircle the Soviet forces
south of Kharkov without worrying about its northern flank.[45]

This order sealed the fate of the 69th and 40th Armies, which were
struggling to reach new defense positions. *Grossdeutschland* lunged at
the junction of the two armies. Late on the afternoon of March 13,
Grossdeutschland secured Graivoron and turned northeast, up the
Vorska Valley to Borisovka. As a result, the 40th Army was forced back
to positions north of Graivoron. By March 15, the 40th Army was not
only cut from the 69th Army, but it was also split in two by
Grossdeutschland's advance. Meanwhile, the 167th and 320th Infantry
Divisions mopped up Russian resistance in the wake of
Grossdeutschland.[46]

On March 15, the 4th Panzer Army began its attacks to eliminate
remaining Russian resistance in the Kharkov area. The 6th Panzer
Division pushed north and east across the Udy River, while *Das Reich*
thrust southeastward along the Kharkov-Chuguyev road and turned
south across the Udy near Vesenskoye. *Totenkopf* also continued to
pressure Soviet forces along the Kharkov-Chuguyev road. The following day, elements of the 6th Panzer Division established contact with
the 11th Panzer Division, advancing from south of Kharkov, driving
the Russians toward the German blocking forces around Chuguyev.[47]

While the 4th Panzer Army smashed Russian resistance east of
Kharkov, elements of the German 2nd Army and Corps Raus consolidated the success of *Grossdeutschland*. Tomarovka fell to
Grossdeutschland on March 15. By March 18, German units held positions on both sides of the Vorskla River, from Krasnopolye to west of
the town Udy. Together with the 167th and 320th Infantry Divisions,
elements of *Grossdeutschland* attacked to reduce the 69th Army salient
from south of Borisovka to Udy (the Udy pocket).[48]

By March 18, the Kharkov area was secured. Two days earlier,
Manstein had ordered the 4th Panzer Army to "strike with strong
forces (at least three divisions between the Donets and Kharkov-Belgorod road to break up the enemy forces [the 2nd Guards Tank Corps]
moving on its north flank and to mop the area west of the Donets."[49]
Das Reich and *LSAH* were to concentrate north Kharkov and attack on
March 18, with *Totenkopf* following on the right rear.[50]

The Russians were powerless to stem the German advance. Sweeping aside the 2nd Guards Tank Corps, *LSAH* took Belgorod on March
18, and turned west to establish blocking positions along the railroad
south of the city facing the Udy pocket. Trapped between the SS

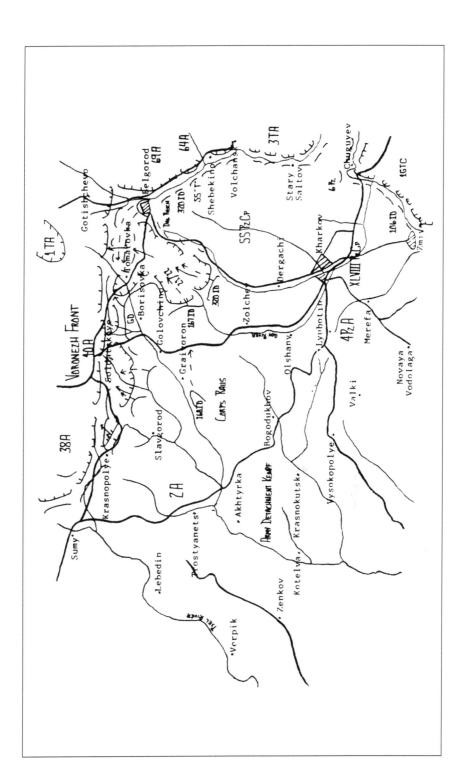

Panzer Corps and Corps Raus, Soviet forces in the Udy pocket struggled for survival. Although many of the Russian troops escaped, all
of their heavy equipment was left behind.[51]

By March 20, the Russians abandoned the western bank of the
Donets between Belgorod and north of Chuguyev, leaving only isolated pockets to be mopped up by the Germans. Meanwhile, Corps
Raus and SS Panzer Corps consolidated their positions in the
Belogorod-Tomarovka area. At the same time, STAVKA poured reinforcements into the Belgorod-Kursk region to support the 69th, 40th,
and 3rd Tank Armies. The 21st Army began arriving on March 22, and
took up positions north and west of Kharkov. The same day, the 64th
Army arrived to take over the 69th Army's sector southwest of Belgorod.[52]

On March 23, Manstein declared an end to active operations in the
Kharkov-Belgorod area. In thirty-three days, February 18-March 23,
Army Group South successfully eliminated the danger to its line of
communications across the Dnieper, wrecked Soviet plans to bottle up
Army Group South and isolate the southern flank from the rest of the
front, and delivered a crushing counterblow which reversed the trend
of events that had threatened the entire German position on the
Eastern Front for nearly four months. In the process, the Soviet 6th
Army and 3rd Tank Army and Mobile Group Popov were wiped out.
Considerable parts of the 1st Guards, 40th, and 69th Armies were
either destroyed or rendered useless. Total Russian losses for the
period were in excess of 600 tanks, 1,200 field pieces, 14,000 prisoners,
and over 46,000 men dead.

Manstein's counterstroke had regained the initiative for the German
side and brought German forces back to the approximate line they
held in the summer of 1942.[53]

Notes

1. Glanz, pp. 232–233.
2. Ibid., pp. 233–234.
3. Ibid., pp. 238–239. Erickson, pp. 46–47.
4. 4 PZ AOK Anlg. 1 KTB, February 25, 1943, Roll 365, Frame 8,651,015.
5. Ibid., February 28, 1943, Frame 9,651,180.
6. II SS Panzer Corps Anlg. A II KTB 4, February 3, 1943, Roll 118, Frames
   3,751,523, 3,751,525. February 4, 1943, Frame 3,751,540. Glanz, pp. 242–246.
7. II SS Pz Cp. Anlg. A II KTB 4, February 8-10, 1943, Frames 3,751,594,
   3,752,015, 3,751,540. Glanz, pp. 247, 252.

8. Glanz. pp. 253–254.
9. II SS Pz Corps. Anlg. A II KTB 4, February 10, 1943, Roll 118, Frame 8,650,861. Glanz, p. 254.
10. Glanz, pp. 255–256.
11. 4 Pz AOK Anlg. 1 KTB, February 13, 1943, Roll 365, Frame 8,650,861.
12. Glanz, p. 259.
13. Ibid., pp. 259–260.
14. Ibid., pp. 232, 261–262. II SS Pz Cp. Anlg. A II KTB 4, February 17, 1943, Roll 118, Frame 3,751,689.
15. Glanz, p. 263.
16. 4 Pz AOK Anlg. 1 KTB, February 19, 1943, Roll 365, Frame 8,650,902.
17. Ibid.
18. Glanz, pp. 264–265.
19. 4 Pz AOK Anlg. 1 KTB, February 28, 1943, Roll 365, Frame 8,651,180.
20. Panzer Armeeoberkommando 4 Ia, Anlagenband C 3 z. KTB nr. I u. II, February 1–July 31, 1943, Microcopy T 311, Roll 367, March 2, 1943, Frame 8,653,215. March 3, 1943, Frame 8,653,226. Cited henceforth as 4 Pz AOK Anlg. 4 KTB with date, roll, and frame number. II SS Pz Cp. Anlg. A II KTB February 28, 1943, Roll 118, Frame 3,752,003. March 5, 1943, Frame 3,752,084. Glanz, p. 267.
21. 4 Pz AOK Anlg. 3 KTB, March 2–5, 1943, Frames 8,653,215, 8,653,226, 8,563,238, 8,643,255–8,653,256. II SS Pz Cp. Anlg. A II KTB 4, February 28, 1943, Frame 3,752,003. March 5, 1943, Frame 3,752,084. Glanz, pp. 267–270.
22. 4 Pz AOK Anlg. 3 KTB, March 3–4, 1943, Frames 8,653,226, 8,653,228. Glanz, p. 270.
23. Glanz, p. 270.
24. Ibid., pp. 271–272.
25. 4 Pz AOK Anlg. 3 KTB, March 2–4, 1943, Roll 367, Frames 8,653,215–8,653,216, 8,653,226, 8,653,238. II SS Pz Cp. Anlg. A II KTB 4, March 3–4, 1943, Roll 118, Frames 3,752,056, 3,752,142.
26. II SS Pz Cp. Anlg. A II KTB 4, March 5, 1943, Frame 3,752,141.
27. Ibid. 4 Pz AOK Anlg. 3 KTB, March 3, 1943, Roll 367, Frame 8,651,161. March 5, 1943, Frame 8,653,255.
28. II SS Pz Cp. Anlg. A II KTB 4, March 6, 1943, Frame 3,752,187. 4 Pz AOK Anlg. 3 KTB March 6, 1943, Frames 8,653,267–8,653,268. Glanz, p. 273.
29. II SS Pz Cp. Anlg. A II KTB 4, March 6–7, 1943, Frames 3,752,187, 3,752,211. 4 Pz AOK Anlg. 3 KTB, March 6–8, 1943, Frames 8,653,267, 8,653,280, 8,653,288.
30. II SS Pz Cp. Anlg. A II KTB 4, March 7, 1943, Frame 3,752,211. 4 Pz AOK Anlg. 3 KTB, March 7, 1943, Frame 8,653,280. Glanz, p. 274.
31. 4 Pz AOK Anlg. 3 KTB, March 8, 1943, Frame 8,653,288.
32. Ibid., March 9, 1943, Frame 8,653,296. Glanz, pp. 275–276.
33. Glanz, p. 276.
34. Ibid., pp. 277–279.
35. 4 Pz AOK Anlg. 3 KTB, March 10, 1943, Roll 367, Frames 8,653,313–8,653,314. II SS Pz Cp. Anlg. A II KTB 4, March 11, 1943, Roll 118, Frame 3,752,282.
36. 4 Pz AOK Anlg. 3 KTB, March 11, 1943, Frame 8,651,291.

37. II SS Pz Cp. Anlg. A II KTB 4, March 11, 1943, Frame 3,752,301.
38. Ibid., Frame 3,752,302.
39. Ibid., March 12, 1943, Frame 3,752,313. 4 Pz AOK Anlg. 3 KTB, March 12, 1943, Frame 8,653,336.
40. II SS Pz CP. Anlg. A II KTB 4, March 14, 1943, Frame 3,652,336. 4 Pz AOK Anlg. 3 KTB, March 13, 1943, Frame 8,653,353.
41. Glanz, pp. 280–281.
42. II SS Pz Cp. March 14–15, 1943, Roll 118, Frames 3,752,363, 3,752,379, 3,752,381. 4 Pa AOK Anlg. 3 KTB, March 14–15, 1943, Roll 367, Frames 8,653,364–8,653,365, 8,653,371–8,653,372.
43. Glanz, pp. 280–281.
44. Pz AOK Anlg. 3 KTB, March 12, 1943, Roll 367, Frame 8,651,305.
45. Ibid.
46. Glanz, pp. 281–282. 4 Pz AOK Anlg. 1 KTB, March 16, 1943, Roll 365, Frames 8,651,341–8,651,342.
47. 4 Pz AOK Anlg. 3 KTB, March 14, 1943, Roll 367, Frame 8,653,385. March 16, 1943, Frame 8,653,386.
48. Glanz, p. 285.
49. 4 Pz AOK Anlg. 1 KTB, March 16, 1943, Roll 365, Frame 8,651,341.
50. II SS Pz Cp. Anlg. A II KTB 4, March 16, 1943, Roll 118, Frame 3,752,406.
51. 4 PZ AOK Anlg. 3 KTB, March 17–18, 1943 Roll 367, Frames 8,653,401, 8,653,411.
52. Ibid., March 20–21, 1943, Frames 8,653,439–8,653,440, 8,653,450. Glanz, p. 287.
53. 4 Pz AOK Anlg. 3 KTB, March 23, 1943, Frame 8,653,411. March 23, 1943, Roll 365, Frame 8,651,399.

CHAPTER 6

The Genius of Manstein

The recapture of Kharkov and the subsequent German drive to the Donets River marked the end of the winter campaign of 1942–1943. In four weeks, Manstein's counteroffensive achieved a dramatic reversal that seemed inconceivable after the 6th Army had been trapped in Stalingrad the previous November. Repeatedly attacked and under continuous pressure by a numerically superior foe, Army Group South had withstood four major Soviet offensives in four months: Operation URANUS, the initial assault to isolate Stalingrad in November 1942; Operation LITTLE SATURN, which blunted the 4th Panzer Army's relief drive and threatened to envelop *Armee Abteilung* Hollidt along the Chir; Operation GALLOP, which menaced Army Group South's line of communications across the Dnieper; and Operation STAR, which also threatened to cut off Army Group South farther up the Dnieper on either side of Kremenchug. These Russian blows were delivered in rapid succession without any respite for the defending Germans.

Battered, reeling, and teetering on the brink of disaster, Army Group South bent but never broke. That the German Army managed to survive the winter campaign of 1942–1943 is a testimony to the ability and fighting qualities of the private soldiers, NCOs and officers of the *Wehrmacht*. However, these characteristics had already been displayed during the first winter in Russia, when the cold was as great an enemy as the Red Army.

With the war entering its fifth year, many of the formations fighting with Army Group Don by now had a proud history. Veterans remembered the days of glory when they had marched victoriously through Poland, France, and the Balkans, as well as the early days of the Russian campaign. Unit pride instilled in these veterans, and the replacements that would soon join them, a fighting spirit that enabled them to carry on when resistance seemed hopeless. However, without the proper leadership, the esprit of the enlisted ranks would have been lost.

While the courage and skill of the German soldier played an important part in Army Group South's survival, it was the combination of luck and superior leadership that proved to be the decisive factors. Although thrust into an unpromising situation in November 1942, Manstein was fortunate that he was faced initially with only a limited Soviet offensive. The Russian attack on November 19, 1942, against the Rumanian 3rd and 4th Armies, shattered the front and threatened to unhinge the entire German southern flank. There was virtually nothing to prevent a Russian drive to Rostov after the front had been broken. *Armee Abteilung* Hollidt showed great skill and determination in piecing together its front along the Chir, but by then the Russians had already turned most of their forces toward Stalingrad to ensure the encirclement of the 6th Army. As a result, the Germans were granted a reprieve and given just enough time to solidify the front.

Manstein's reputation ensured him of the respect of his subordinates. Nevertheless, he was fortunate enough to be in a position where his commanders not only respected him, but were men of ability. Moreover, these men also understood and respected the abilities of each other and, in many cases, had served together in previous campaigns. Kempf, Funck, Knoblesdorff, and Raus had all been divisional commanders under Hoth. Wenck had been chief of staff to a panzer corps under Hoth, while Kirchner had served as a corps commander, and Huhnersdorff had been Hoth's chief of staff.

Many of Manstein's commanders had also served under him previously. Busse had served on his staff at 11th Army and had since become indispensable as Manstein's operations officer. Hoth had been Manstein's predecessor at the 18th Infantry Division and Hollidt's 50th Infantry Division had been part of Manstein's 11th Army during the Crimean campaign. These earlier relationships contributed to the smooth functioning of Army Group Don during its period of crisis.

Not only were many of these men familiar with each other, but each was or proved to be an outstanding leader in his own right. Hermann Hoth had already established a reputation as a capable panzer leader. Hollidt and Wenck proved to be great improvisers and motivators. Kirchner was a solid professional, while Knoblesdorff understood the need to closely coordinate infantry and armored operations. Even those who were relatively new to their commands (Raus and Huhnersdorff were commanding an entire division and regiment for the first time, respectively) showed superior ability.

That these men were capable commanders was also reflected in their subsequent careers. Hollidt and Fretter-Pico would later lead the new German 6th Army. Knoblesdorff would rise to command the 1st Panzer Army, while Hausser would later command the 7th Army in Normandy. Balck and Raus would also eventually command armies.

The vigor, energy, and ability even of these exceptional men might have been lost were it not for Manstein, who provided the guiding hand and firm foundation that transformed defeat into victory. Manstein's arrival at Army Group Don headquarters on November 27, was a major step toward the eventual recovery of the German southern flank. Prior to his arrival he had already concluded that the Soviets would make Rostov their primary objective; an assumption that remained the basis of all of Army Group Don's subsequent operations.

From the time he assumed command in November 1942, until the 4th Panzer Army's counterstroke in February 1943, Manstein never lost sight of the fact that the Russians were making their main effort against Army Group Don, with the aim of severing the southern wing from the rest of the front, which, if successful, would precipitate the collapse of the entire German position on the Eastern Front. Manstein's foresight and his resolve not to be distracted from his fundamental task, the maintenance of the southern flank, were the single most important factors in determining the outcome for the Germans. Manstein's foresight and determination are also two of the major characteristics that qualify him for greatness, if not genius.

The ability to foresee the enemy's actions and to divine his intentions is not unique among military leaders great or small. For any commander to be successful, he must be able to anticipate the enemy so that his own troops can gain the advantage. What separates Manstein from the others and possibly elevates him to the level of genius is the fact that he was able to anticipate the enemy consistently, under tremendous pressure. Given enough time, even an armchair general might arrive at the proper solution to a tactical or strategic problem. In war, however, one is seldom afforded the luxury of enough time. In the case of Manstein and Army Group Don, there was virtually no time to labor over decisions. The correct decision had to be made and made quickly.

The survival of Army Group Don was due as much to Manstein's foresight as to its fighting skill. This foresight was most in evidence as Manstein planned his counterblow. If the counteroffensive was to be successful, Manstein had to assure that his panzer divisions would be in a position not only to block a further Russian drive toward the Dnieper, but also to pinch off the Russian salient bulging to the southwest.

Manstein's genius must be credited with allowing him to put together his counterstroke "on the run." The formulation of an operational plan is not an easy task under any circumstances. Many factors and variables must be weighed, including relative troop strength, disposition of forces, the area of the main attack, the axis of advance, supply, intelligence, and a score of other major and minor details. The entire process is greatly simplified if the front is relatively stable or inactive, or if the attacker already has the initiative. Manstein, however, was operating with neither condition in his favor.

Manstein developed his plan while Army Group South was struggling to keep the Russians at bay along the Donets. Moreover, the Germans had been in nearly continuous retreat for almost the entire winter, falling back 250 miles in three months. What Manstein now proposed was not only to stop the German withdrawal, but to launch an offensive to eliminate substantial enemy forces and at the same time regain considerable territory. Except for the SS Panzer Corps, this reversal was to be accomplished using tired and worn-out men and machines. In this respect, Manstein's sense of timing, his shifting of troops, and his balancing of means and ends have no equal.

Manstein always had to think several steps ahead of the Russians, weighing every option and variable and playing out each scenario in his mind so that when the time came to act, he could do so swiftly and decisively. This process was greatly complicated by the fact that all of Manstein's decisions had to be cleared through Hitler, making it necessary for Manstein to make allowances in his plans for any time it might take Hitler to grant his permission.

If nothing else, Manstein's daily bouts with Hitler, in addition to discharging his other duties as an army group commander, are an indication of Manstein's physical strength and stamina. If Manstein is to be considered a military genius, then at least part of his genius derives from his ability to deal effectively with Hitler. On more than one occasion, Manstein demonstrated skill and determination in arguing his points with the dictator. This was especially true in face-to-face encounters, when considerable moral courage was needed to withstand Hitler's harangues and intimidating outbursts. Hitler was not without his charms, and Manstein would not have been alone had he succumbed to Hitler's talk of new weapons, moral superiority or will power.

Invariably, Manstein has been compared to other well-known German commanders, including Rundstedt, Bock, Guderian, Hoth, and Kleist. Albert Seaton goes so far as to conclude of Manstein that:

> In the first half of the war, against outdated high commands, inexperienced field generals, and poorly trained troops, the victories were remarkable. But these successes could not be repeated indefinitely, for such audacity too little account of the feasible, factors such as climate, distance and terrain, and the steadily improving quality of enemy troops and high command.[1]

This evaluation is unjust and misses the mark. Manstein's advocacy of the *Sichelschnitt* plan for the invasion of France demonstrated his insight into strategic planning. His appreciation of the possibilities of the plan also demonstrated his foresight and a keen understanding for the application of the new methods of mobile warfare.

A comparison of Manstein to Rundstedt and Bock reveals that their success in Poland was achieved against an ill-prepared and ill-equipped foe. More significant is the fact that Rundstedt's victory in France was a direct result of Manstein's support of the *Sichelschnitt* plan! The victories enjoyed by Bock and Rundstedt in the early part of the Russian campaign were also achieved against "outdated high commands, inexperienced field generals, and poorly trained troops."

By contrast, the achievements of Army Group South were the result of Manstein's foresight and determination. Moreover, Manstein's victory came not against an inexperienced foe with inept leadership, but against an enemy who was equally determined and capably led. By the time of the winter campaign of 1942–1943, the Red Army had demonstrated its ability to conduct strategic operations. By this time, too, most of the incompetent commanders had been either killed in combat or shot. Rising to take their place were men like Vasilevsky, Rokossovsky, Yeremenko, and Zhukov. Not only was the Soviet command improved, but so was the Russian soldier. In addition, the Soviet Army was being reorganized along improved and more efficient lines and also equipped with superior weapons.

Given the situation on the German southern flank from November 1942 to February 1943, it is doubtful that any commander other than Manstein could have brought Army Group South safely through the winter. While Guderian and Hoth were both excellent panzer leaders, neither showed the imagination of Manstein.

Guderian's development of the panzer arm and the tactics for its employment certainly qualify him for greatness. His leadership and the outstanding work he performed in reinvigorating the panzer force prior to the battle of Kursk, as Inspector General of Panzer Troops, demonstrate his organizational abilities. However, like Rundstedt and Bock, Guderian's success in the field came early in the war. Whether or not he would have been Manstein's equal under similar circumstances will never be known.

In his discussion on military genius Clausewitz states that:

Two qualities are indispensable: first, an intellect that, even in the darkest hour, retains some glimmering of inner light which leads to truth; and second, the courage to follow this faint light wherever it may lead. The first of these qualities is described by the French as *coup d'oeil*, the second is determination.[2]

Clausewitz further refines the definition of *coup d'oeil* as "the quick recognition of a truth that the mind would ordinarily miss or would perceive only after long study and reflection."[3] He also refines the definition of determination as courage aroused by the intellect, "which then supports and sustains it in action."[4]

As commander of Army Group South, Manstein never lost sight of the "inner light." His perceptive mind and quick intellect enabled him to assess the situation rapidly and accurately and allowed him to take swift action. The inner light also enabled Manstein to foresee an opportunity for a German counterattack. At the same time, whether in pressing for additional reinforcements, in his persistent messages to *OKH*, or in his arguments with Hitler, Manstein was sustained by determination. But not even the genius of Manstein could prevent the last victory from becoming a lost victory.

Notes

1. Albert Seaton, "Erich von Manstein," in *The War Lords*, ed. by Michael Carver (Boston: Little, Brown and Company, 1976), p. 243.
2. Carl von Clausewitz, *On War*, ed. and trans. by Michael Howard and Peter Paret (Princeton, New Jersey: Princeton University Press, 1976), p. 102.
3. Ibid.
4. Ibid.

Bibliography

Primary Sources

Oberkommando des Heeres (T 78)
Operationen Abteilung I/N Band I Nord, Roll 337.

Heeresgruppe Don (T 311)
Ia, Anlagenband, 2 u. 3 z. KTB, November 27–December 14, 1942, Roll 268.
Ia, Anlagenband 4 z. KTB, December 15–23, 1942, Roll 269.
Ia, Anlagenband 5 z. KTB, December 24, 1942–January 3, 1943, Roll 270.
Ia, Anlagenband 6 z. KTB, January 4–12, 1943, Roll 270.
Ia, Anlagenband 7 z. KTB, January 13–20, 1943, Roll 271.
Ia, Anlagenband 8 z. KTB, January 21–29, 1943, Roll 271.
Ia, Anlagenband 9 z. KTB, January 30–February 6, 1943, Roll 272.
Ia, Lage der Heeresgruppe Don. Maps (1:100,000), November 27–December 31, 1942, Roll 272.
Ia, Lage der Heeresgruppe Don. Maps (1:100,000), January 1–31, 1943, Roll 272.
Ia, Lage der Heeresgruppe Don. Maps (1:100,000), February 1–28, 1943, Roll 272.

Panzer Armeeoberkommando 1 (T 313)
Ia, Anlagenband z. KTB Nr. 10 February 1–28, 1943, Roll 42.

Panzer Armeeoberkommando 4 (T 313)
Ia, Anlagenband C 2 z. KTB Nr. 5, Teil III, August 19–December 31, 1942, Roll 356.
Ia, Kriegstagebuch I u. II, March 25–April 25, 1943. February 1–July 31, 1943, Roll 365.
Ia, Anlagenband C 1 z. KTB Nr. I u. II, February 1–July 31, 1943, Roll 365/366.
Ia, Anlagenband C 2 z. KTB Nr. I u. II, January, 1–July 31, 1943, Roll 366.
Ia, Anlagenband C 3 z. KTB Nr. I u. II, February 1–July 31, 1943, Roll 367.

XLVIII Panzer Corp (T 314)
Ia, Kriegstagebuch, November 1–30, 1942, Roll 1160.
Ia, Anlagen z. KTB. November 1–30, 1942, Roll 1160.

Ia, Kriegstagebuch, December 1–31, 1942, Roll 1160.
Ia, Anlagen z. KTB, December 1–31, 1942, Roll 1160.
Ia, Kriegstagebuch, January 1–31, 1943, Roll, 1164.
Ia, Anlagenband z. KTB, January 1–31, 1943, Roll 1164.
Ia, Kriegstagebuch, February 1–June 30, 1943, Roll 1165.

LVII Panzer Corps (T 314)
Ia, Kriegstagebuch 5, October 1–December 31, 1942, Roll 1480.
Ia, Anlagenband 5 z. KTB 5, September 30–December 29, 1942, Roll 1481.
Ia, Anlagenband 6 z. KTB 5, December 21–31, 1942, Roll 1481.
Ia, Anlagen z. KTB 4 u. 5, September 1–December 31, 1943, Rolls 1481 and 1482.

II SS Panzer Corps (T 314)
Ia, Anlagenband A I Teil z. KTB, January 1–February 9, 1943, Roll 118.
Ia, Anlagenband A II Teil z. KTB 4, January 3–March 27, 1943, Roll 118.

6th Panzer Division (T 315)
Ia, Anlagenband 5 z. KTB, December 6–10, 1942, Roll 341.
Ia, Anlagenband 6 z. KTB, December 16–20, 1942, Roll 342.

11th Panzer Division (T 315)
Ia, Kriegstagebuch 6, November 1–December 31, 1942, Roll 594.
Ia, Anlagenband 1–4 z. KTB 6, November 1–December 31, 1942, Rolls 594 and 595.
Ia, Kriegstagebuch 7, January 1–31, 1943, Roll 596.
Ia, Anlagenband 1–2 z. KTB 7, January 1–31, 1943, Roll 596.
Ia, Kriegstagebuch 8, February 1–28, 1942, Roll 597.

Foreign Military Studies Series

Ms C050 *Conduct of Operations in the East, 1941–1943*. General Walter Kruger.
Ms D282 *Employment of a Furlough Detachment for Rear Area Security (Don Donets, Winter 1942–1943)*. Lieutenant General Wilhelm Russwurm.
Ms P060g vol. 2, part 3 *Unusual Situations, the Stalingrad Area*. General Erhard Raus.
Ms P114c vols. 1–2, part 4 *Die Operationen der Deutschen Heeresgruppen and der Ostfront, 1941 bis 1945, Sudliches Gebiet: Die Russich Gegenoffensive bis zum Mius und zum Donets, November 1942–March 1943*. General Friedrich Hauck.
Ms T10 *German Defense Against Russian Breakthroughs*. General Erhard Raus.
Ms T15 *Reverses on the Southern Wing, 1942–1943*. General Friedrich Schulz et al.

Memoirs and accounts by participants

Balck, Hermann. *Ordnung im Chaos, Erinnerungen, 1893–1948*. Osnabruck: Biblio Verlag, 1981.
Guderian, Heinz. *Panzer Leader*. New York: Ballantine Books, 1957.
Hoth, Hermann. *Panzer Operationen*. Heidelberg: Scharnhorst Buchkameradschaft, 1965.
Knoblesdorff, Otto. *Geschichte der niedersachsischen 19. Panzer Division, 1939–1945*. Bad Hauheim: Verlag Hans-Henning Podzun, 1958.
Manstein, Erich Von. *Lost Victories*. Edited and translated by Anthony G. Powell. Novato, California: Presidio Press, 1982.
Mellenthin, F. W. Von. *Panzer Battles: A Study of the Employment of Armor in the Second World War*. New York: Ballantine Books, 1971.
Wenger, Carl. *Heeresgruppe Sud: Der Kampf in Suden der Ostfront, 1941–1945*. Bad Nauheim: Podzum Verlag, 1966.
Zhukov, Georgi K. *The Memoirs of Marshal Zhukov*. New York: Delacorte Press, 1971.

Secondary Sources

Allen, W.E.D., and Muratloff, P. *The Russian Campaigns of 1941–1943*. Harmondsworth: Penguin Books, 1944.
Brett-Smith, R. *Hitler's Generals*. San Rafael, California: Presidio Press, 1977.
Carrel, Paul. *Hitler Moves East, 1941–1943*. Boston: Little, Brown and Company, 1964.
———. *Scorched Earth: The Russian-German War, 1943–1944*. New York: Ballantine Books, 1966.
———. *Unternehmen Barbarossa im Bild*. Berlin: Verlag Ullstein GmbH., 1967.
Carver, Michael, ed. *The War Lords: Military Commanders of the Twentieth Century*. Boston: Little, Brown and Company, 1976.
Chant, Christopher. *Hitler's Generals*. New York: Chartwell Books, 1979.
Clark, Alan. *Barbarossa: The Russian-German Conflict, 1941–1945*. New York: William Morrow and Company, 1965.
Clausewitz, Carl. *On War*. Edited and translated by Michael Howard and Peter Paret. Princeton, New Jersey: Princeton University Press, 1976.
Cooper, Matthew. *The German Army, 1933–1945*. New York: Stein and Day Publishers, 1978.
Craig, William. *Enemy at the Gates: The Battle for Stalingrad*. New York: Ballantine Books, 1974.
Donhauser, Anton J., and Drews, Werner. *Der Weg der 11. Panzer Division, 1939–1943*. Bad Worishofen: Holzmann-Deuck-Service, 1982.
Downing, David. *Devil's Virtuosos: German Generals at War, 1940–5*. New York: St. Martins Press, 1977.
Dunnigan, James. *War in the East: The Russo-German Conflict, 1941–1945*. New York: Simulations Publications Incorporated, 1977.

Erickson, John. *The Road to Berlin: Continuing the History of Stalin's War With Germany.* Boulder, Colorado: Westview Press, 1983.

———. *The Road to Stalingrad: Stalin's War With Germany.* London: Westview Press, 1975.

Heibert, Helmut, ed. *Hitler's Lagrbesprechen: Die Protokollfragemente seiner militarischen Konfrenzen 1942–1945.* Stuttgart: Deutsche Verlags-Anstalt, 1962.

Humble, Richard. *Hitler's Generals.* New York: Doubleday and Company, 1973.

Guillaume, A. *The German Russian War, 1941–1945.* London: The War Office, 1956.

Irving, David. *Hitler's War.* New York: Viking Press, 1977.

Keegan, John. *Waffen SS: The Asphalt Soldiers.* New York: Ballantine Books, 1970.

Kehrig, Manfred. *Stalingrad: Analyse und Dokumentation einer Schlact.* Stuttgart: Deutsches Verlags-Anstalt, 1974.

Lederrey, E. *Germany's Defeat in the East: The Soviet Armies at War.* London: The War Office, 1955.

Mellenthin, F. W. Von *German Generals of World War Two as I Saw Them.* Norman, Oklahoma: University of Oklahoma Press, 1977.

Mitcham, Samuel. *Hitler's Legions: The German Order of Battle in World War II.* New York: Stein and Day Publishers, 1985.

Paget, R. T. *Manstein: His Campaigns and His Trial.* London: Collins, 1951.

Schiebert, Horst. *Zwishchen Don und Donets, Winter 1942–1943.* Neckargemund: Kurt Vowinckel, Verlag, 1961.

Schwarz, Eberhard. *Die Stabilisierung der Ostfront nach Stalingrad, Mansteins Gegenschlag zwischen Donez und Dnjepr im Fruhjahr 1943.* Gottingen: Munster-Schmidt Verlag, 1985.

Seaton, Albert. *The Russo-German War, 1941–1945.* New York: Praeger Publishers, 1970.

Stein, George. *The Waffen SS.* New York: Cornell University Press, 1977.

Syndor, Charles W. *Soldiers of Destruction: The Death's Head Division, 1933–1945.* Princeton, New Jersey: Princeton University Press, 1977.

Taylor, Telford. *Sword and Swastika: Generals and Nazis in the Third Reich.* Chicago: Quadrangle Paperbacks, 1969.

Trevor-Roper, H. *Blitzkrieg to Defeat: Hitler's War Directives, 1939–1945.* New York: Holt, Reinhart and Winston, 1964.

United States Military Intelligence Service. "Order of Battle of the German Army, 1943." Washington, D. C.: United States War Department General Staff, 1943.

———. "Order of Battle of the German Army, 1945." Washington, D.C.: United States War Department General Staff, 1945.

Werth, Alexander. *Russia at War, 1941–1945.* London: Barrie and Rockliffe, 1964.

Ziemkie, Earl. *Stalingrad to Berlin: The German Defeat in the East.* U.S. Army Center of Military History, Washington, D.C., 1968.

Ziemkie, Earl, and Bauer, Magna. *Moscow to Stalingrad: Decision in the East.* New York: Military Heritage Press, 1988.

Miscellaneous

Center for Land Warfare, U. S. Army War College. *1984 Art of War Symposium, From the Don to the Dnieper: Soviet Offensive Operations, December 1942– August 1943.* Transcript by Lieutenant Colonel David Glanz.
Historical Division Headquarters, USA, Europe, Foreign Military Studies Branch. "Panzer Retreat to Counteroffensive: Change-over from Withdrawal to Pursuit Tactics." Transcript of lecture given by General Fridolin von Senger and Etterlin.
———. "Failure of a Relief Mission." Transcript of lecture given by General Fridolin von Senger and Etterlin.
Newton, Steven A. *Hitler's Generals: A Biographical Register of German Generals, 1939–1945, Including Senior Luftwaffe and Waffen SS Commanders* (unpublished manuscript).

Index

Maulwurf (Mius) position: importance of, 102, 116, 117; mentioned, 90, 97, 99, 100, 101, 103, 109, 110, 115

Operations:
  GALLOP, 91, 126, 133
  SATURN (BIG/LITTLE): delayed, 33; mentioned, 67; objective of, 6, 32, 44; revision, 34; success of, 41, 45, 48, 58
  STAR, 91, 92, 96, 108, 134
  URANUS, 4-7

Paulus, Friedrich, 2, 33, 43, 45, 46, 48

Rokossovsky, K., 4, 5, 33, 153
Rostov: defense of, 60, 63, 66, 67, 77, 78, 81, 82; importance of, 3, 48; mentioned, 44, 53, 56, 72, 75, 76, 78; as Russian objective, 6, 18, 30-33, 54, 55, 80; vulnerability of, 13, 59, 62, 63, 65
Rumanian 3rd Army: destruction of, 8, 12; holds Chir bridgehead, 19, 21; mentioned, 4, 18, 20, 24, 27, 29, 30, 31, 39
Rumanian 4th Army, 3, 5, 22, 29, 30, 43, 47
Rundstedt, Gerd, 10, 152, 153
Russian Armies:
  1st Guards: and GALLOP, 84, 91, 92, 95, 103, 105, 106, 113; and German counterattack, 122-126, 146; mentioned, 6, 61, 96, 117, 118, 133; and SATURN, 32, 34, 58
  2nd Guards: commitment of, 3234, 45, 47, 55; mentioned, 60, 63, 76, 83; threatens Rostov, 65, 67
  3rd Guards: and GALLOP, 84, 92, 95, 96, 103; mentioned, 60, 68, 82; and SATURN, 32, 43, 58
  3rd Tank: and German counterattack, 122, 125, 126, 139, 140, 143, 146; mentioned, 141, 142; and STAR, 91, 94, 96, 134, 137, 138
  5th Tank: mentioned, 24, 28, 33, 34, 39, 55, 60, 82, 84; and SATURN, 32; and STAR, 92
  5th Shock: 33, 34, 55, 60
  6th: and GALLOP, 83, 84, 91, 92, 94, 96, 106, 109, 113, 116; and German counterattack, 117, 120-126, 134, 139, 146; mentioned, 74, 95, 108, 133; and SATURN, 6, 34, 58
    13th: 74
    17th: 6
    21st: 5, 6, 146
    24th: 6
    28th: 5, 55, 60, 62, 65, 66, 76, 80
    38th: 74, 91, 134

    40th: and German counterattack, 140-142, 144, 146; mentioned, 74, 84; and STAR, 91, 96, 134, 137-139
    47th: 55
    51st: 5, 29, 33, 34, 46, 55, 56, 60, 65, 76, 80
    57th: 5, 34
    58th: 33
    60th: 74, 91, 134
    62nd: 5
    63rd: 5
    64th: 5, 146
    65th: 6
    69th: and German counterattack, 122, 138-140, 142, 144; mentioned, 84, 137; and STAR, 91, 96, 134, 146
Russian Corps:
  1st Guards, 80
  1st Guards Cavalry, 113, 125
  1st Guards Mechanized, 59
  1st Guards Motorized, 68
  1st Guards Tank: and German counterattack, 109, 120, 121, 123, 126; mentioned, 80, 133; and STAR, 92-95
  1st Tank, 40 n.76
  2nd Guards, 55
  2nd Guards Motorized, 63, 67, 72, 76, 80
  2nd Guards Tank, 72, 76, 80, 143, 144
  2nd Tank, 72
  3rd Guards, 55
  3rd Guards Mechanized, 80
  3rd Guards Motorized, 56, 59, 61, 76
  3rd Guards Tank, 63, 67, 72, 76, 80
  3rd Tank: and German counterattack, 114, 118, 122-124, 126; and STAR, 94, 95, 104-106
  4th, 33
  4th Cavalry, 77
  4th Guards: mentioned, 80; and STAR, 95, 104-106
  4th Guards Tank: and German counterattack, 112-116, 118, 122-124, 126; and STAR, 95, 104-106, 111
  4th Mechanized, 34, 36
  4th Tank, 74, 80
  5th Guards Motorized, 56, 67, 76, 80
  5th Guards Tank, 138
  5th Motorized, 40 n.76, 80
  5th Tank, 80
  6th Guards: mentioned, 76, 80; and STAR, 95, 106
  6th Guards Cavalry: and German counterattack, 140-142; mentioned, 126, 134, 137
  6th Motorized, 55, 56, 59
  7th, 77

About the Author

Dana V. Sadarananda, a native of Baltimore, graduated from Villanova University and received his doctorate from Temple University, both located in Philadelphia, Pennsylvania. While at Temple, he studied under noted military historian Dr. Russell F. Weigley.

This is Dr. Sadarananda's first published book. It is the result of over four years of research, including many hours reading and translating the war diaries of the German army group commands available at the National Archives in Washington, D.C.

Dr. Sadarananda spends much of his free time with computer war game simulations, playing in amateur racquetball tournaments, and coaching Little League baseball. He has traveled extensively in the Far East and lives in Harrisburg, Pennsylvania with his wife Michele.